Total Facilities Management

Second Edition

Brian Atkin PhD, MPhil, BSc, FRICS, FCIOB

Adrian Brooks BSc (Hons), MBA, MRICS

Blackwell
Publishing

© 2000 by The Further Education Funding Council
and Blackwell Science Ltd – First edition
© 2005 B. Atkin & A. Brooks – Second edition

Blackwell Publishing Ltd
Editorial offices:
Blackwell Publishing Ltd, 9600 Garsington Road,
Oxford OX4 2DQ, UK
  Tel: +44 (0)1865 776868
Blackwell Publishing Inc., 350 Main Street, Malden,
MA 02148-5020, USA
  Tel: +1 781 388 8250
Blackwell Publishing Asia Pty Ltd, 550 Swanston
Street, Carlton, Victoria 3053, Australia
  Tel: +61 (0)3 8359 1011

First edition published 2000 by Blackwell Science Ltd
Second edition published 2005 by Blackwell
Publishing Ltd

Library of Congress Cataloging-in-Publication Data

Atkin, Brian.
   Total facilities management / Brian Atkin &
Adrian Brooks.— 2nd ed.
   p. cm.
   Includes bibliographical references.
   ISBN-10: 1-4051-2790-2 (pbk. : alk. paper)
   ISBN-13: 978-1-4051-2790-5 (pbk. : alk. paper)
   1. Real estate management.   2. Facility
management.   3. Building management.
I. Brooks, Adrian.   II. Title.
HD1394.A86 2005
658.2—dc22   2004026966

ISBN-10: 1-4051-2790-2
ISBN-13: 978-14051-2790-5

A catalogue record for this title is available from the
British Library

Set in 10/12pt Palatino
by Graphicraft Limited, Hong Kong
Printed and bound in India
by Gopsons Papers Ltd, Noida, India

For further information on Blackwell Publishing,
visit our website:
www.thatconstructionsite.com

Total Facilities Management

Contents

Preface

The first edition of *Total Facilities Management* was, at the time of its publication, the latest phase in a collaboration that had begun five years earlier. This collaboration was illustrative of how serious research into an ill-defined problem can yield not only improved and even new insights, but also how it can provide answers for practitioners who need guidance based on tested theory. The original work was 'a study of value for money in facilities management' in a key area within the public sector in the UK. The study helped us understand how real organisations were coping with issues such as best value, customer satisfaction and the development of the professional discipline of facilities management. From this work, we were able to set out practical guidance which we were pleased to see published by the UK government through the Stationery Office (formerly known as HMSO). The guidance was written for practitioners, not an academic readership, and was well received by the public sector and, to our delight, by many organisations and individuals in the private sector. This reaction was instrumental in taking the decision to draft *Total Facilities Management* as a means for others to access our research findings and practical guidance.

The success of the first edition encouraged us to update and expand the treatment of the subject and to draw in a broader appreciation of how facilities management is practised in parts of the world other than the UK and North America. In this connection, we are especially grateful to Dr Keith Futcher, Managing Director of EastPoint Management Services Limited, and his colleagues for providing access to so many examples of best practice facilities management. The location of EastPoint – part of the international conglomerate Jardine Matheson – in Hong Kong has added a further dimension, one of managing a different organisational culture and context to that found in the UK and North America. What is also interesting about EastPoint is that it has taken and applied, tested and refined, many model practices and procedures. This has allowed us, as authors, to establish this broader international appreciation and to enable readers to access material from a market leader.

We are also grateful to several organisations in the UK that have helped us deepen our treatment of a number of issues which we introduced into the first edition. Important changes have taken place in the UK during the past five years and these are reflected in an expansion of our concern for human resources management, change management, workplace productivity and the dramatic growth in public-private partnerships. Particular thanks go to Karen Gunther of Sun Life of Canada (UK) Limited, a prominent life assurance and pensions provider, and Ruth Saunders of Diageo plc, one of the world's leading premium drinks businesses, for allowing us to incorporate case studies of their in-house activities. Finally, we should like to thank Dr Roine Leiringer for his input on public-private partnerships, drawing as it does from his doctoral research in this area.

We trust this second edition of *Total Facilities Management* will go some way towards satisfying a market need for balanced guidance based on best practice underpinned by robust theory. If it does, it will demonstrate the important connection between research and practice, as well as offering something for everyone with a professional interest in facilities management.

Brian Atkin   *Adrian Brooks*
Reading   London

Introduction

Managing non-core business services enables an organisation to function at its most efficient and effective level. Implicit in this management role are the issues of customer satisfaction and best value. The focus for these issues is facilities management, which has traditionally been seen as the poor relation of the main real estate and construction disciplines. The significance of facilities management is now recognised and this book offers a progressive look at how facilities management applies to organisations of all kinds. The book contains many examples of how facilities can be better managed; these are largely derived from practices known to work well, although the approach is not intended to be prescriptive.

The organisation

This book is directed at organisations within both the public and private sectors. The types of organisation addressed might therefore range from colleges to entertainment complexes, from manufacturing companies to airports. The structure, management and accommodation of these organisations will vary widely; nevertheless, the information contained in this book is intended to have a correspondingly wide application. It is necessary, of course, for each organisation to consider the relevance to itself, its sector and its country of each of the points raised. Thus, where specific public sector regulations, or UK and European legislation, are referred to, it is the principles embodied within that legislation that should be noted if the legislation itself is not directly applicable.

The customer

In the broadest sense, the customer is the client organisation acting as a purchaser of services. These will sometimes be procured in-house and sometimes from external providers. Although the distinction between purchaser and provider is more obvious in the case of external provision, it is important that the same distinction is recognised within in-house provision. The customer in this instance might be an internal department being served by the organisation's facilities management team, with a financial exchange between the two different cost centres. The relationship between the two parties therefore remains a formal one requiring guidelines and procedures for its formulation and implementation.

In most organisations, customers will therefore be the organisation's employees and constituent departments, as the principal building users. In some, such as leisure centres or department stores, the external user of the organisation's facilities becomes an additional type of customer whose needs must be considered within facilities management planning and operation. This book generally refers to the former type of customer (internal user), with these users typically providing the interface between the external user and the facilities management service providers.

Abbreviations

B2B	business to business
B2C	business to consumer
BIFM	British Institute of Facilities Management
BPR	business process re-engineering
CAFM	computer aided facilities management
CCT	compulsory competitive tendering
CCTV	closed circuit television
CDM	Construction (Design and Management) Regulations 1994
CIOB	Chartered Institute of Building
CIPS	Chartered Institute of Purchasing and Supply
COSHH	Control of Substances Hazardous to Health Regulations 1988
CPD	continuing (or continuous) professional development
CSF	critical success factor
DBFO	design, build, finance and operate
EBITDA	earnings before interest, taxes, depreciation and amortisation
EC	European Commission
EU	European Union
EVA	earned value added
FM	facilities management
HRM	human resources management
HSE	Health and Safety Executive
ICF	informed (or intelligent) client function
IFMA	International Facility Management Association
ICT	information and communications technology
ISO	International Organization for Standardization
JCT	Joint Contracts Tribunal
KPI	key performance indicator
M&E	mechanical and electrical
NEBOSH	National Examinations Board in Occupational Safety and Health
OJEC	Official Journal of the European Communities
PACE	Property Advisers to the Civil Estate
PDA	personal digital assistant
PEST	political, economic, social and technological
PFI	private finance initiative
PPE	personal protective equipment
PPM	planned preventive maintenance
PPP	public-private partnership
QA	quality assurance

RIDDOR	Reporting of Injuries, Diseases and Dangerous Occurrences Regulations 1995
SBS	sick building syndrome
SLA	service level agreement
SMEs	small and medium sized enterprises
SWOT	strengths, weaknesses, opportunities and threats
TFM	total facilities management
TUPE	Transfer of Undertakings (Protection of Employment) Regulations 1981

1 An Introduction to Facilities Management

Key issues

The following issues are covered in this chapter.

- There are a number of definitions of facilities management. One that is commonly used is 'an integrated approach to operating, maintaining, improving and adapting the buildings and infrastructure of an organisation in order to create an environment that strongly supports the primary objectives of that organisation'.

- In any discussion of facilities management it is, however, necessary to stress the importance of integrative, interdependent disciplines whose overall purpose is to support an organisation in the pursuit of its (business) objectives.

- The proper application of facilities management techniques enables organisations to provide the right environment for conducting their core business on a cost-effective and best value basis.

- If buildings and other facilities are not managed, they can begin to impact upon an organisation's performance. Conversely, buildings and facilities have the potential to enhance performance by contributing towards the provision of the optimum working and business environment.

- In practice, facilities management can cover a wide range of services including real estate management, financial management, change management, human resources management, health and safety and contract management, in addition to building maintenance, domestic services (such as cleaning and security) and utilities supplies.

- There is no universal approach to managing facilities. Each organisation – even within the same sector – will have different needs. Understanding those needs is the key to effective facilities management measured in terms of providing best value.

- Quality of service or performance is a critical factor in any definition of value, and the relationship between quality and cost or price has to be better understood in this respect.

- Cost savings cannot be looked at in isolation from value. Organisations must be able to demonstrate what they are getting for their money and should not assume that paying less today is proof of better value for money.

- The many risks involved in the search for best value should be recognised and transferred to those who are able to manage them effectively. This means that organisations should examine all options carefully and adopt those that are most likely to achieve best value.

Background

As recently as forty years ago there was only fleeting mention of facilities management. Buildings were maintained, serviced and cleaned: that was largely it. A united concept was far from broad acceptance in the real estate (or property management) sector. Few common procedures were in circulation and it was left to innovative organisations – many of them in the fast-growing banking, telecommunications and media sectors – to devise ways of effectively managing their buildings and burgeoning portfolios. Since then facilities management has not only emerged as a service sector in its own right, it has helped to establish a new professional discipline with its own codes, standards and technical vocabulary. This introductory chapter sets the scene, by discussing the importance of facilities to an organisation (acting as client) and how approaches to facilities management can differ between organisations, even within the same sector. There is no single formulation of facilities management that will fit all situations. Nonetheless, the concept of the informed client function is common to all situations and is described and discussed in this chapter. It is a theme that runs throughout this book, reflecting a deliberate focus on the client organisation, its values, culture and needs. The reader is introduced to the necessity of securing best value in the provision of services and is acquainted with some of the attendant risks – more are to be found listed in the appendices. The context for facilities management is first described and an overview follows in the form of a simple functional model. This is developed in the text to show the distinction between core and non-core business – something that is essential to understanding the correct focus for facilities management.

Rationale for facilities management

Most buildings represent substantial investments for organisations and usually have to accommodate and support a range of activities, taking into account competing needs. Within those activities is the organisation's core business, for which an appropriate environment must be created in buildings that may not have been designed for the purposes for which they are now used. Yet, no matter how well focused an organisation might be on its core business, it cannot lose sight of the supporting services – the non-core business. The relationship between the two is shown in Fig. 1.1.

Organisations may have already considered the distinction between their core business and non-core business (such as security, payroll or cleaning) as part of the drive to deliver customer satisfaction and achieve best value.

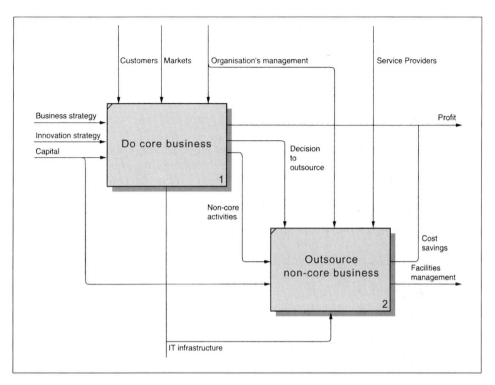

Fig. 1.1   Basic relationship between core and non-core business.

Since running costs account for a significant part of annual expenditure, there is bound to be pressure to look for savings in non-core business areas. Cutting operating budgets may be financially expedient, but may not favour the organisation's long-term development. Since the running of an organisation involves complex, coordinated processes and activities, it is necessary to take an integrated view. A piecemeal approach to cutting costs is unlikely to produce the required savings and may impair the organisation's ability to deliver high-quality services. For this and other reasons, we can begin to see why facilities management is a more powerful concept than real estate (or property) management, because it takes a holistic view of the dynamics of the workplace – between people and processes and between people and their environment.

Facilities management can therefore be summarised as creating an environment that is conducive to carrying out the organisation's primary operations, taking an integrated view of the services infrastructure, and using this to deliver customer satisfaction and best value through support for and enhancement of the core business. We can develop this definition to describe facilities management as something that will:

● Support people in their work and in other activities
● Enhance individual well-being
● Enable the organisation to deliver effective and responsive services

- Sweat the physical assets, that is, make them highly cost effective
- Allow for future change in the use of space
- Provide competitive advantage to the organisation's core business
- Enhance the organisation's culture and image

Defining facilities management

Facilities management has traditionally been regarded as the poor relation within the real estate, architecture, engineering and construction (AEC) professions. This is because it was seen in the old-fashioned sense of caretaking, cleaning, repairs and maintenance. Nowadays, it covers real estate management, financial management, change management, human resources management, health and safety and contract management, in addition to building and engineering services maintenance, domestic services and utilities supplies. These last three responsibilities are the most visible. The others are subtler, although of no less importance. For facilities management to be effective, both the 'hard' issues, such as financial regulation, and the 'soft' issues, such as managing people, have to be considered.

The International Facility Management Association (www.ifma.org) defines facility[1] management as 'a profession that encompasses multiple disciplines to ensure functionality of the built environment by integrating people, place, process and technology'. This definition clearly illustrates the holistic nature of the discipline and interdependence of multiple factors in its success. Elsewhere, the British Institute of Facilities Management (www.bifm.org.uk) promotes the development of facilities management as a critical, professional and strategic business discipline.

An oft-cited definition of facilities management is provided by Barrett and Baldry (2003) who see it as 'an integrated approach to operating, maintaining, improving and adapting the buildings and infrastructure of an organisation in order to create an environment that strongly supports the primary objectives of that organisation'. They continue by reminding us that 'the breadth and scope of facilities management are not constrained by the physical characteristics of buildings. For many organisations the effectiveness and behaviour patterns of the workforce and the effectiveness of their information technology and communication systems are of considerable importance and the profession of facilities management continues to evolve to reflect this.' Whatever is adopted as a definition, either in this book or by practitioners communicating with their clients and customers, it should stress the importance of integrative, interdependent disciplines whose overall purpose is to support an organisation in the pursuit of its (business) objectives.

---

[1] The word 'facility' is used instead of 'facilities' in some parts of the world. Whilst the authors appreciate the distinction that other authors and authorities might attach to the former, we consider such distinction largely a matter of individual preference.

Approaches to facilities management

Organisations may not be aware of the extent to which value for money in facilities management can be improved – the search for best value. This suggests that it is not the outcome that needs to be scrutinised, but the decision-making that leads to it and the assumptions upon which it is based – see Fig. 1.2.

There are common themes and approaches to facilities management, regardless of the size and location of buildings, although these may not necessarily result in common solutions to problems. In some cases, estates-related and facilities services are contracted out – a form of outsourcing – and in others retained in-house for good reasons in each case. There are also many organisations that operate what might be described as a mixed economy, where some services, even the same services, are partially outsourced as well as being retained in-house. Whichever course of action has been taken, the primary concern is the basis for the decision. Where the organisation's decision has been arrived at for entirely proper reasons, such as demonstrating better value for money from one approach as opposed to the other, facilities management can be regarded as working effectively.

Informed client function

Organisations need to act as informed or 'intelligent' clients if they are to be sure of delivering customer satisfaction and achieving best value. The informed (or intelligent) client function (ICF) is a requisite irrespective of how facilities are procured. The following outlines the scope of the ICF.

- Understanding the organisation, its culture, its customers and needs
- Understanding and specifying service requirements and targets
- Brokering the service amongst stakeholders
- Managing the implementation of outsourcing
- Minimising risk to the organisation's future – risk management
- Agreeing monitoring standards
- Managing contractors and monitoring their performance
- Benchmarking performance of outsourced service(s)
- Surveying users for satisfaction with the service
- Providing relevant management reports to users
- Reviewing service levels/requirements to ensure they still meet user needs
- Developing, with service providers, delivery strategies for services
- Agreeing, with service providers, changes to service requirements
- Maintaining the ability to re-tender, as and when required
- Understanding the facilities management market and how it is developing
- Undertaking strategic planning
- Safeguarding public funds, where relevant
- Developing in-house skills through education, training and continuing professional development (CPD)

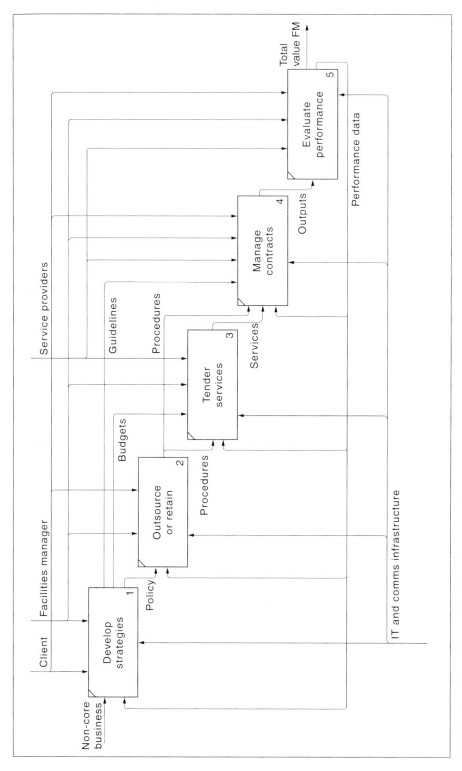

Fig. 1.2   Overview of the top-level functions within facilities management.

Concept of best value

Value for money is a term long used to express satisfaction with the cost of a good or service of given quality. The term 'best value' extends the concept of value for money to imply a need to strive continually for something superior at the lowest practicable cost.

The 'best value decision' is generally cited as the determinant of whether to outsource a service or to retain it in-house. Despite this, many organisations are likely to be unaware of the extent to which they can improve value for money. Value is about the relationship between cost or price, and quality or performance. However, value for money is often simply equated with achieving a reduction in cost. Organisations may believe they are achieving value for money if they are paying less for a given service this year compared with the previous year. Whereas cost is easier to measure, value for money is concerned with quality of a service and the economy, efficiency and effectiveness with which it is delivered. Organisations should therefore set themselves cost and quality objectives for the management of their facilities, the cost objective only taking priority where financial constraints are severe.

When choosing options for service provision and service providers, organisations therefore need to include an assessment not only of cost implications but also of quality (see Chapter 6 for cost and quality evaluation and the cost/quality mechanism). They should choose the approach and service provision that offer best value, not simply lowest cost, and measure performance against both cost and quality. Benchmarking can help in checking performance (see Chapter 14).

Normally, the achievement of best value is demonstrated by acceptance of the lowest tender price in a competition where all other criteria (quality, performance, terms and conditions) are equal. Best value can also be achieved through collaborative arrangements with suppliers and service providers. Economies of scale offered by bulk purchasing of utility supplies – see below and Chapter 12 – are an obvious example. An additional benefit from collaboration is that risks are also shared.

Supplier relationships

There are a number of options open to organisations beyond simply entering into a price competition each time a new supply or service is required or a contract is renewed. For instance, collaboration with other organisations can often enable more favourable terms to be leveraged from suppliers, because negotiation and procurement powers are improved. In fact, there is a wide range of possible relationships from which to choose the one(s) that fit the requirements of the (client) organisation.

At one end of the scale, both client organisation and supplier may be concerned primarily with optimising their immediate interests without making long-term commitments. Such relationships are typical of many commodity markets. At the other end, both parties may look for a long-term, cooperative partnership. The type of relationship that will produce the greatest benefits will depend upon circumstances such as the nature of the market and the demands of the service to be provided. Choosing the right relationship with suppliers and managing it well requires skill, judgement and experience.

The best contribution that organisations can make to the raising of supplier competitiveness is to manage their own procurement intelligently. An important element of this will be to combine competition and cooperation to optimal effect. Mutually satisfactory relationships between buyers and sellers are fundamental to successful procurement activity. Yet, whatever the chosen relationship with suppliers, organisations should avoid taking an adversarial or unaccommodating approach. Relationships should be as open and supportive as possible – given the need to maintain competition and to treat suppliers even-handedly – and should be based on mutual respect. Organisations should recognise that it is in their interests to help suppliers develop in ways that make them better able to provide what is required by the organisation and to do so to the desired quality and at a competitive price. The relationship should be one that encourages continual improvement.

Sourcing services based on partnering or partnership has become a popular (even established) basis for relationships with suppliers. Partnering is another type of arrangement for procuring services that offers the chance to develop a strong relationship with a service provider who can ensure that best value is achieved whilst risks are better managed at the same time. Customers and suppliers decide to collaborate closely in order to deliver requirements such as cost reduction, improved quality or innovative solutions, rather than to conduct their business at arm's length. Essentially, partnering is acceptable in terms of accountability – particularly important in the public sector – if the following apply:

1. There is competition at the outset in the choice of partners and periodic re-competition.
2. The partnering arrangement is established on the basis of clearly defined needs and objectives over a specified period.
3. There are specific and measurable milestones for improved performance as part of the contract in order to demonstrate, through the use of benchmarking (see Chapter 14), that best value is being achieved.

Partnering is likely to bring greater benefits than other approaches in certain circumstances, for example, where there is a poorly developed or highly specialised market or where the requirements of the purchaser are complex and continuously developing. Purchasing (or procurement) managers should consider carefully whether or not a partnering arrangement would best suit the needs of their organisation in each particular case – see Chapter 12 for further discussion of partnering.

Matters of risk

In managing any organisation, there are innumerable risks involved in meeting business objectives. These risks have the potential to hinder, even negate, attempts at achieving best value. Table 1.1 indicates some risks that

Table 1.1   Risks faced by organisations in their facilities management.

1. Inadequately resourced or inexperienced client function (Chapters 1, 2, 13, 15 and Appendix B).

2. Inadequate planning of the implementation – no analysis of implementation or allocation of related responsibilities (Chapters 2, 3, 5, 6, 7, 13 and Appendix D).

3. Misapplication of Transfer of Undertakings (Protection of Employment) Regulations 1981 (TUPE) (Chapter 5).

4. Poor relationship between service provider and contract manager (especially if the latter was once involved with preparing an in-house tender) (Chapters 6 and 13).

5. Conflicts of interest when dealing with in-house tenders, arising from inadequate split between purchaser and provider personnel (Chapters 6 and 7).

6. Unclear or imprecise roles, responsibilities and targets for effective teamworking (Chapters 3, 5, 6, 7 and 13).

7. Possible loss of control over the facilities management function and ownership of, and access to, documents and knowledge (Chapter 6).

8. Lack of standard forms of facilities management contracts or inadequate conditions of contract (Chapter 6).

9. Inappropriate allocation of risks and rewards between the client organisation and service providers (Chapters 6, 7 and 15).

10. Inadequate definition of the scope and content of services (Chapter 8).

11. Lack of consideration of all stakeholders in the facilities management sphere (Chapter 8).

12. Specifications that are over-prescriptive and/or concentrate on procedures not outputs (Chapter 8).

13. Stakeholders 'gold plating' their requirements (Chapter 8).

14. Poorly controlled changes to user requirements (Chapters 8 and 13).

15. Excessive monitoring of contractor performance (Chapter 8).

16. Absence of, or poor system for, providing incentives for performance (Chapter 8).

17. Inflexible contracts unable to accommodate changes in user requirements during the contract and work outside specification (Chapter 8).

18. Failure to take account of relevant health and safety legislation at the correct time, leading to excessive cost later (Chapter 9).

19. Redundancy in the supply chain where cost is added without necessarily adding value (Chapter 12).

20. Poor bundling/grouping of activities to be outsourced (Chapter 11).

21. Absence of shared ownership of outcomes (Chapter 12).

Table 1.1   Cont'd.

22. Poor cashflow position for client organisation and for service providers (Chapter 13).

23. Financial failure of chosen service provider during contract period (Chapter 13).

24. Absence of benchmarks of cost and quality against which to measure performance and improvement (Chapter 14).

25. Lack of education and training in facilities management (Chapter 16).

26. Fraud or irregularities in the award and management of contracts (Appendix B).

organisations face in their facilities management. The relevant chapters of this book, in which the underlying issues are considered, are indicated in the table. Some of these risks may be easier to address than others. In certain cases, organisations will need to acquire new skills or insights into how problems can be tackled.

In pursuing more efficient and effective facilities management, organisations should also be aware of the opportunities that stem from a greater awareness of potential risks. To a large extent, the opportunities mirror the risks and counter their influence, as Table 1.2 shows.

Table 1.2   Opportunities arising from a greater awareness of potential risks.

1. Enhancing client capability and quality of provision, and proper assessment of requirements for the scope and content of services (Chapters 3 and 5).

2. Identification and allocation of risks on a rational basis to help clarify relationships between contractors and facilities managers (Chapters 3, 6 and 11).

3. Proper separation of duties between purchasers and providers (Chapters 3, 6 and 7).

4. Clear responsibilities and targets for effective teamworking (Chapter 5).

5. Proper contract documentation with appropriate conditions of contract for both in-house and outsourced services (Chapters 6 and 13).

6. Proper allocation of risks and rewards (Chapter 3).

7. Improved response to customer and market requirements (Chapters 2 and 3).

8. Improved performance with proper incentivisation (Chapters 6, 7, 12 and 13).

9. Health and safety legislation incorporated into facilities management policies at the appropriate time (Chapter 9).

10. Shared ownership of outcomes (Chapters 6 and 7).

11. Proper monitoring of contract performance (Chapters 6, 7 and 13).

12. Improved cashflow forecasting and budgeting (Chapters 2 and 3).

13. Opportunity to build up quality and cost benchmarks against which to measure performance and improvements (Chapter 14).

14. Properly focused education and training for in-house personnel in facilities management matters (Chapters 5, 7 and 16).

15. Proper assessment of activities to be grouped/bundled for outsourcing (Chapters 6 and 8).

16. Efficiency gains enabling resources to be released for the improvement or expansion of core-business provision (Chapter 2).

Conclusions

Facilities management is about providing support to an organisation's core business. To benefit most, organisations need to understand that they must be informed clients in managing their facilities. This requires a focus on service delivery that provides customer satisfaction and best value in an environment in which risks abound. Effective facilities management comes from being able to devise and implement practices that reduce or eliminate the risks and that add value to the core business.

CHECKLIST

This checklist is intended to assist with the management review and action planning process.

		Yes	No	Action required
1.	Does facilities management have a sufficiently high profile in the organisation, i.e. is it connected to the business objectives of the organisation?	☐	☐	☐
2.	Has senior management articulated a workable definition of facilities management?	☐	☐	☐
3.	Could the organisation be considered an informed client?	☐	☐	☐
4.	Is the organisation able to determine whether or not it is achieving best value in relation to its facilities management services, however provided?	☐	☐	☐
5.	Are relationships with suppliers considered on a needs basis or is a blanket approach to procurement adopted?	☐	☐	☐
6.	Has the organisation undertaken a formal risk assessment of its facilities management and then implemented a risk response method?	☐	☐	☐

2 Developing a Strategy for Facilities Management

Key issues

The following issues are covered in this chapter.

- The development of a facilities management strategy is a project in its own right and must be undertaken rigorously using appropriate techniques and tools. The organisation should follow three stages – analysis, solution and implementation – to produce an effective strategy for the management of its facilities:
  - *analysis* – all relevant facts are assembled, including the organisation's objectives, needs and policies, a review of resources, processes, systems and the physical assets, together with their attributes in terms of space, function and utilisation
  - *solution* – criteria for judging options are defined and evaluated against the objectives of the organisation to produce the facilities management strategy
  - *implementation* – this completes the strategic planning and development process through the establishment of an implementation plan that incorporates the key elements of procurement, mobilisation, training, communication, review and feedback.

- On completion, the facilities management strategy should become an integral part of the organisation's strategic and operating plans. The facilities management strategy document should incorporate:
  - financial objectives
  - goals and critical success factors (in terms of quality, cost and time objectives)
  - targets for potential efficiency gains and quality improvements
  - customer-focus strategy
  - technical strategy
  - in-house/outsourcing strategy
  - procurement strategy
  - human resources plan
  - business processes
  - methodology for managing change
  - information and communications technology (ICT) strategy.

- The organisation needs to see its facilities management strategy as the cornerstone of its accommodation (or space) strategy, not as an adjunct to it.

- Facilities management needs to encompass a diverse range of issues that impinge on the success of the organisation's core business. As such it will have to base much of its decision-making on the expectation that change is a constant feature of the workplace today and into the future.

- The rise in the use of ICT and the integration of other forms of technology into buildings – especially 'smart' sensors and controls – imply that facilities management strategies must be tied directly to the organisation's ICT strategy, as well as its business strategy.

Introduction

There are basically two ways of looking at the management of facilities. The first is to consider what must be done to maintain current services or even to improve upon them – a largely short-term perspective. The second adopts a longer-term view that takes into account the potential changes likely to be faced by the organisation into the future and how these will impact upon the services required. Clearly, a desire to improve current service provision is not wrong, but does overlook the inevitability of change occurring and perhaps invalidating earlier decisions. Facilities and the demands placed upon them are unlikely to remain static in all but the most stable of organisations, which is why an approach must be devised to manage the process of moving from where the organisation is today to where it wishes to be at some point in the future. In other words, a strategy is employed to deal with a dynamic situation in which major business decisions – perhaps affecting the very viability of the organisation – are connected with the organisation's existing facilities' provision and forecast requirements. The approach is implicitly top-down, otherwise current operations would be effectively dictating the organisation's business development – a sure route to failure.

The starting point for managing the facilities is, therefore, the organisation's business plan together with its accommodation (or space) strategy. Combined, they embody the goals of the organisation and make clear what is needed to support the organisation's development. Naturally, these key documents should be kept up-to-date so they are always available for assessing the nature and level of services support required by the organisation. This chapter reviews the approach to developing a strategy for facilities management that will reflect the organisation's business objectives, needs and policies, as well as the practicalities imposed by its accommodation (or space). It will consider the successive stages in the process and reveal that a wide range of techniques and tools are at the disposal of managers to help them in their work. In this respect, the approach is one of applying accepted theories of strategic business planning and development to the facilities management 'problem'.

Developing a facilities management strategy

In order to manage facilities efficiently and effectively, robust strategies must be developed within the context of the organisation's strategic business plan and accommodation (or space) strategy. These should include development of strategic objectives and a business plan for the facilities management function, with proper reference to the organisation's business plan and accommodation strategy in which it might be contained. A business plan for facilities management should have the following goals.

- Consider the needs of the organisation, differentiating between core and non-core business activities.
- Identify and establish effective and manageable processes for meeting those needs.
- Establish the appropriate resource needs for providing services, whether obtained internally or externally.
- Identify the source of funds to finance the strategy and its implications.
- Establish a budget, not only for the short term, but also to achieve best value over the longer term.
- Recognise that management of information is the key to providing a basis for effective control of facilities management.

This process of developing a facilities management strategy is illustrated in Fig. 2.1 and shows three main stages with their contributory elements. The three main stages in the development of a strategy are:

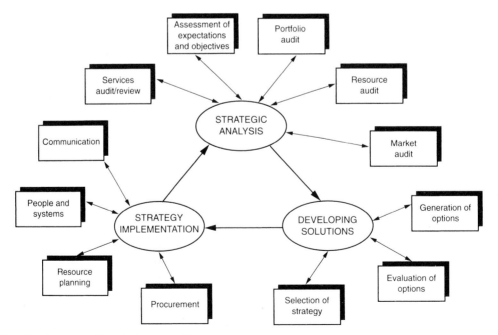

Fig. 2.1   Process of developing a facilities management strategy.

1. Strategic analysis
2. Developing solutions
3. Strategy implementation

Table 2.1 presents possible management techniques and tools that are available.

Strategic analysis of facilities' requirements

The aim of the analysis is to establish a thorough understanding of the present state of the organisation's real estate and its approach to facilities management. This means assembling all relevant facts including:

- Organisational objectives, needs and policies (from the organisation's strategic plan).
- Physical assets and space utilisation achieved (from the organisation's accommodation (or space) strategy).
- Review of resources, processes and systems to provide a broad picture of the current provision of services.
- Detailed breakdown of costs involved in the form of a cost analysis.

Services audit and review

The organisation should be in the position of having already identified and differentiated between its core and non-core business activities. This differentiation is necessary to ensure that effort can be concentrated where it is needed most, that is in developing the best working and business environment. General examples of non-core business activities, in addition to those mentioned in Chapter 1, are catering, printing, vehicle maintenance and conference facilities. Important in this respect is to appreciate that since no two organisations are the same, there is the likelihood of some organisations (of an apparently similar nature) regarding certain activities as core business, whilst others would class the same activities as non-core. It is not for the authors to say which activities are core and which are non-core business. These are matters for the senior management of the organisation and, in most instances, are likely to be decisions upon which the future of the organisation is predicated.

The organisation should critically review the operation of services provided by considering:

- *Policy* – examining existing policies in terms of corporate guidelines and standards, performance standards, quality assurance, health and safety and other statutory requirements, human resources, financial and other approvals.
- *Processes and procedures* – defining business processes, including budgeting, procurement, purchasing approvals and payments.

Table 2.1   Techniques and tools to support development of a facilities management strategy.

Development stage	Phase	Technique or tool
Strategic analysis	Services audit/review	Benchmarking
	Assessment of expectations and objectives	Political, economic, social and technological (PEST) analysis Strengths, weaknesses, opportunities and threats (SWOT) analysis If . . . then analysis Mega trends Quantitative analysis Scenario analysis
	Portfolio audit	Space analysis Real estate register Maintenance plan Risk assessment
	Resource audit	People and skills profiling Service provider audit (existing internal arrangements) Business process analysis
	Market audit	Service providers (external) Real estate availability Market trends
Developing solutions	Generating options	Outsource modelling Business process re-engineering (BPR)
	Evaluating options	Maintenance plan Risk analysis Stakeholder analysis Cost-benefit analysis Lifecycle cost appraisal Feasibility analysis
	Selecting option	Optimisation model Sensitivity analysis
Strategy implementation	People and systems	Change management Training and personnel development Business process re-engineering (BPR)
	Communication	Organisation's intranet Newsletters, noticeboards and memoranda Workshops and seminars
	Resource planning	Project planning, scheduling and control Resource levelling/optimisation
	Procurement/purchasing	Service provider selection Market testing Benchmarking

- *Service delivery* – auditing all aspects of the real estate and facilities management strategy and service delivery, including relationships with customers (especially quality, cost and time objectives).

In carrying out a review of the above aspects, the organisation should make use of benchmarking (see Chapter 14) as a method or tool for measuring current levels of performance and achievement. Measuring a process is also an aid to understanding it, as well as offering valuable insights into how it might be improved.

Assessment of expectations and objectives

The organisation should be able to define its expectations and objectives for its facilities with relative ease. For instance, it might aspire to expand its core business into areas for which different kinds of facilities and services will be required to those currently provided. It would be useful, therefore, to broaden discussion to identify potential extensions and additions, as well as noting where closure of business operations is necessary or likely. These objectives should be embodied in a formal statement as part of the organisation's overall mission statement, or linked to it, and should relate to the business needs as identified in the strategic (business) plan.

Portfolio audit

Implicit in an audit of real estate and related assets is consideration of the necessity for and provision of support services, maintenance plan(s) and an assessment of risks. The organisation also needs to consider its space utilisation and procedures for charging for the use of space. In itself, this kind of auditing can succeed in raising awareness of how space is being used and how economical that use is. However, there is the danger that perceptions of space utilisation will vary within the organisation and across regions, with the result that what is regarded in one location as the norm is seen either as extravagant or inadequate by those elsewhere.

Organisations operating across regions – for example Scandinavia and the UK – are bound to notice differences in the allocation of space per worker. The same company operating in Stockholm and London would likely record quite different figures for space allocation. British workers, because of their acceptance of higher densities, would see their Swedish counterparts as having generous, even too much, space; the Swedes would disagree. Climate and culture can have a significant influence on the amount and quality of space expected by workers. Attempts to normalise standards across regions is likely to prove counterproductive. With the emergence of large regional markets – even global markets – problems can so easily arise from cultural differences, and local customs and practice. Understanding that there are going to be differences – and that such a situation is normal – is a way to avoid problems.

Space is rarely provided freely, even if present use suggests otherwise. An evaluation of the true cost of providing space, that is, the cost of providing support services, must always form part of any assessment. This will help to establish which spaces are providing best value and which are not. In this connection, it is necessary to look at the value (to the organisation) of activities against the cost of locating them. For example, it would make little economic sense to house a printing press – no matter how convenient it is – in prime real estate that attracts a premium rent. In such a case, relocation should be actively considered.

Practice Point 2.1   Spaced out.

Key-point: the organisation must have an up-to-date picture of its use of space and the extent to which it is satisfying customer needs.

When a health care facility decided to audit its use of space and establish a basis for charging, some departments expressed concern. In one case, a department felt that it was paying far too much for the space it had and was determined to seek a reduction. In another case, the department was complaining that its rooms were overcrowded and lacked certain amenities. Worse, it might have to restrict the number of patients it could see, which would lead to longer waiting lists. The case was strengthened by the department's threat to go public on the length of its waiting list and the associated risks to proper medical care and attention. These matters were resolved only after management was able to make an informed decision based on an up-to-date statement of the use of space, the need for space and the availability and cost of space elsewhere. The subsequent circulation of a space plan and analysis helped to make everyone aware of who had what, as well as helping to pinpoint priority needs for changes to space allocation.

Resource audit

Part of this top-level analysis should include a review of personnel employed in the provision of facilities and support services. This will, of necessity, cover both in-house and contracted out (outsourced) arrangements. The organisation should also review the extent of available human resources, information about which should be available from its human resources planning (see Chapter 5). Additionally, the organisation must analyse the processes that are contained within its facilities to determine, amongst other things, patterns of use, areas of intensive use and areas of under-use. Methods for determining these factors are increasingly supported by ICT, but should always be based on *good* science and ethical practice. Many organisations now routinely survey their facilities using CCTV for reasons of security, and general health and safety. When used for the right motives, this kind of technology can provide proof of a particular need or the lack of it.

The resource audit should concentrate on:

- *People* – determine skills profiles and identify gaps
- *Providers* – assess capability, scope and terms of engagement
- *Systems* – establish the status of all procedures and technology by process analysis and systems audit

Market audit

The organisation should consider undertaking periodic audits to establish the state of the real estate market (should acquisition or disposal become an option) and the position regarding service providers (see Chapter 11) in all the categories affected. It is possible this kind of information will be available from market audits carried out when preparing the accommodation (or space) strategy and from the valuation of assets for financial accounting purposes.

Developing solutions

Once information from the analysis stage has been assembled, a robust and structured approach to the interpretation of the information must be adopted. It is essential that the interpretation of information derived from the analysis is open, without bias and allows new ideas and innovative solutions to flow. The recommended approach is:

- Generation of options
- Assembly of criteria for evaluating options
- Evaluation of options
- Selection of preferred option, that is, the organisation's actual facilities management strategy

Generation of options

There are many ways in which organisations can establish options, for example, consultation with stakeholders and invitations to external experts. The strategic analysis stage should have highlighted precisely how well the organisation's accommodation or space and other attributes of its facilities match up to its needs. This means that options should be considered for bridging identified gaps as well as for aligning innovative solutions with present and future needs. Creativity is a useful commodity to have at this stage and should even extend to 'thinking the unthinkable'. Important also is the need to avoid prejudging the merits of any option as this runs the risk of corrupting the process: evaluation should be left until later. If an option proves unworthy then that will become evident later, so little purpose is served here in trying to complicate matters.

Criteria for evaluating options

Before any attempt is made to consider the relative merits of options, it is essential to identify and agree the criteria for judging them. Moreover, there needs to be a very clear separation between the assembly of criteria and their application to options to ensure objectivity. All criteria must, however, include assessments of best value and likely customer satisfaction. Options should be evaluated consistently against the set criteria to ensure objectivity, parity and accountability. Criteria should therefore be explicit and open to review. Sometimes the options will not be mutually exclusive and, on occasion, senior managers may find that a combination of two or more, or a variation in one, provides a better way forward. If this does happen, it may be evidence of a failure in the 'generation of options' stage and worth noting for future occasions.

Selection of the preferred option(s)

In many respects, this is a fairly straightforward matter. If the tasks in the preceding stages have been undertaken rigorously the preferred option or options will be clear enough. Should the position be otherwise, it is likely that a failure either in identifying relevant criteria or in applying them correctly is to blame. At the conclusion of this stage, a facilities management strategy can be reflected both in the organisation's overall strategic plan and in its accommodation (or space) strategy. The strategy should contain the following elements:

- Financial objectives
- Goals and critical success factors (in terms of quality, cost and time objectives)
- Targets for potential efficiency gains and quality improvements
- Customer requirements
- Technical issues
- Risks and areas of uncertainty
- In-house and outsourcing strategy (see Chapter 3)
- Methodology for managing change (see Chapter 4)
- Human resources plan (see Chapter 5)
- Procurement strategy (see Chapter 6)
- Business processes
- Supporting ICT strategy

Strategy implementation

Once established, broad policy statements should be developed into operational plans and implemented through a process that is capable of managing change. A change management process should therefore be instigated (see Chapter 4), incorporating best practice in human resources management (see Chapter 5). The implementation plan should include timetables, milestones and details of the organisation's risk management as it relates to its facilities. The risks to successful implementation should be identified and responsibilities for managing them assigned (see below for an approach). The plan should encompass people and systems, communication, resource planning and procurement, each of which is discussed below. Senior management must be committed to the successful implementation of the resultant strategy. Where this involves the decision to outsource, attention should be paid to the demands of the informed client function – discussed in Chapter 1.

A risk assessment should be performed to identify risks arising from the implementation of outsourcing, particularly the impact on core operations, and how to address them. Responsibilities for dealing with them should then be assigned on the basis of a full understanding of the ability of the party (or individual) to handle the risk(s) in question. Assignment of risk without regard to the capacity of a party or individual to handle it can lead to increased exposure for the organisation, when the objective is to mitigate or eliminate risk.

Typical of the risks that can occur are the following:

- Unclear definition of roles and responsibilities
- A timetable that is too demanding
- Insufficient time allowed for contract negotiation
- Insufficient expertise in the negotiation of contracts and drafting of service level agreements (SLAs)
- Lack of definition of requirements before contract award
- Too short a transition period between the award and start of contract

Whilst we have yet to consider the position regarding outsourced services, there are some issues that need to be addressed. For example, the effect of a major breakdown in a key service area could threaten continuity of operations for the organisation and should be examined at this point. Contingency plans must be drawn up and validated. In some cases, it may be necessary to introduce trials or another kind of 'run through' to test the efficacy of the proposed arrangements and their ability to cope with various eventualities.

The organisation should also plan and run through the arrangements for managing the transition period. For example, it should plan the handover of information to any newly appointed service providers and other contractors. Sufficient time must be allowed for this activity – two to three months – as this will generally set the tone of the relationship between the organisation and its service providers. The accuracy and completeness of information to be handed over must also be verified.

In the transition period before any new contract starts, the service provider (as contractor) should visit users (the customers) and discuss the new arrangements and what might be expected from them; for example, changed goals and new procedures must be communicated.

People and systems

The most important aspect of an implementation strategy, when bringing about any change, is to carry it through in a controlled way. In order to achieve this, organisations need to develop employees' skills and understanding so that they are fully conversant with the meaning and practice of facilities management. Education and training, together with the mentoring of individuals, will achieve these aims and enhance competence. Close monitoring and control of systems and procedures will help to ensure that these, too, develop in the ways intended. This is not a one-off exercise; there has to be a culture of continual improvement with periodic checks on performance.

Communication

Effective communication between the organisation (acting as an informed client) and service providers is essential to ensure that the implementation of a strategy is both understood and acted upon (see Chapters 1 and 4–6). It is important to involve all stakeholders in the discussion about organisation and structure. Failure to do so is bound to lead to complications later.

A stakeholder is anyone who has a legitimate interest in a business or process; this includes, but is not limited to, customers, employees, statutory authorities, neighbours and the public, to varying extents. Employees need to recognise that facilities management is an especially active process and not one of simply reacting to problems as and when they arise. In organisational terms, this demands a structure that is flat, so that employees with decision-making powers are in close contact with other internal and external users to head off problems before they have the chance to develop. Cultivating relationships is really only possible by communicating clearly and often.

Resources planning

Planning and controlling the use of resources in an efficient and effective manner is a job in its own right. Where organisations are large employers (of either in-house personnel or external service providers), it makes good sense to plan for the optimal use of resources. When management teams are small and the demands on them appear modest, it is still necessary to take formal steps to plan resources. Even the best managers cannot keep everything in their heads, besides which there will be absences when others have to assume responsibility. ICT can help here through the use of low-cost project planning and scheduling software to allocate resources to individual tasks and provide a means for measuring progress and performance. Important in this respect is to avoid unnecessary levels of detail that serve to do little more than show off the features of the software in use.

Procurement

Finally, the point is reached where procurement of services can be considered and, as appropriate, partners can be selected (see Chapters 3, 6, 7, 11 and 12 for a detailed treatment of this subject). Procurement may seem a rather inflated term for what might be seen by some as largely a purchasing decision. The purpose in using the word procurement is to make it clear that we are dealing with a broader set of considerations than the act of obtaining quotations and placing orders. A wide range of issues must be taken into account that, more often than not, requires technical knowledge of the area in question.

Relationships between client organisations and service providers

There will be changes of personnel and other aspects of an organisation's management over time. Arrangements and agreements, with respect to facilities management, may well outlast the terms of employment of key personnel. It is important, therefore, that organisations recognise the need for:

- The purchaser – i.e. the organisation – to be an informed client
- A purchaser–provider relationship to develop between those commissioning the service and service providers (both in-house and outsourced)

In coming to terms with these needs, organisations might benefit from a better understanding of the new tasks that this role as an informed client represents (see Chapter 1). This function will need a significant degree of operational knowledge and experience, not only of the client organisation's own business, but also of the services being provided.

The success of any change initiative in the delivery of services will depend on two main parties:

1. The (client) organisation's representative (facilities manager, estates manager or other senior manager).
2. Service providers, whether internal or external to the client organisation.

Both parties need to share the common objective of delivering best value. To be successful in achieving this goal, the potentially divergent interests of individuals within the two parties also need to be recognised. A cooperative approach, which recognises individuals' interests and aligns efforts with the goals of the organisation, has the potential to deliver the greatest benefit. A cooperative approach (for example, partnering) is also one of the recommended arrangements for managing external service providers (see earlier note in Chapter 1 and Chapter 12; also see Chapter 5 on human resources management implications).

Case study – Developing a strategy

This case study considers how a facilities management consultant worked with a client to increase awareness of the benefits of facilities management and to develop a robust facilities management strategy for the present and the future. The approach involved raising the profile of facilities management within the client organisation and working in partnership to re-engineer and support business processes to enable the client to operate in a strategic and effective way. The case study also considers the need for the facilities management consultant to protect its own business interests, not least to ensure that it is fit to provide the most appropriate service to the client organisation.

External factors leading to a significant drop in the air travel market fuelled the need for a well-known airline to reduce its fixed cost base. The company decided to outsource its maintenance activities, for the majority of its operational portfolio, to a single provider. In so doing, the property function within the airline changed from a large in-house resource of engineers and supervisors to a small number of contract managers. This in turn led to the need for a clear definition of the retained roles, significant changes to the supporting business processes and the replacement of legacy systems with up-to-date ICT that could provide meaningful management information.

Recognising that it was in an entirely new position, both functionally and managerially, the airline decided to enlist the help of an external facilities management consultant. The newly appointed head of facilities was instrumental in this decision. Being new to the organisation, the head of facilities was unfamiliar, as yet, with the resources at his disposal and the precise nature of the task ahead of him. As the projected consultancy work could not be specified in detail, being of an unknown quantity and composition, the company chose to approach four organisations with which it was familiar. There was, therefore, a competitive element, although only among organisations identified by the airline as pre-qualified for the role. The four consultants were asked to tender for a three-year period of consultancy aimed at helping the airline to manage the transitional period within its property function. The successful consultant was selected to manage 10 million sq. ft (900 000 m^2) of buildings and, as part of the restructuring of the airline's property department, it was required to provide a breadth of support services through an expert team of facilities managers, project managers, procurement specialists, contracts managers, electrical and mechanical engineers, building and quantity surveyors, administrative personnel and health and safety specialists.

Facilities management had scarcely been a recognised discipline within the organisation, being considered more as a maintenance function. The nomenclature attached to posts, such as 'head of maintenance', reflected the fact that the requirement to manage facilities, particularly within the wider context of the organisation's overall business needs, was not fully recognised. Similarly, the type of reactive approach that dominated maintenance activities was evidence of a lack of strategic thinking and of a failure to recognise facilities as something more than a cost; that is, to appreciate their ability to add value to the core business.

The profile of facilities management within the organisation was therefore very low and it was this that the consultant set out to address, by educating the client as to the full role of the discipline, what it required of the organisation and what it could offer in return. Part of this education involved the development of the informed client function (ICF), vital if the airline were to stand on its own after the three-year period of support. As things stood, there was essentially no recognition of a client role within services provision. Work was requested and performed on a reactive basis, with no element of strategy or evidence of an overall facilities plan related to wider organisational needs. The property department was used to managing its own labour under this sort of regime, but now line managers were required to be contract managers and had no existing framework for this kind of management.

The airline and the consultant formed a partnership through a framework agreement based on an open-book approach. Remuneration was not linked to output, because it was not clear at the outset what that output should be. Instead, the consultancy and operational services were reimbursed at base costs plus an agreed mark-up. The airline was free to draw on the expertise of the consultant as it found necessary. As we shall see below, although the venture proved to be a success for both parties, the consultant was obliged to protect its own wider business interests as the airline's demands threatened to draw too heavily on the former's resources. The partnership did not involve the sharing of risk and reward, both of these accruing to the airline, but the monitoring and measurement of performance and benefits played a key part in the agreement and the pursuance of common goals was central to its structure. Openness and trust, which are an essential element of partnering, also played a part in this less formal, temporary business partnership.

Outlining what those common goals were was an early challenge. As noted above, neither established personnel at the airline nor the new head of facilities knew what would ultimately be required or desired. It was therefore necessary for the consultant's personnel to work alongside the airline's management to ensure a complete understanding of its business objectives, changing needs and organisational culture. From this it could develop a comprehensive facilities management strategy to suit the company's particular requirements in the specific context of its current and future core business needs.

Current reality also played a part in providing the guidance and impetus for change. When the airline realised that it simply did not have the ability within its current set-up to manage the input of a major contractor, it became obvious that a re-engineering programme would have to be undertaken. In order to allow forward movement, therefore, the consultant adopted a re-engineering approach to the property department's business processes, which had already proved to be unwieldy and based upon a model which had supported a large in-house resource of more than 400 employees. Initially, existing business processes needed to be re-engineered, but subsequently the development of a new process model was required and the design and procurement of a new property management information system.

In the ICT field, therefore, re-engineering involved establishing a central and accessible information system, capable of coordinating the disparate information sources and systems into an intelligible format which could make visible the connections between different elements not only of the facilities management function but also of the overall business. In the human resources management (HRM) field, clarity of role, responsibility and accountability were required, particularly for newly created, or relabelled, positions. Contract managers became senior facilities managers and ultimately property managers, each step involving more than simply a change of title. It was the consultant's role to help the airline perform this initial step in such a way as would ensure that the change was not only sustainable but also incorporated a system capable of continuous adaptation to changing business and economic circumstances.

In parallel with this project, and with other corporate initiatives aimed at restructuring the organisation, was the further definition of the property and facilities function, a facilities management strategy for the airline and, as part of that strategy, the identification of service levels and appropriate service delivery mechanisms. As discussed above, the department's operational managers had found themselves operating in a reactive way, which in turn left them little time to plan strategically with their customers within the airline the direction of their own business and the optimal support for their customers. The consultant quickly adopted a role as a business partner that gave the senior managers some initial 'breathing space' in which the property department's business plan could be developed. This plan reflected their aspirations for the new business. This was a fundamental step, as the facilities management function wanted to bring about significant change in a way that caused the least disruption to the airline's core business. This required the secondment of a number of the consultant's personnel into operational roles while the airline spent time recruiting a number of suitably qualified permanent employees to take over from them. With these front line roles occupied, time was then made available to shape the future business strategy.

A series of collaborative senior management workshops took place, involving personnel from both sides' management teams, through which the open exchange of knowledge and information was enabled and coordinated. By this means, a re-engineering project was initiated and an execution plan prepared. Initially, the project sought to identify goals and objectives together with tangible measures following the *Balanced Scorecard* (Kaplan and Norton, 1996) approach. Once this had been completed, key processes were identified linked to the goals and objectives by these measures. The four key processes were identified as follows:

1. Customer-relationship management
2. Estates-related and facilities management planning
3. Service delivery
4. Service and organisational development

Work progressed through a number of small teams, each led by a senior airline manager, to redesign these processes. Once completed, a clear set of deliverables was defined related to each of these processes:

● Customer property plans
● Customer profiles
● Customer feedback
● Service level agreements
● Service delivery feedback
● Cost and charging
● Property portfolio details
● Property guidance
● Project management framework
● Master schedule
● Low-value catalogue items

Through the development of appropriate key processes and their core deliverables, work was started on the specification of a management information system, the first phase of which was focused on the management and maintenance of the airline's corporate assets.

As noted above, the whole period of change, both prior to and during the consultant's involvement, raised HRM issues. When the new head of facilities came in, personnel were required to reapply for their redefined jobs, where those existed. This action and the general atmosphere of change inevitably made personnel unsettled and anxious about the future. One of the consultant's roles was to use its expertise to manage the process of change within the HRM context on behalf of the airline. In order to do this, the consultant used an input–output model devoid of references to names or existing mechanisms, in order to analyse the revised personnel requirements, both in terms of numbers and roles, without any threat of bias from vested interests. The consultant also became involved in TUPE issues within contracts being procured on the airline's behalf.

Performance was judged annually on the basis of the consultant's costs and the savings that it had delivered to the airline. Each project or initiative was scoped in order to make its success measurable. The incorporation of targets or milestones over the three-year period was considered important as a defence against the complacency which can develop within a long-term relationship founded on trust, and which may lead the consultant to feel too much at home in the client organisation. The division between operational and consulting divisions within the consultant also guarded against this. Although quality is difficult to measure, it was deemed to have improved and, more tangibly, during this period the partnership identified and achieved annually recurring savings in excess of £2.5 million.

As shown above, the form of the partnership agreement was such that the airline could draw on the resources of the consultant as it saw fit, with reimbursement being made accordingly on an open-book basis. As a result, from an initial six people from the consultant being involved with the project, the numbers rose at one point to 70; this was potentially detrimental to the consultant's wider business interests. It therefore set up a separate company to safeguard the interests of the parent company and to cope more appropriately with the changing demands being made by the airline in response to its developing situation.

Over the initial three-year period the task set for the consultant was subject to continual change. One response, as discussed above, was to establish a separate business, which reflected its origins and purpose by drawing in two employees from the airline. After three years, the period of the initial contract, the emphasis had moved from facilities management to project management. The shape of support required therefore differed, and to accommodate and reflect this change, as well as to protect the primary business interests of the consultant, a separate project management organisation was established. This enabled the consultant to recruit more project management personnel to fit the redefined task. Meanwhile, the facilities management function set up by the consultant was handed over to the airline's own in-house team, incorporating not only the latter's employees but also several former employees of the consultant.

In retrospect, those involved at the consultant's end of the partnership felt that the biggest problem faced was encouraging the airline's personnel to spend the time and make an effort in areas the consultant saw as important. It was felt necessary to work against the given reactive approach and to replace it with the reality of strategic thought and a fuller understanding of its significance within the facilities management role.

Overall, the project enabled the airline to initiate change in a controlled and systematic way with a clear set of deliverables and has subsequently delivered a support function that is customer-focused and responsive to the support needs of the airline. Operating on the basis of a partnering relationship meant that personnel from both organisations worked collaboratively in an open and trusting way, which enabled rapid progress to be made towards common goals. Subsequent changes within the airline have occurred with increasing frequency; however, the fundamental changes begun by the partnership, and the strategy set out, have stood the test of time, allowing the property department to adapt more readily to these frequent changes.

Conclusions

Organisations need to see their facilities management strategy as the cornerstone of their accommodation (or space) strategy, not as an adjunct to it. By identifying the kind of accommodation and facilities currently provided and required in the future, an organisation will be able to quantify the gap that has to be bridged. There are, however, other aspects relating to facilities management that have to be considered carefully if the most appropriate strategy is to be developed. Various tools and techniques are available to support a rigorous process of analysis, solution development and implementation, success in which will lead to a workable strategy for effective facilities management.

CHECKLIST

This checklist is intended to assist with the review and action planning process.

	Yes	No	Action required
1. Does the organisation accept the importance of a proper facilities management strategy within the context of the strategic plan and accommodation strategy?	☐	☐	☐
2. Has the organisation completed a strategic analysis of its facilities requirements?	☐	☐	☐
3. Have new ideas and innovative solutions been considered in the context of the facilities management strategy?	☐	☐	☐
4. Has the organisation's senior management avoided the temptation to prejudge options before they have been systematically evaluated?	☐	☐	☐
5. Have criteria for judging options generated in the strategic analysis been prepared objectively?	☐	☐	☐
6. Has the broad strategy been developed into an operational plan addressing the issues of managing change?	☐	☐	☐
7. Has the organisation considered its relationship with service providers in all areas and at all levels?	☐	☐	☐

3 Retaining Services In-house vs Outsourcing

Key issues

The following issues are covered in this chapter.

- The organisation must identify the key attributes of the services it requires so that a balanced view of needs is established as the basis for evaluating available options within the decision to retain in-house or to outsource.

- The organisation should define its own evaluation criteria with respect to these attributes of service so that the importance or weight given to options is truly reflective of the organisation's accommodation and facilities management strategy and policies.

- Consideration must be given to direct and indirect costs of both in-house and outsourced service provision so that a complete financial picture is gained, with comparison made on a like-for-like basis to enable a decision to be taken on best value.

- Support services should represent best value on the grounds of affordability for the organisation in the implementation of the objectives of its strategic plan, irrespective of the cost of those services.

- Evaluation criteria for the sourcing decision must embrace 'hard' and 'soft' measures and compare all costs with the required quality.

- Roles and skills must be derived from the services to be provided, with specialist skills highlighted.

- Since the factors affecting the choice of in-house or outsourced facilities management may change, the route by which services are procured should be reviewed at appropriate intervals by market testing.

Introduction

This chapter considers the issue of whether to retain services in-house or to outsource them. There can be many possibilities open to organisations and each has to be considered carefully if the route that leads to best value is to be followed. It is not a simple choice between retention in-house or outsourcing. The choice between in-house and outsourced services is not always clear-cut, which is why there has to be a proper understanding of requirements. If the procedure advocated in Chapter 2 has been followed, the organisation will have not prejudged the situation; instead, it will have determined its requirements precisely. The first step is to consider the attributes of each service that are seen as important. Realism has to prevail so that attributes are stated in terms that are 'within range' and not so demanding of service providers that they are unlikely ever to be fulfilled. Many of the attributes will seem obvious; others will be less so. The issue of cost is bound to be a prominent factor for many organisations – it may have been the main motivation for considering outsourcing as an option. However, as we shall see, it is important to understand how cost is generated. Finally in this chapter, the organisation is presented with the means by which it is able to determine the arrangements through which service provision can take place. This step is a significant one and has many implications for the quality of service as well as cost. However, it is not a 'once and for all time' situation, but one that has to be revisited periodically as conditions change in the market for services and supplies.

Attributes of service

The organisation is free to determine those features of a given service that are important to it: to do otherwise would not make sense. Even so, the organisation must be realistic, both in terms of the features demanded and the ability of others to deliver them. For any given service, there will be a number of features (referred to as attributes) that can be considered significant and/or important to the organisation. They can include, but are certainly not limited to:

- Customer service
- Uniqueness of service
- Priority, flexibility and speed of response
- Management implications and indirect cost
- Direct cost
- Control

Customer service

The organisation will have established the scope and standard of services it requires. In addition to the many 'hard' measures that are usually associated with them (for example, responding correctly to a need) a number of 'soft' measures must also be considered (for example, the level of customer service provided). These become particularly important when dealing with people who are external to the organisation, although are still important when dealing with people within it. Soft measures might include:

- A courteous and responsive helpdesk in preference to a logbook in which faults are simply noted.
- Call-back to the customer to verify that the work has been carried out.
- Adoption of performance measures for courtesy, response, presentation and tidiness.

Practice Point 3.1   A helping hand.

Key-point: the organisation needs to have a helpdesk or central coordination point if it is to deal effectively with customer enquiries about facilities and related services.

The organisation in question did not believe that, given its relatively small size, it warranted a helpdesk. After all, the facilities manager appeared to know what was going on and he always seemed to be receiving calls from various people to tell him if there were problems. In fact, over a six-week period, the facilities manager was so overwhelmed with the number of calls and visits he received that he managed to do little other work. Furthermore, there were complaints that some problems were not being resolved. In the end, he discussed the matter with his senior management and obtained permission to set up a helpdesk on a three-month trial basis. Its scope was to cover security, transport, catering, cleaning, porterage, maintenance, mail services and room bookings. In the first two weeks, the helpdesk attracted 500 enquiries most of which were dealt with promptly and to the satisfaction of the individual enquirer. In establishing the helpdesk, the organisation had created a focal point for dealing with problems. This meant that personnel were generally able to resolve problems immediately, rather than allowing them to escalate.

Uniqueness of service

When contemplating different ways of providing a service, the special demands of that service must also be considered. While most tasks will not represent an undue challenge to providers within the facilities management sector, the organisation might, for example, possess specialist plant and equipment unfamiliar to maintenance operatives. This may restrict the potential choice of the provider of maintenance and supplier of spares. In some cases, legislation will ensure that only certain qualified persons and firms are authorised to perform maintenance. The maintenance of lifts and elevators is an obvious example. Generally, issues can include:

- The number of external service providers that can potentially offer the service.
- Location of the service provider and its distance from the organisation's facility in question.
- Cost of, or premium charged for, the service.
- Average delivery time, i.e. waiting time and time for undertaking the service.
- Level of specification needed to place orders.

Priority, flexibility and speed of response

The priority of services to be provided must be expressed clearly, so that critical services can be highlighted and the required level of response taken into account. A risk assessment should be undertaken for high-priority services, so that the consequence of failures is made clear and the appropriate level and speed of response can be planned. This can be undertaken as follows:

- Identify all sources of risk that might affect service provision
- Undertake a preliminary analysis to establish the probable high-priority risks for further investigation
- Examine these high-priority risks to assess the severity of their impact and probability of occurrence
- Analyse all risks to predict the most likely outcome
- Investigate alternative courses of action
- Choose the course of action deemed necessary to hold, avoid, reduce, transfer or share risks, as appropriate
- Allocate responsibility for managing risks – these should be placed with those best able to manage them

High-priority services and their related risks must be identified and assessment made of the probability and consequences of such risks. The management team can use questionnaires and checklists to identify risks. These could then be scored as shown in Table 3.1.

Risks scoring a total of 5 or more would be unacceptable and consideration would need to be given to how such risks might be avoided, reduced or transferred. Thus, risks can be recognised and assessed so that appropriate action can be taken. In the process of doing this, risks impacting on services provision may be ranked to allow the organisation to look objectively at how they can best be managed.

For example, the occurrence of a significant failure in the heating system during the winter months might be improbable (score 1), but the consequences could be serious (score 3). The full impact of this risk is rated as 4 and is something that the organisation might be prepared to accept (hold). This can be contrasted with the 'as likely as not' event that fuel oil will not be delivered on time (score 3). If this were so, the consequences

Table 3.1   Risk scores.

Probability	Chance of occurrence (%)	Score	Consequence	Score
Improbable	10	1	Insignificant	1
Unlikely	25	2	Marginal	2
As likely as not	50	3	Serious	3
Probable	75	4	Critical	4
Highly probable	90	5	Catastrophic	5

for heating the buildings could be serious (score 3). This gives a total score of 6. In other words, fuel oil deliveries are a high priority service and, as such, must be made at the required time. The organisation should take steps to reduce the chance of non-delivery on specified dates or to hold a reserve fuel supply, whichever is more appropriate in terms of cost and practicality.

The organisation should also consider the level of flexibility required for each of the services provided. Variable demand for some services, such as porterage[2] and transport, which may peak at certain times of the year, can cause difficulties in maintaining a constant resource level. In such instances, the ability to call off labour from an external provider at short notice can help and is also likely to provide a cost-effective way of delivering those services.

The speed with which a service provider can, under each service approach, respond to orders or requests is a factor for further consideration. For example, the response time of an external provider in the case of an emergency call-out, may or may not be longer than that of an in-house resource. In the case of a remote site, the response time for a maintenance contractor may be significant and a premium to reduce this time might prove prohibitive. Alternatively, if an emergency were to escalate, a large external provider may be preferred to the in-house alternative, because of ready access, out of hours, to necessary equipment and labour.

Management implications and indirect cost

The decision to outsource or provide services in-house must take into account both the capability of service providers and the effort required to manage them. An organisation that takes the decision to outsource can delegate the direct supervision of work and service operatives to the provider. The role for the organisation's representative then becomes the management of the output from the service provider. The representative should act as an informed client (see Chapter 1) managing performance against specifications and service level agreements (see Chapter 8). Organisations need to consider their approach to this new management role carefully.

When contemplating a mix of support services such as cleaning, security, building and mechanical and electrical maintenance, it is easy to see the diversity of tasks involved. This may mean that a manager or supervisor who is trying to cope with such a range of services may not be proficient in all. This could prove to be a problem for smaller organisations where, although the tasks are not extensive individually, their diversity is great, requiring the manager or supervisor to be multi-skilled. For larger organisations, specialist management and supervision may be cost-effective and efficient, because more of it is required.

---

[2] The word portering is also commonly used.

A further consideration is that of the expertise available within the organisation for the management of these services if retained in-house. Whilst accommodation services such as cleaning and porterage do not require high levels of expertise, statutory equipment testing and maintenance of major appliances do. For a manager whose remit includes the management of such services on a part-time basis, the initial learning and the continuing professional development (CPD) to keep abreast of legislation and industry practice, represent a significant investment in time and effort. Consequently, in-house service provision may not be the most cost-effective choice.

In choosing the approach to service provision, total cost is frequently misreported. In evaluating the comparative cost between an in-house or outsourced service provision, organisations should identify all costs, both direct and indirect. A common mistake is for direct costs only to be reported. Indirect costs include those incurred in the internal management of external contracts and the ongoing training and development of in-house personnel. Furthermore, the full administration of the services such as permit-to-work procedures, competent and approved person regimes, together with the technology to operate them, all attract a cost that must be recorded.

The organisation also needs to consider the cost of financial administration. For instance, a small number of labour and material contracts means that invoices can be processed more cost-effectively than in situations where invoices are many and frequent. Clearly, the method of procurement has an implication for the accounting function.

Direct cost

By way of contrast, direct cost is easier to ascertain than indirect cost. In the case of an outsourced service, the contract sum is a clear figure that is readily available. For in-house provision, the direct cost calculation would include employees' salaries and benefits. As noted above, these more obvious costs should not be looked at in isolation from the associated indirect costs.

Control

Linked closely to the management variable is the issue of control. For many organisations considering outsourcing, the greatest concern is that of a perceived loss of control. The level of control that can be achieved is closely correlated with the method of procurement and the contractual relationship established between the organisation and the service provider. Through a more traditional contract the level of control is limited. For more control, a partnering arrangement may be appropriate (see Chapter 12).

Table 3.2   Illustration of options and their implications.

Attributes of service of importance to the organisation	In house	Special company/ business unit	Managing agent	Managing contractor	Managed budget	Total FM	Off-the-shelf/ agency
Customer service	+	+	++	+	++	+	–
Uniqueness of service	–	+	+	+	+	+	–
Priority, flexibility, speed of response	++	+	++	++	++	+	++
Management implications/indirect cost	–	+	+	+	++	++	–
Direct cost	+	–	–	–	–	–	–
Control	++	++	++	+	++	–	+

++ = an attribute is most likely to be satisfied; + = may be satisfied; and – = unlikely to be satisfied.

Whatever arrangement is put in place, ICT has a part to play in the delivery of reliable management information. It is through available and accessible management information that many of the control issues can be resolved. Value can also be added if management information is delivered as a consequence of service provision and is, therefore, available without cost or, at least, for a nominal sum.

Overview of options and implications

Choice is not limited to in-house provision or outsourcing. Table 3.2 shows six options (defined subsequently in Table 3.3) that an organisation might consider and how the different attributes of service of importance to the organisation can be scored against each option. The particular interpretation represented by this model is hypothetical and based on the authors' experiences. Moreover, it should be used only at the early stages when determining an approach to the overall provision of services. Many of the attributes listed will, at a later stage, be used in the assessment of tenders.

The organisation should always consider its own evaluation criteria to determine the importance or weight that might be given to an option in terms of its potential to add value to the core business. Although plus and minus signs are used in the example based on the authors' perceptions and experience, a numerical system could have been used to arrive at similar, if not the same, results. Whichever approach is adopted, the basis for each

Table 3.3   Definition of options.

In-house – The retention of the organisation's employees for the delivery of estates-related and facilities services.
Special company/business unit – The reconstitution of the in-house team into an independent company, with the objective of expanding its business by gaining contracts from other clients.
Managing agent – The appointment of a specialist to act as client representative. This person (or organisation) is then responsible for arranging the appointment of service providers.
Managing contractor – The appointment of an organisation to manage all service providers as though part of one large contracting organisation. The contractor is paid a fee for providing this service, usually as a percentage of the value of the expenditure managed.
Managed budget – A variation on the *managing contractor*, where a contractor takes responsibility for the payment of all suppliers and provides a consolidated invoice at the end of each month. The contractor's fee is related to the contractor's own resources as deployed.
Total facilities management (total FM) – The responsibility for providing services and for generally managing the facilities is placed in the hands of a single organisation.
Off-the-shelf/agency – The contractual employment of personnel through a specialist or general recruitment agency. Agencies provide variable standards of selection expertise, personnel support and training, and customer support.

score must be made explicit so that there can be no misunderstanding of the relative weighting of attributes. Furthermore, the exact interpretation of options will differ from one organisation to another, but the adoption of such an approach should enable objective comparison to be made and for it to be transparent to all stakeholders.

Market testing

Going to the market should be an honest attempt at establishing the attraction or otherwise of outsourcing. This does not, however, imply frequent tendering exercises, where in-house providers compete for work alongside external contractors. It is preferable for clear-cut choices to be made between internal restructuring and outsourcing, wherever possible, particularly within the public sector. This avoids the counterproductive effects that the anxiety caused by market testing, or the demoralisation caused by an unsuccessful tender, may have on the in-house team and its subsequent dealings with its new, external employers.

Appropriate use of the market would include regular comparisons of current prices and rates for services using published data, participation in a benchmarking club (see Chapter 14) or indicative quotations from potential service providers. An awareness of the state of the market for services means that at any time a judgement can be made as to whether or not a preferred option is the most appropriate. Some of the requisite information, however, may already be contained within market audits carried out during the preparation of the accommodation strategy.

It is the performance of the service provider that should be reviewed on an annual basis, rather than the decision to outsource or retain services in-house. Once that decision has been taken it should not be subject to continuous review. The organisation should try to avoid letting contracts on less than an annual basis. Longer-term contracts for three or more years can be let with break clauses. Annual reviews should, in any case, be incorporated into contracts running for two or more years. In some countries, legislation may still force re-tendering on an annual basis for public sector contracts. This can add to cost, as well as limiting the performance of the service provider. In such cases, it can only be hoped that the institutions concerned eventually recognise the short-sightedness of their approach and move to an arrangement that is capable of achieving best value. It is surely not beyond the ability of those institutions in question to draft contracts that incorporate annual reviews and break clauses to cover the eventuality of poor performance by the service provider. The mechanisms for reviewing performance are dealt with in Chapters 8 and 13.

Other implications of outsourcing

Should an organisation decide to outsource, it is then faced with a further decision as to how the outsourcing will be organised and structured. How will the contracts be let? Will there be separate or bundled individual contracts, a total facilities management package or a management contract (see Chapter 11)? What might make sense for the organisation might not prove attractive to service providers – much can depend on the market at a given time. If the option of a management contract is exercised, the organisation will need to consider whether this should be undertaken for a fee or on the basis of service performance.

Conclusions

The decision to outsource can be made rationally and objectively, based on attributes of service that are realistic. At any time, organisations can apply the evaluation model shown in Table 3.2 to help determine whether or not to outsource a service. They should do so having regard to those attributes of service that are meaningful and relevant to them. The benefit in using a model of this kind is that specific options can be evaluated with sensitivity and the correct decision for the organisation at any point can be made. Time is an important factor, since needs change and sometimes the most appropriate option is the one that can be adapted over time to suit new circumstances. Limited and periodic market reviews are useful for information gathering, but habitual market testing is not considered best practice and may be counterproductive. There will be advantages and disadvantages to providing services either in-house or by outsourcing. The organisation must decide the route that provides the best value for itself in the long term. This is achieved by taking full account of the implications, especially the true cost of all options.

CHECKLIST

This checklist is intended to assist with the review and action planning process.

	Yes	No	Action required
1. Has the organisation established the scope and standard of customer services required and compared it to its current provision of facilities management services?	☐	☐	☐
2. Do the current facilities management arrangements properly address priorities and provide flexibility and speed of response?	☐	☐	☐
3. Have the management implications of outsourcing services as opposed to retaining them in-house been considered?	☐	☐	☐

		Yes	No	Action required
4.	Have both the direct and indirect costs of service provision been properly identified?	☐	☐	☐
5.	Has the level of control required been properly integrated with the methods of procurement and the contractual relationships that might be established between the client organisation and the service provider?	☐	☐	☐
6.	Do contracts run for more than one year, with the provision of annual reviews and break clauses to enable poorly performing service providers to be removed?	☐	☐	☐
7.	Is market testing undertaken periodically irrespective of the route taken to the provision of services?	☐	☐	☐

4 Change Management

Key issues

The following issues are covered in this chapter.

- Change is normal, but its consequences can be abnormal for the people affected by it.

- Organisations need to adopt an intelligent approach to planning, co-ordinating and controlling a process of change that ensures continuity of operations, whilst injecting new energy and impetus into the 'business' and its social infrastructure.

- A recognised methodology exists for guiding organisations and individuals towards implementing a change management process – something that can be defined, detailed and determined.

- Change management is rarely, if ever, a linear process; instead it is likely to involve some degree of iteration and/or reworking.

- Planning is key to success and, in many respects, there cannot be too much of it. Organisations should not underestimate the time required to plan (and then implement) a change management project.

- Facilities management provides a mechanism for handling routine change, but it cannot deal with wholesale change – other approaches must be taken, perhaps drawing on key project management skills.

- Consultation with all stakeholders is essential, otherwise just one disaffected party could ruin the chance of success.

- Targeted change management can lead to results that dramatically improve the viability of the organisation and its competitiveness, where the latter is a relevant factor.

Introduction

The idea that things – and that includes organisations – must change has become abundantly clear over the last few decades. From a world in which stability was the norm, we have come to a time where normality itself is a state of change. This apparent paradox serves to make us realise that in order to progress we have to do things differently – we have to do them better. The point is that change has always been present: it is simply that the rate of change nowadays is so great as to be visible to all. Change management can be defined as a set of techniques that aid in evolution, composition and policy management of the design and implementation of an object or system. However, this starkly abstract view overlooks the human dimension that is a fundamental condition of facilities management. Another view is that it is an organised, systematic application of the knowledge, tools and resources of change that provides organisations with a key process to achieve their business strategy. Clearly, the introduction of a focus on business strategy helps to contextualise the definition, but in order to humanise it we must go further. By incorporating the 'people-side' of business and coupling it to the workplace, we can offer the following definition for the purpose of this work: 'the process, tools and techniques to manage the people-side of business change to achieve a required outcome and to realise that change effectively within the social infrastructure of the workplace'. This sharper focus on the problem with which we are faced helps when exploring the approach that organisations must take. This chapter therefore examines change management in an organisational setting, where the objects of change are the facilities to serve the core business and the subjects are the people who will deliver this new order.

Change in an organisational setting

As we have seen from earlier chapters, facilities management is about, *inter alia*, helping organisations to manage change. Facilities management moves an organisation from where it is today to where it needs to be in the future to meet its business objectives. In practice, this may mean the requirement for more or better accommodation and pressure on the organisation to adapt what it has already. Such are the symptoms of a rapidly changing business world. Organisations can be sure of one thing – the nature of work and business will be different tomorrow. The difficulty is in predicting how and in what ways things will be different. For some organisations, the need to change may be one of extreme urgency and a consequence of events past or in anticipation of those to come. Organisational change can, thus, be the result of the need to:

- *Refocus* – reduce diversification of activities
- *Re-engineer* – redesign business processes
- *Downsize* – concentrate on core business
- *De-layer* – remove redundant levels of management

Organisations face other pressures for change and these can stem from a variety of causes:

- Organisational structure/relationships – as mentioned above
- ICT
- Productivity demands

- Human skills and resources
- Time pressures
- Comfort and welfare

Change can therefore occur in various ways and at various levels, and is often influenced by decisions and behaviour that are people-oriented. Change management is about where an organisation aims to be, how it will get there and how it will involve people.

Managing change in practice

Later in this chapter – through the means of a case study – we shall introduce the notion of an organisation venturing towards a project management style of operation for its facilities management. As we shall see, some actions can be translated into projects, enabling them to be subject to an established discipline with a proven methodology, techniques, tools and metrics. The attraction is in the control that can be exercised over delivery to quality, time and cost objectives. This thinking does, however, fall short of advocating a project-managed approach to facilities management and it is important to avoid mixing concepts. Even so, there is the possibility of gaining benefit from looking at different approaches from which, hopefully, one can find better ways of delivering objectives. Any new insights that might be provided would justify the time expended.

Bringing about change in a controlled way will draw on many skills, not least social skills in dealing with the people affected by alterations in some aspect of their work. The potential for failure, or a less than satisfactory outcome, looms large and demands attention to be directed to those factors that might threaten success. A later case study – see Chapter 5 – shows how it is possible to help people make the transition from an established and, therefore, familiar situation to one that is unfamiliar and potentially threatening. The need for early involvement of all stakeholders cannot be overemphasised. These are the people upon whom the outcome rests.

Change as a process

First and foremost, change management should be seen in terms of a process – something that is eminently capable of being 'defined, detailed and determined'. Fig. 4.1 shows the essential form of the change management process.

By using the device of an explicit, shared model of the process, it is possible to obtain feedback and, importantly, 'buy-in' from stakeholders. Used as the starting point for the redesign or re-engineering of an organisation's business processes, the model avoids drawing people into descriptions where reading between the lines is one of many drawbacks. A process model, as an abstraction of the real world, can be used to focus attention on the sequence

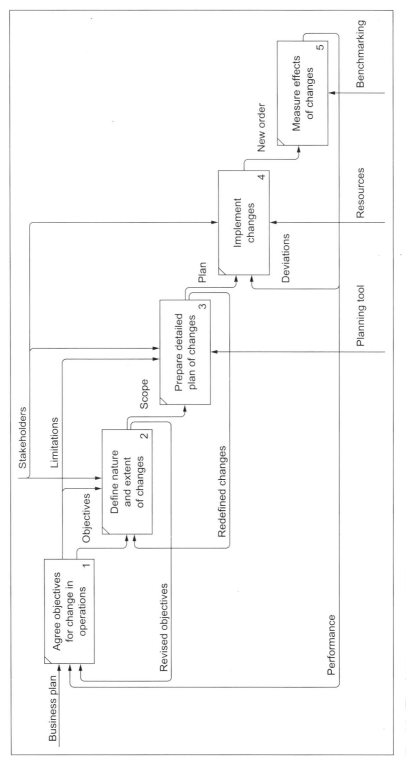

Fig. 4.1   The change management process.

and logical relationship between activities that must be performed to deliver change. Moreover, the standard conventions adopted in the model can be used as a checklist of 'who shall be involved', 'where' and 'with what information and/or control?' The protocol thus helps to define the process.

Since the modelling approach is implicitly top-down, it is possible to breakdown (decompose) higher level activities into their constituent tasks. In this way, the authors of the model – change managers – have total control over the level of detail that is required to portray the process (or any part of it) adequately. The golden rule is to decompose the model to a level that is consistent with the requirements of the job in hand. The level of detail is, therefore, that which is necessary and sufficient, and no more since more would mean waste.

Building such a model is an exercise in creating a single, integrated view of the process. When supported by appropriate ICT tools, it is possible to check the integrity of the model. Put another way, it is possible to see if the process is 'all joined up'. Measuring the process, that is determining its performance and outcome, completes the exercise. The process has now been 'defined, detailed and determined'.

Change management is however rarely, if ever, a linear process; instead it is likely to involve some degree of iteration or reworking. A further benefit of a process model is that it allows sequence and logic to be scrutinised – most of which can be accomplished from simple visual inspection – and adjustments made to improve, even optimise, the outcome. Like other techniques, such as project planning and scheduling, it is not so much the benefit of creating the plan (or model) in the first place, but the ability to be able to test different scenarios and to identify a superior plan. Without such techniques, one risks striving for the exact attainment of an inferior plan. This outcome is likely when processes are described in words and not shown as deeds.

Change management, and the approach advocated above, has much in common with the principles of 'action research', where scenarios are generated, tested and fed back into the organisation where their effects are observed. These results are then used to modify the approach or model until it produces the desired outcome. The intention here is not, however, to dress up the application of a management technique into some kind of quasi-scientific theory; rather the aim is to show that there are always parallels from which one can gain useful insights.

Planning is key to success and, in many respects, there cannot be too little of it. Time spent 'up-front' is usually amply rewarded by certainty of delivery; in other words, there are no surprises. Organisations should not underestimate the time required to plan a change management project. Unless it is taken seriously it will not produce the desired effect and the entire approach may be needlessly discredited. Facilities management can provide a mechanism for organisations to manage routine change; however, it cannot deal with wholesale change – other ways must be found such as outlined above. Whatever approach is taken it is vital to consult with all stakeholders: their input is necessary and their support may be too. Since implementing change generally involves alterations in the organisation's structure and tasks of the employees concerned, these factors will need to be looked at both at an organisational and individual level.

Communicating change

It is important that those involved in the changes – employees and other stakeholders – are informed and that they are involved in decision-making. Communication is the means by which important messages are put across and commitment is returned. Failure here will mean that strategic planning (including resources planning) and the organisation's development and growth will be impeded as the change process becomes stalled. People can often be influenced by education and persuasion. Education is the milder form of social influence because it can help in presenting several, different viewpoints, some of which will be unbiased. In this way, the target audience is offered a choice. On the other hand, persuasion can be targeted directly at employees conforming to one viewpoint. It can be used to get employees to accept change such as new working methods and new technology. Other forms that are available include propaganda and indoctrination, although the former is unethical and the latter is extreme and unacceptable in a democratic society. Nonetheless, it may help to be aware of these extreme measures, so ensuring that they are avoided.

Practice Point 4.1   Been there, done that.

Key-point: meant with the best of intentions, it is possible for personnel who have been used to a particular way of working to want to continue as before believing that their experience will prove them right.

A college had decided to retain its facilities management in-house after a long process of consultation and some market testing. The main argument given in support of retention was that personnel in the new facilities division had amongst them tens of years of experience of managing the college buildings and grounds. Whilst this was the case, some personnel clearly had entrenched views. Typical of this problem were comments like, 'we tried that in the 80s and it didn't work then, so why is it going to work now?' It was not so much that the personnel concerned were being deliberately obstructive; rather, they had closed their minds to any alternative. If anything, the passage of time had reinforced their own belief in the limited value of doing certain things, because this was the easier alternative. The major challenge for the head of facilities – a newcomer – was to coax them into discussing the reasons why it failed in the past and how they had felt at the time. By persisting with a process of exploring the conditions surrounding a given event, the head of facilities was able to turn the situation around. Now, it was more likely to be a case of, 'we tried that in the 80s, it didn't work then because we were not able to do it this way. Now we can. I am sure that if we gave it a try we would succeed today.'

The process view of change management discussed earlier deserves further elaboration. Clearly, not everyone will be comfortable with graphical or pictorial representations of something they see all around them in the richness of the working environment. In extreme cases, they may see a process model as a crude device that strips away all that is human about work and the workplace. In one sense they are right – models *are* abstractions of reality. To complete the exercise we need to embellish the model, portraying the new order with information that will help people to understand sufficiently what is involved. No process model should, therefore, be posted as the blueprint for the future unless it is accompanied by supporting descriptions of activities, the human and other resources required to perform them, the tools that can be applied to assist in this task and the controls that will be exerted to ensure that the process delivers. Communicating a complete package of information is critical to success.

Responsibilities of those managing change

Implementing planned change brings the change manager directly to the all-important task of protecting the budget. The budget will have presumably been set according to an accepted plan and is an especially challenging situation when the changes involve outsourced services. These will be subject to contracts in which change – sometimes referred to as variations – may be accommodated. There are a number of reasons why change can be necessary, but most significantly we should think about the circumstances where a change can lead to increased cost.

Some changes can be anticipated and resources provided for them, whilst there may be no possibility of predicting others. Circumstances can include:

- Changing needs in the (client) organisation's programme.
- Unforeseen requirements of external authorities.
- Unforeseen conditions in the workplace.
- Designers or other specialists requiring additions to complete work.
- The change manager simply failing to include certain work.

Arguably, the most important point to bear in mind is that change is generally not welcomed by the client and is distrusted. It is therefore important that changes are allowed for in terms of quality (or performance), cost and time before project initiation so that the client's representative can be forewarned. It is conceivable that the client will understand and accept the need for a change. Change managers must also consider the needs of subcontractors in addition to those of the client organisation. The former should be treated even-handedly to ensure their commitment to the project. In overall terms, certainty and speed are of the essence in change management for ensuring a smooth transition and minimal disruption in workflow. Ensuring the commitment of everyone increases the probability of success.

Resolving cultural conflict

There can be many reasons why change projects fail. Some of the reasons have been touched upon already, but there are others lurking that must be brought out into the open. In these times of international business, travel and worker relocation, it is necessary to consider both the needs of foreign workers and the impact on work of conflict that can arise from different cultures.

The study of cross-culture and its impact on work practices is well documented, certainly at the level of the organisation – see, for example, Hofstede (1991). There is an expanding body of knowledge and literature to support it. Where there is a real weakness is in understanding cultural differences in the setting of a project, particular major projects involving a multi-national team or workforce. When international corporations wish to embark upon change projects in any of their overseas sites they would do well to increase the time and resources allocated to planning – see also Chapter 17.

Case study – EastPoint Property Management Services Limited

EastPoint emerged from a property management department within Colliers Jardine (Hong Kong) Limited with a heritage of more than two decades of business in Hong Kong as a Jardine Matheson company behind it. Over that period it had focused on traditional operations with every day being treated the same as any other. Today, as a property, asset and facilities management business, EastPoint employs 3 200 people to undertake professional management, security and technical duties on a wide range of property infrastructure projects throughout Hong Kong, in Macau, and currently as consultants in China. It manages over 100 million sq. ft of property – nearly all of this is the 'common area' of multi-strata, multi-ownership properties typical of urban Hong Kong. These common areas are the frameworks, the approaches and the adjacent areas of buildings that contain a much greater area of residential, commercial and industrial units of accommodation. The organisation estimates that 7% of the population of Hong Kong lives or works in these units and are in its care. It is an important statistic – the organisation has always been concerned about professionalism in managing property, but now it has more to do with caring for the communities of people within these properties. EastPoint is repositioning and innovating within its business to get closer to the heart and soul of these communities.

The innovations that EastPoint have accomplished, through a process of controlled managed change, can be summarised as follows:

- Process re-engineering – delivering tangible products of change that include improved processes for governance, risk assessment, effectiveness and efficiency.

- Business re-structuring – redistributing responsibilities and breaking down the walls that had traditionally existed between the established divisions in the organisation.
- Management by projects – adding project management skills and techniques as a prerequisite for business management and for leadership at all levels.
- Documentation to technical publishing standards – striving for clarity, comprehension, visual impression and quality impression.
- Use of proven technology – building information systems and electronic communications that integrate its dispersed business and reduce administrative and transaction costs.
- In-house open learning programmes and mentoring – providing personal workforce training without loss of productivity and with enhanced team effectiveness.
- Young Executive Training Programme – bringing bright minds to bear on research and development issues under seasoned leadership and obtaining tangible results – see also Chapter 16.
- Empowering executive personnel – responsibility for creative leadership in the form of enterprise task groups.

Some of these innovations are now discussed.

Process re-engineering is a broad set of coordinated activities to establish continual process improvements in business governance, risk management, quality standards and performance, and business metrics. As a result, a number of tangible products and techniques have become firmly implanted in the organisation's business. The office policy manual, quality manual and derivative products are best-in-class examples of procedural instruction. Risk assessments of tender submissions are based on Monte Carlo simulation and used to provide upside and downside appreciation of the risks inherent in the tender and pricing sensitivities in real terms.

Business re-structuring has taken place in two stages. The property management department was reorganised early to redistribute responsibilities and to break down the walls that had traditionally existed between the established divisions in the organisation. It has given greater emphasis and new direction to the business support functions – for example quality control has been replaced by performance management and work improvement. This has created space for accelerating the development of up-and-coming talent within the organisation. Executive director roles have been defined and are used to empower specific individuals to take up a leadership role in one of three key enterprise areas of the organisation: commercial, operations and business administration. All executive directors report directly to the Managing Director and thereby to the Board.

Management by projects has become the norm for the planning and execution of the actions, small or large, that are required to bring about change in the organisation. Personnel holding strategic roles are given training in project management to an internationally accredited qualification so they are practically equipped to deliver projects on time and within budget.

The Open Learning Programme (OLP) is used to provide property management training to all 3 200 employees, using a technical manual and derivative open-learning workbooks which were developed as part of a mentoring approach to on-the-job training. The organisation adopted a two-stage approach to producing improved documentation that would provide technical instruction for all personnel. A production team was formed with participation from various grades of operational personnel.

The first task was to refine existing procedures by weeding out non-productive activities and processes, and by ensuring that customer satisfaction was given prominence in operational processes. For these reasons, the paper trails required for ISO quality assurance were discarded if they failed to contribute directly to productivity or customer satisfaction. Performance monitoring was by exception rather than by rule. All pro-forma were reviewed for service need, standardised in readiness for porting to electronically-enabled processes on the organisation's intranet. The intention was to cut operational procedures to the minimum or otherwise validate them as essential to the business. The second task was to author new documentation that would serve as a technical reference for the organisation. At this stage, a consultant was appointed to design a standard template for the organisation's documentation. These guidelines adopted clear, straightforward English and uncluttered text in readiness for the later production of open-learning workbooks and work instruction guidelines.

The task-force effort in the first review of existing documents and editorial rework into new material amounted to 1 800 man hours. This produced the draft of 'lean' organisational procedures. A technical writer was employed to author a technical manual from this material, corresponding workbooks for open learning and job specific guidelines for site personnel. Final format according to the layout template and final revisions were done in-house.

Twelve operational areas were identified for the open-learning training programme. Each workbook was produced for easy reading. They included simple learning exercises to reinforce the learning process. As such, they are a personal study aid designed by experienced personnel in the organisation. Each workbook relates to sections in the technical manual. It is a reference book on the 'who, what, where, when and how' of the work process. Workbooks are not used in isolation. Users are encouraged to discuss them, to get answers on their questions from more experienced colleagues such as supervisors, or peers, and to make reference to the technical manual.

The OLP is complemented by an in-house training centre, which was introduced in 2001 as a cost saving and work improvement measure. Previously, the organisation's on-going need for security-related training of building personnel was outsourced. Establishing the training centre has provided:

- An upgrade in the quality of training and on-the-job performance
- A cost saving equivalent to £30 000 annually
- Substantial improvement in the organisation's reputation with the police authority which imposes controls over how property is managed

EastPoint recognised the improved efficiency and effectiveness that would be achieved by organising its business around workflow management and re-engineered business processes. This action had the added benefit of creating tangible new products and processes that clearly demonstrated business change. It has enabled the organisation to focus on reducing transaction costs within its business operations.

The organisation has also recognised that the nature of the business was changing to community care and, increasingly, the delivery of services at the personal level. Especially important in the context of relationship management is a distribution network that enables delivery of collateral items or messages on a personal basis to 7% of the population of Hong Kong. For EastPoint, the physical distribution network already exists, so the organisation is busy building the electronic network that will enable communications based on B2C intranet technology. Providing personal messaging to individuals to keep them informed and to demonstrate the organisation's commitment to a personal service is seen as offering strategic competitive advantage. It is also one step closer to creating an e-distribution network for the sale of services and commodities that can be distributed by EastPoint's physical distribution network.

Reducing transaction costs through e-enabled integration of a differentiated and decentralised business is likely to add significant value to EastPoint's procurement chain and offers better ways of deploying on-site operational resources. The organisation thus sees strategic competitive advantage from its B2C communications with the people in its communities and from B2B communications with its suppliers and other stakeholders in the business.

As evidence of EastPoint's successful implementation of its planned changes, the organisation has recently reported a 37% increase in revenue, a 47% increase in profit (EBITDA) and a 92% increase in EVA.

Conclusions

Change is bound to be a major concern and one that can be a force for good and bad. Organisations that are able to apply themselves differently and do so quickly may have an advantage over their competitors. However, this comes at a cost. Time and resources must be invested in planning – there can never be too much. Tools and techniques are available to help in the formalisation of the change process. Change managers do, however, need to ensure that they involve all stakeholders from the outset. Producing a workable plan for change is no fluke; it is the result of hard work that has clear objectives, which can be measured. Change management can be seen therefore as a powerful tool in itself, as it helps the organisation maintain focus on its strategic business objectives whilst identifying and bringing about the operational transformations that will help to deliver them. As the dynamics of the workplace change, so too will facilities management have to change to enable organisations to implement strategies that assume change as a normal feature of business life.

CHECKLIST

This checklist is intended to assist with the review and action planning process.

	Yes	No	Action required
1. Does the organisation have an explicit methodology for managing change?	☐	☐	☐
2. Is this methodology transparent, i.e. does it make the plan for change explicit and will it enable stakeholders to 'buy-in' to it?	☐	☐	☐
3. Is it the organisation's policy to involve stakeholders from the outset?	☐	☐	☐
4. Are major change projects given special status, i.e. do they have separately identified resources and time plans?	☐	☐	☐
5. Is there a communication network for adequately disseminating and gathering information with respect to proposed changes?	☐	☐	☐
6. Is the potential for conflict, arising from cultural differences, recognised by the organisation?	☐	☐	☐
7. Are there policies and/or procedures for dealing with variations to the implementation of a planned change?	☐	☐	☐

5 Human Resources Management Implications

Key issues

The following issues are covered in this chapter.

- HRM issues need to be considered during the development of the organisation's strategic plan and accommodation strategy as an integral part of managing the provision of its support services and facilities.

- Senior management's goal of achieving best value for the organisation needs to be shared by all employees.

- Significant changes in the extent of outsourcing will have an impact on the roles and responsibilities of those concerned, requiring changes to HRM policy and procedures.

- Where applicable, the organisation must make clear its position on the transfer of employees to another employer. Legislation exists in many countries to ensure that employees are not treated unfairly.

- Performance appraisals are needed across the length and breadth of the organisation – there should be no discontinuity between senior management and operatives – and must be linked to the organisation's strategic business objectives.

- Remuneration and rewards for personnel should stem from performance appraisal and the overall success of the organisation – they must not be detached from it.

- Developing the skills and expertise of the workforce can be achieved by providing opportunities for personnel that are identified from performance appraisals.

Introduction

Adopting any significant change to the way in which estates-related and facilities services are provided will have an impact on the culture of the organisation and the nature of relationships with both internal and external parties. This chapter highlights those aspects of human resources management (HRM) that need to be addressed when developing a strategy to improve the value of support services required by the organisation. A key determinant of success for any organisation is the performance of its personnel. For this reason, performance appraisal has become the norm, yet is not always implemented so that remuneration and reward are linked to it and the overall health of the organisation. Here, we deliberately avoid the issue of why some organisations feel it is necessary to steer clear of the connection by showing, through a current example, how performance can be used to forge a closer bond between employer and employees. Developing the skills and expertise of the workforce is touched upon in this chapter, though this is covered more fully in Chapter 16. A case study is used to illustrate the breadth of problems that can be encountered when attempting to bring about change within an organisation that appears to have gone relatively unchanged for many years. Finally, an area of particular concern for HRM professionals and senior management is the transfer of employees from the (client) organisation to external service providers under an outsourcing arrangement. Legislation exists in many countries to safeguard the interests of employees to the extent that they are not treated unfairly as the result of their employment being transferred to another employer. The chapter concludes by illustrating, through a case study, how employees can be successfully transferred from the (client) organisation to a service provider, whilst including some notes of caution.

Dealing with shifting demands for resources

This chapter does not seek to provide a broad treatment of the subject of human resources management (HRM) as this can be found in many other books. Instead, it deals with issues and questions that arise from changes to the current organisational structure and its direction, as would occur if previously retained services were now to be outsourced.

The need for changes in the organisation's current HRM practices will depend upon the extent to which in-house services are to be outsourced to external service providers, as well as the type of policies and practices that are currently in place. Most organisations will probably have already considered many of the issues highlighted in this chapter. The sections that follow act primarily as a check against the main aspects of HRM that need to be reviewed when change is being considered. Particularly important is the need to consult with a competent legal authority on the current position in regard to the transfer of employees from the (client) organisation to external service providers, and this is outlined in a later section.

Appropriate management structure

Any significant change in the number of services that are outsourced will have an impact on the structure of the department or organisation; in the case of outsourcing all estates-related services and facilities management, a core management team is required to control and coordinate the activities of the external parties. In this instance, the role of management changes from direct or hands-on management to the management of the output of others, that is, the performance measurement of deliverables. The main management tasks then become the management of the respective contracts and the definition and development of policy and procedures. In this connection, it is essential to ensure that there is a split between purchaser and provider, regardless of whether or not services are outsourced, with the purchaser acting as the informed client in order to monitor the performance of in-house or outsourced service delivery. These policies and procedures, along with relevant standards, are vital if the respective contracts are to meet the expectations of customers and are not to encourage malpractice or some other kind of irregularity.

The most appropriate management structure will be the one that ensures both control and economy for the organisation over its facilities. This means that organisations will need to determine exactly the number of employees and their functions for managing the provision of services, whether they are outsourced or retained in-house. Clearly, the management of contractors is different from the supervision of directly employed personnel and should not demand the same level of resources. It is acceptable that some personnel will have to be retained even where the organisation has opted for total facilities management by a single contractor (see Chapter 11) since the informed client function (ICF) must be maintained (see Chapter 1). Under these circumstances, there is a need for someone to be able to manage the client–service provider interface. The duties involved here can be summarised as:

- Maintaining and enhancing the ICF.
- Defining estates-related and space standard policies and monitoring space utilisation.
- Understanding and monitoring client requirements and likewise keeping clients informed.
- Planning projects involving new or additional works.
- Managing the approvals process and payments to service providers.
- Measuring the performance of service providers.

Case study – Practical human resources issues

This case study illustrates the potential HRM issues faced by an organisation when outsourcing some or all of its non-core business. It is evident that considerable expertise is required to manage these issues in a way that satisfies both legal and ethical requirements, and avoids alienation and dissatisfaction among the remaining workforce, as part of an enduring focus on optimising the environment for core business interests. The case study is intended to provide a stimulus for the reader to develop a prior understanding of the HRM implications of certain changes in the provision of facilities management services and to exercise the judgement

required to cope with a situation such as that illustrated here. With such prepara-
tion it should be possible to consider HRM implications in conjunction with the
initial decisions regarding service provision, rather than as a separate issue to be
handled after such decisions have been taken.

The resolution to outsource some or all facilities management services must
always be taken in this wider context, for which the fullest possible awareness and
understanding is essential, as the case study reveals. Where the client organisation
is aware that it lacks the expertise to manage such complexity, it can choose to
enlist the help of a facilities management consultant at an early stage. In the case
illustrated, many decisions had been made prior to the involvement of the facilities
management consultant. The consultant was therefore brought in to manage, in
particular, the HRM consequences of the earlier, relatively uninformed, decision-
making process within the client organisation.

Northen plc has been established for over a hundred years as a mutual
building society, having transferred more recently to full banking status.
After a series of acquisitions and a very successful share flotation it is now
one of the largest retail banks in the UK with assets of over £150 billion. It
provides a full range of financial services through a network of over 3 000
retail outlets across the country. There is a Northen plc bank in every major
UK town and city and the organisation has become a household name
attracting well over three million customers. In line with its competitors,
Northen plc has undertaken a series of projects to outsource areas of its
non-core business.

The bank's facilities management department group premises is split
into two divisions: 'network premises' and 'head office premises'. Each has
adopted a different approach to its facilities management, creating within
the organisation a 'mixed economy' of service provision.

The network premises section looks after the building maintenance of
all retail branches and a large number of business (administrative) centres.
The management of facilities services has been kept in-house, but all
services have been outsourced at the operative level. A central telephone
helpdesk allows building users to request services and it also monitors
costs and other management information to allow budget management
and forecasting.

The head office premises section carries out a similar task for the bank's
20 or so head office buildings, all located in large cities. Head office premises
runs a mainly in-house operation and provides specific services as follows:

- Engineering – mechanical and electrical (M&E) engineering services
  maintenance and projects, including heating, air-conditioning, lighting,
  cable laying, generators and installations.
- Building maintenance – building fabric maintenance and projects,
  including condition surveys, decorations, repairs, minor works and
  new build.
- Accommodation services – facilities services including porterage, furniture management and handyman services.

Head office premises has contracted out services such as lift maintenance, specialist equipment maintenance, pest control, feminine hygiene, grounds maintenance, cleaning and internal plants. Contracts had been let in bits and pieces for about 10 years; as a result there are currently over 200 contractors working in head office buildings. Other facilities services such as catering, security, conference room booking, chauffeur services, mail and messenger services are provided by the central services department. They do not fall within the scope of any group premises outsourcing project.

Head office premises provides services split into two geographical regions: west and east. Each region is managed by a facilities manager, with responsibility for about 10 sites. There are three main buildings in each region, with each having a resident senior engineer, who manages all engineering services within the buildings. Of engineering personnel, 50% are Northen plc employees, 40% are employed by a local engineering contractor and 10% are employed by a local plumbing contractor. Contracted personnel have been employed full time by Northen plc for between five and ten years, and are managed by Northen's senior engineers. The engineering, building maintenance, health and safety and environmental managers report directly to the head office premises manager. They provide policy, expert advice, quality control and a specialist management resource both to head office and network premises.

An accommodation services manager reports directly to each of the facilities managers and manages a mixed workforce of porters and handymen. The latter's role is furniture management, 'churn' and minor works. About half of the handymen are employed by a local joinery contractor and have been employed for a period similar to other contracted personnel. A workshop is also managed by one of the regions and consists of 10 self-employed shopfitters, who have worked for Northen plc for up to 15 years. They carry out office re-fits and, on occasion, make hand-built furniture.

There are currently two helpdesks, one for each of the regions, but not all buildings are covered by the helpdesk facility. The helpdesks allow building users to call in and report repair requirements or request services. Typical requests include: porters required to move desks, broken lights that need fixing and heating not working. The helpdesk also processes invoices from external contractors and records limited financial data. Management information is not fully recorded and it seems impossible to measure historical costs for service provision.

Generally, the culture in Northen plc is hierarchical and resistant to change. The notion of a 'job for life' was ingrained in the business. In addition to this, the east region was originally part of a smaller bank that was merged with Northen plc some years earlier. Its systems are compatible with Northen plc but there are communication problems between the regions. There is also resistance to the idea that there may be other ways of doing things.

Northen plc has its own internal union, of which all employees are members. The union is strong, but also has a reputation for working closely with management to resolve personnel issues. Communications can sometimes be difficult, as line management must liaise with the union via the employee relations department. There is also a tradition of communicating to employees on major issues through the union.

Northen plc has always paid its personnel above market rates and has been generous with overtime. Additionally, employees enjoy preferential mortgage and loan rates, extended sick leave, a share scheme, performance-related bonuses and a high employer contribution pension plan. Redundancy packages are particularly high. Group premises employees are proud to work for Northen plc and consider themselves part of the banking sector as opposed to representatives of other professions and occupations acting within it.

An earlier outsourcing exercise involving security officers was mismanaged. This was not only expensive, but also led to a fragmented security department comprising a combination of in-house and contracted personnel with top-heavy management and inconsistent procedures. As a result, outsourcing is an unpopular concept with management and employees alike.

Group premises went through a series of structural reorganisations in the past and there are a number of rumours circulating about outsourcing and personnel lay-offs. Derogatory graffiti started to appear on noticeboards and spurious advice has been generated on the rights of personnel under employment law. Although performance at work is high, morale has steadily fallen.

Deregulation of financial services has increased market competition dramatically and Northen plc has embarked on a restructuring programme to increase effectiveness and reduce costs. The decision to outsource the facilities services provided by head office premises has been made at board level and the head office premises manager has been asked to look at the options and make recommendations for providing a more effective and efficient service. Although costs must be reduced it is essential to maintain current high quality standards in the provision of an outsourced service to building users (customers).

Past experience and recognition of the need to manage change effectively have led the head office premises manager to retain a team of facilities management experts to provide advice on outsourcing and the HRM issues involved. The appointed facilities management consultant is therefore faced with two related areas requiring expert help: the continuation of the outsourcing process and its HRM impact. The first area involves helping the client to determine the levels at which outsourcing could be carried out, and advising on the advantages and disadvantages of different options and the appropriate bundling of outsourced contracts. The second area concerns identifying the key HRM issues and advising on how they might be handled. These include deciding who should be consulted concerning the outsourcing exercise, whether TUPE is relevant and, if so, to which employees, and the development of a communication plan.

The particular expertise of the facilities management consultant will be used to supplement the client's existing HRM function, by bringing an awareness of issues in specific relation to the concerns of the facilities management function and, by implication, to the core business which that function aims to support and enhance. From this perspective, the careful and appropriate management of personnel during such changes becomes an essential element in facilities management providing the optimal environment for an organisation's core business.

Employment obligations

Labour markets around the world are subject to varying degrees of control. Increasingly, governments and the legislature are applying more socially-minded principles to the matter of employment. The responsibility of employers for their employees has come in for serious attention in efforts to safeguard the latter's rights. In Europe, EC Directives are applicable to all EU member states and prescribe policy and procedures covering the transfer of employees. In the UK, the relevant legislation is the Transfer of Undertakings (Protection of Employment) Regulations 1981 (TUPE). Organisations must establish how TUPE affects their policies, procedures and actions to ensure that they comply with the legislation. Although, for simplicity, the current discussion is set in the context of the UK, the intentions embodied in TUPE do have a far wider application.

Employment obligations, both legal and moral, need to be considered carefully before outsourcing. TUPE stipulates that, in the case of directly employed personnel, there should be a consultation period before services are outsourced. In the case of contract personnel, organisations should pass their details to the firms tendering for the contracts. The scope of TUPE extends to cover all subsequent situations where the employment status of personnel is subject to change. It is essential, therefore, for organisations to establish how TUPE affects their policies, procedures and actions to ensure that they comply with the legislation.

The obligation to consult employees is an obligation to consult with elected representatives of those employees, or with any recognised trade union. If there are no recognised trade unions and no elected representatives, the employer has a duty to procure the election of representatives. It is not only representatives of employees subject to transfer who must be consulted, but also representatives of any employees who may otherwise be affected by the transfer. The duty to inform and consult is, therefore, broad and the intention is to involve stakeholders. The information that must be passed to the employee includes details of the measures the transferee (that is, the new employer) intends to take with regard to the individual's employment.

This is a complex area of legislation and specialist advice should be sought. Consideration should be given both to the management of the process as well as to the inclusion, within tendering documentation, of necessary clauses in order that the mechanism by which TUPE operates can be put in place. In cases where TUPE does not apply, a redundancy situation may arise, and different procedures will have to be observed (and, of course, selection for redundancy must be fair).

Common sense suggests that the best approach to dealing with the transfer of employees is to involve them fully in discussion about their future employment. There are bound to be cynics amongst those facing potential transfer – many will feel threatened – but the only way forward is to keep to a path that strives for fairness. Failure to do so may not only risk a backlash, it might also incur criminal prosecution for those who have disregarded the correct procedures.

Case study – Sun Life of Canada (UK) Limited

Sun Life of Canada (UK) Limited is a life assurance provider that closed to new business in the UK in 2001. The organisation operates out of a 9 500 m² building in the South of England that is occupied by its outsourcing partners and will remain so for the next 20 to 25 years as the existing book of business runs out.

Sun Life outsourced its ICT support and ongoing administrative responsibilities, whilst entering into a sale and lease-back arrangement on the building itself in 2002. The building is effectively, therefore, a multi-let environment with an occupancy profile that includes four separate tenants. Under the individual lease terms, responsibility for running the facility remains with Sun Life, which raises a recovery service charge to the other tenants. The building has been maintained to a very high level, befitting the corporate headquarters of a prominent financial services organisation.

In 2003, Sun Life entered into a partnering agreement with Acuity Management Solutions under an initial three-year agreement for facilities management services. Acuity managed a transition process that included the transfer of 20 Sun Life employees and the novation of an extensive range of supply chain agreements. Following the transition process, Acuity took responsibility for the delivery of facilities services throughout the building, including all demised areas. This includes the management of the tenant relationships and agreement of annual service charges. Described here is the process by which Acuity carried out this transfer and the benefits delivered through the approach that was adopted.

The process of outsourcing the facilities management function for any client has the potential to create tensions that could increase risk of business interruption with a consequential increase in costs. For this reason, Acuity considered it vital to the success of the contract that a carefully managed transition programme was designed and implemented. The programme translated the vision and objectives of outsourcing into a new set of philosophies, processes and systems, and applied them in a systematic way to ensure successful implementation without risk of business interruption.

The overall transition process began during the mobilisation phase, but continued throughout the first six months of the contract. During this important phase, the facilities management team was strengthened by

Acuity's own human resources to provide specific skills and experience in the management of change. Taking the outsourcing concept as the starting point the team covered the following:

- Implementation and communication planning
- Operational audits of existing processes and procedures
- Process re-engineering of the existing processes and procedures
- Employee surveys to establish skill levels and identify development requirements
- Risk and benefit analyses
- Detailed reviews of the specialist supplier base
- Asset management and assessment of the building improvements that were required, together with the associated business cases and their prioritisation

The whole transition process was the subject of an intensive change management regime to ensure that all the issues raised were dealt with appropriately in a proactive manner.

One of the main objectives of this process was the ability to deliver high quality services continuously. These services could have been impaired by low employee morale, particularly when the attention of individuals was distracted by their becoming more concerned about the changes and impact on themselves, rather than on the delivery of services. Acuity recognised that managing people through any change process inevitably has its high and low points. Often, expectations are set too high by the new provider wishing to rally its newly acquired personnel. When these high expectations are subsequently not met an already fragile situation is exacerbated.

Recognising the impact and adopting a proactive approach mitigated this threat. Proactive management of the change process ensures that momentum is maintained, particularly as it is a fundamental component in the successful achievement of strategic direction. Whilst a degree of overt or covert resistance is almost inevitable from some affected employees and, to a lesser extent, certain stakeholders, the introduction of a change agent can provide direction and assist in the overall achievement of progress in a shorter timeframe. Whilst senior management commitment is essential, without an identified driver to own and push the change through, progress can, all too often, be slow and painful. Acuity's Account Director adopted this dual role of 'agent and driver'.

The success of the mobilisation process was particularly critical for Sun Life as this represented a first generation outsourcing exercise, with TUPE implications and a relatively short timescale involved. Acuity provided a dedicated mobilisation team that operated in addition to and in parallel with the existing facilities management team. The intention was to establish and document fully the processes, procedures, communications, information and reporting requirements, so that the team could focus on the continuous delivery of high quality services.

The first step was to establish and confirm with Sun Life the detail of the mobilisation plan. A detailed task list was prepared which allowed both parties to track and report on progress against the plan, in weekly communication meetings, until both parties agreed that the process was complete.

Mobilisation was led by the Acuity Account Director who took responsibility for managing the client relationship from the 'go live' date. The Account Director was also supported by a fellow director who was involved in one-to-one interviews with each employee. This approach was adopted by Acuity to allow employees access to a director who would not be directly involved in the contract subsequently, but who could act as a mentor should any of the transferring employees have anxieties or concerns which they were uncomfortable raising with their new line manager, the Account Director. In addition, further support personnel were also involved to assist with the technical, health and safety and human resource related issues.

Acuity ensured that a full and open communication process to help employees understand and adjust to the change was followed. A detailed communication plan was adopted and a five-stage process was implemented. Initially, an *Introduction to Acuity* meeting with affected employees was arranged. This meeting described the organisation, its goals, clients and organisational structure; it covered the process, clearly describing the path to be followed and a set of frequently asked questions.

Following this initial meeting, discussions with individual employees were scheduled to explain their position within the organisation, its policies and practices, terms and conditions of employment, and to give each individual the opportunity to raise any queries or concerns. This meeting was conducted in two parts. The first part, with the Account Director, discussed the job, any predicted changes and how work would be managed by Acuity. In the second part, the Acuity Consulting Director discussed terms and conditions, how Acuity manage people and procedural changes, and finally dealt with any queries or concerns.

The time spent with the employees at this stage helped them understand the change and the reasons for it, and was critical in managing their morale during the transition. The objective throughout was to avoid surprises and to ensure that all employees fully understood the process they were going through.

Once the individual meetings were completed, transfer documentation was sent to each transferring employee. This included a statement of principal terms and conditions and the Employee Handbook. In addition, each employee was sent a welcome letter from the Board of Directors. Acuity's induction process was then implemented. Events were organised formally and informally to welcome the transferring employees and to complete the induction process. At every stage of the process, the transferring employees had open access to at least two senior personnel and this open approach reduced any lingering suspicion that might have remained from the initial decision to outsource.

Once the transfer had been effected, work continued in reviewing practices and the roles and responsibilities of all personnel, who were given the opportunity to contribute ideas and to identify areas where activities could be carried out more effectively. The Account Director continued to spend a significant amount of time coaching the senior site personnel, providing the support and assistance needed to move from an in-house cost centre to a contributing profit centre.

Twelve months later, the same personnel remain with a site based manager who has developed his skills and successfully made the transition to a broader operations manager with responsibility for a profit and loss account. In addition, the performance management regime implemented by Acuity has demonstrated improving performance month on month together with sustainable savings representing over 10% of the annual budget.

The facilities management team at Sun Life has accepted and met the challenges it faced with commitment and good humour. Whilst initial thoughts of transfer were filled with apprehension, the approach adopted not only reduced anxieties, but allowed individuals to contribute to a process where they could identify the value they were adding. Once the initial trust was established, respect and commitment followed.

Functions, job descriptions and skills

As changes occur in the mode of managing facilities, it is likely that the functions to be performed by personnel will also change. This will mean that job descriptions have to be revised for those with responsibility for managing services. The content of these revised job descriptions will dictate the selection of appropriate individuals for positions. In assigning individuals to positions that require interaction with service providers, including in-house teams, an understanding of operations and performance issues will be required, as well as strong interpersonal skills and knowledge of contracts.

All job descriptions should incorporate a means for evaluating the performance of employees. It is important that job descriptions are accompanied by role-evaluation procedures so that employees and management are aware from the outset what is expected.

The issues highlighted in this book introduce novel ways of operating in a number of areas. These may require managers to develop existing skills further or to learn new skills in order to implement changes effectively. In particular, introducing new information management procedures and systems – many of which are heavily ICT dependent – will require additional training. Difficulties can arise because of the need for employees to adjust to new working practices. Through sensitive handling, the organisation should be able to overcome problems that might arise, using briefings, seminars and training programmes (see Chapter 16).

Managers also need to be aware of the prevailing market for estates-related and facilities services, and what is required to manage service providers effectively. The managers who deal directly with service providers need different skills to those in a line management position. This should be recognised so that training and development needs can be identified (see Chapter 16). In fact, the entire organisation should be subject to continuing professional development (CPD) as an example of its commitment to life-long learning and a drive for continual improvement.

Practice Point 5.1   Worth one last try.

Key-point: the organisation must be prepared to invest in its people, by providing them with opportunities to retrain for new roles and responsibilities.

When a large city-centre organisation decided to overhaul completely its facilities management, it was faced with some tough choices: make everyone redundant and start over again; transfer everyone on the payroll to a new service provider; or invest in the retraining and reskilling of the workforce. After much discussion behind the scenes, it was agreed that it would be more prudent, at least at the time, to opt for retraining and reskilling. There were many cynics, not only in the organisation's management, but also amongst the workforce. For them, it was a case of having heard it all before. Undeterred, the newly appointed facilities manager decided to take the matter into his own hands. First, there were awareness seminars at which everything was brought out into the open. Next, the workforce was regrouped and refocused on its new challenges and goals. Finally, a permanent communication centre was established and charged with the responsibility for making everything in the facilities directorate, as it was now known, much more visible for everyone. A regular newsletter is now published and distributed to everyone.

Performance appraisal

Management at all levels should be subject to performance appraisal, including those managers who either work for or are part of a service provider organisation. The assessment of the performance of service providers in particular is discussed in Chapter 8. Client representatives (facilities managers and estates managers) who deal with service providers should be set performance objectives that reflect the management relationship with those service providers, along with the actions taken to monitor performance and deal with any shortcomings. This could, for example, take the form of targets for tasks planned and completed over a given period, percentage of response times met and number of tasks needing to be reworked. Where performance depends on the efforts of a group of people, performance at group level should also be addressed either through individual appraisals or at group sessions.

There are many ways in which the performance of individuals can be measured and used to create incentives and to reward excellent performance.

A compelling example is provided by EastPoint – an organisation that was the subject of a major case study in the last chapter. There is a fundamental belief on the part of senior management that all personnel should have a vested interest in the performance of the organisation. With that in mind, personal appraisals are undertaken annually and based upon core competences and key performance indicators (KPIs), which are aligned with the organisation's business objectives. The results of the appraisals have a material bearing on the promotion of individuals and the apportionment of performance bonus payments. These KPIs are in addition to core competences measured as part of a standardised appraisal process. The KPIs for associate directors or heads of divisions and above are customised to suited their specific role and responsibilities. Generic KPIs have been introduced for other grades of professional and managerial personnel, where they are based on business measures linked to the properties being managed and, thus, to customer satisfaction.

Examples of generic KPIs for personnel in support roles are based on five fundamental performance areas and attract the same weight:

1. Core skills – ICT ability, planning and foresight, organisation and team participation
2. Knowledge management – expertise, consistency, maintenance and time management
3. Communication – telecommunications, contacts, manner and expertise
4. Technical documentation – production expertise, adherence to standards and multimedia
5. Procedures – ISO compliance and office policies

These can be compared with the KPIs for professional grade personnel, which are also weighted equally:

- Customer satisfaction – ISO compliance rating, customer satisfaction rating and retention/increase in business
- Professional management – tele-protection compliance, upkeep/satisfaction of manager's diary and director's property inspection report
- Company performance – debtor control rating, audited accounts and participation in business development
- Interpersonal skills – communications, turnover of employees, leadership, motivation and self-improvement

The organisation promotes the development of further skills amongst its personnel through its Training Sponsorship Scheme. This is used to motivate and encourage personnel to upgrade their skills continuously by accredited academic study on a part-time basis in their own time. The Scheme is beneficial to the organisation as it increases the knowledge and expertise of its personnel. A subsidy is offered, but paid only when the candidate passes the course examination.

Another approach to accelerating the development of up-and-coming talent is the *Tall Poppies* programme, which has a multi-faceted approach covering:

- The development and faster promotion of high performers.
- Increasing the ratio of internal to external promotions.
- Modifying the appraisal process to differentiate individuals by performance.
- The recruitment of a few outstanding graduates as executive trainees to be used as a core resource in process re-engineering, innovation and the production of tangible products for deployment in the business.

The organisation has taken positive action in favour of internal promotion. Approximately 75% of vacancies have been filled through internal promotion, with external recruitment reduced from 75% to about 50% of all vacancies.

The organisation introduces young managerial talent into the business through the vehicle of an Executive Trainee Programme, with the aim of creating a new generation of young executives appropriately trained for promotion to management positions. These personnel enjoy career development through a combination of productive assignments and participation in an Executive Development Scheme within the wider group of which the organisation is a part. These people have proved a highly productive asset to the organisation, having been deployed on a number of business assignments. These are designed to be meaningful to the individual and productive for the organisation. Each assignment is intended to challenge the individual to be creative and to produce new products or re-engineer processes. Their work must be documented and include implementation in the workplace. Two early entrants have since been promoted to assistant manager roles and are pursuing further management qualifications.

Conclusions

HRM is a sensitive area for all organisations. Increasing legislation has added to the burden on organisations to have clear policies and procedures in place, no more so perhaps than in the case of TUPE. These have to be complete and must apply regardless of whether or not a service is outsourced or retained in-house. Organisations need to adopt a management structure that is appropriate to the mode of service provision and understand their obligations as employers. Job descriptions and skills requirements must be made explicit and procedures put in place to appraise and reward performance against measurable outputs or outcomes.

CHECKLIST

This checklist is intended to assist with the review and action planning process.

	Yes	No	Action required
1. Is the organisation's management structure appropriate to the delivery of cost-effective and efficient management services?	☐	☐	☐
2. Have job functions, job descriptions and service requirements been properly described in relation to the provision of management services?	☐	☐	☐
3. Are employees involved in defining job functions, job descriptions and service requirements?	☐	☐	☐
4. Do current arrangements properly recognise employment obligations, as well as the underpinning legislation?	☐	☐	☐
5. Is a well-developed method of performance appraisal in place covering all employees?	☐	☐	☐
6. Is performance appraisal linked to the organisation's strategic business objectives and overall success?	☐	☐	☐
7. Are employees provided with incentives to develop their skills and are they rewarded when they succeed?	☐	☐	☐

6 Policy and Procedures for Outsourcing

Key issues

The following issues are covered in this chapter.

- There is a logical sequence to the outsourcing of services, covering strategy, tender documentation, tendering and contract award. A realistic timescale must be allowed if the overall process is to be successful.

- Outsourcing involves many activities and these have to be managed. A detailed programme should be prepared to help manage the process and to keep all interested parties informed.

- Defining the scope of services is crucial to successful outsourcing, by providing the basis for inviting tenders and administering the contract. A poorly defined scope will lead, almost inevitably, to problems in the management of the service.

- All stakeholders must be involved in the process of outsourcing if their needs, as well as those identified earlier during the preparation of the facilities management strategy, are to be fully addressed and communicated – success depends on commitment to the process from all who could possibly contribute.

Introduction

Once the decision to outsource has been reached, the procedures that follow tend to be somewhat prescriptive, though are certainly not mechanistic. This means that senior management can rely upon legislation, guidelines and practice notes from a wide range of sources. There is benefit from this situation, but there can be disadvantages arising from dogged adherence to procedures that may have been designed for a different purpose. Some interpretation is likely in order to take account of local circumstances, for instance custom and practice, as well as the market. Narrow interpretation of legislation in particular – as we shall see later – risks creating anomalies that can thwart the good intentions that lie behind them. The approach taken here will be one of highlighting current best practice, drawing on guidance from various sources and the authors' research in the field. The chapter begins by examining the general approach to the procurement of works, supplies and services, referred to collectively as services. The procedures apply also to situations where currently outsourced services are being re-tendered and/or rationalised. For clarity, the procedures are followed in chronological order as far as practicable. The objective is to ensure that the following critical success factors are achieved: first, the scope of the services and interfaces with related services are defined; second, the service level required by stakeholders from the outsourced team is clearly specified; third, the outsourced team has the capabilities and skills to deliver the service; fourth, internal departments are recognised as customers and treated as such; fifth, outsourced service provision is provided through a team approach, with each member working towards a common goal; and last, service provision is continually reviewed and improved.

Essential approach

General guidance on procurement can be found in many publications relating to project management; in fact, the subject is covered comprehensively elsewhere. Additionally, reference can be made to Chapter 1 on the risks encountered in outsourcing and to Appendix C, which provides an effective checklist. The organisation should consider risk assessment and risk transfer as an integral part of the process for procuring services. This will mean that risk assessment forms part of the policy and procedures for outsourcing. Risk assessment was covered in Chapter 3, with an example of how to apply it in practice. For a detailed appreciation of risk management see, for example, CIRIA (1996) in which detailed guidance, with practical examples and pro-forma, can be followed.

In order to illustrate the outsourcing process, a generic procurement plan is set out in Fig. 6.1 showing the main stages and activities. Each activity is described in more detail below. The plan's aim is to provide an indication of the order and timescales involved in moving from the definition of services to the services actually being provided within the organisation. The plan is divided into three main stages:

1. *Strategy* – covering the definition of services, current arrangements, the position of stakeholders and legislation affecting employment and procurement.
2. *Tender documents* – covering service specifications, service level agreements and conditions of contract.
3. *Tendering process* – covering tenderer briefing and assessment, contract award, pre-contract meeting, mobilisation and review.

The timescales will vary according to the scope and scale of services being outsourced. However, many of the critical periods, for instance dealing with legislative aspects, contractual matters, tenderer briefing, tender period and mobilisation, will remain more or less the same for a wide range of contract types and values. The timescale might reduce for activities such as

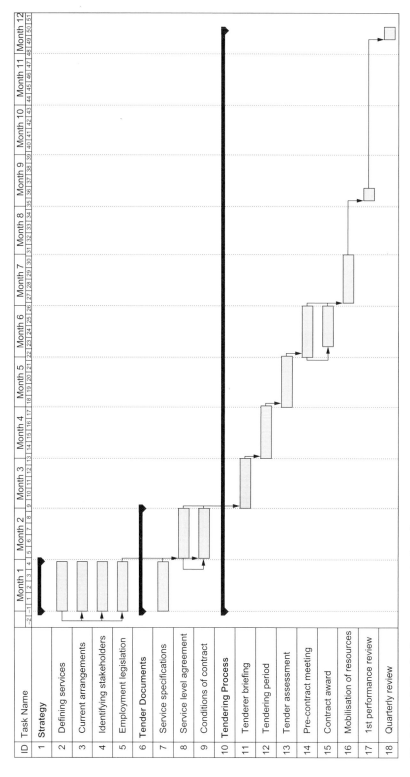

Fig. 6.1 Activities in the procurement of services.

the definition of services, current arrangements, identifying stakeholders, tender assessment and contract award, where the service to be outsourced is of minor economic importance and uncomplicated. As with any exercise of this kind it is easy to underestimate the time required to move from the decision to outsource to the commencement of the service.

Strategy

Defining services

Critical to the success of any outsourcing process is the clear definition of all required services including interfaces – see also Chapter 2. For example, are pest control, waste disposal and sanitary services to be part of the cleaning contract? Such definition is required to ensure that all necessary services are provided and that no gaps exist between the interfaces of each service.

Practice Point 6.1   Falling into the cracks.

Key-point: services must have their scope clearly defined, with special attention paid to instances where some services can fall into the gaps between service contracts.

When infestation of the ceiling void above the kitchens was discovered, the immediate reaction was to call in the cleaning contractor. After all, the contractor was responsible for removal of waste and related duties. In the event, the contractor pointed out that any occurrence of this kind was not his responsibility. The contractor appeared to have acted correctly, but there was the understanding, at least in the mind of the facilities manager, that matters like the one encountered were included in the scope of the cleaning contract. The outcome was that the organisation agreed to pay the contractor to remove the infestation and then formally instructed that the revised scope be included within the contract. Fortunately for the organisation, the service contract contained provision for changes of this kind to be made.

Current arrangements

The following base information should be gathered in relation to current services prior to the initiation of the outsourcing process:

- In-house services – number of employees, their grades and employment details (age, starting date, length of service, experience, special skills, salary and benefits), plant and equipment inventory.
- Outsourced services – contract expiry date, contract value, scope of existing services and special features.

Identifying stakeholders

The importance of stakeholders should come as no surprise – previous chapters have underscored the necessity of their early involvement. Stakeholders are those parties with an interest in the services to be provided, such as internal and external customers. In order to secure the success of the process, it is important that they are identified and their requirements understood, with specifications and service levels aligned to their needs (see Chapter 8). While it may not always be possible, given the constraints that may be imposed on the outsourced team to satisfy every requirement or preference, the needs of stakeholders should be ranked according to their benefit to the organisation to ensure that the more significant ones are met.

Essentially, any individual or group with a legitimate interest in the organisation is a stakeholder and these can include:

- The organisation's employees
- External users and customers
- Service providers and suppliers
- Shareholders and non-executive directors
- Neighbours
- General public
- Community groups
- Local councils
- Statutory authorities

Employment legislation

Prior to proceeding with outsourcing or the re-tendering of services, it is essential to consider the implications of current employment and procurement legislation – see Chapters 5 and 9. In terms of the former, the relevant legislation in the UK is the Transfer of Undertakings (Protection of Employment) Regulations 1981 (TUPE), which is derived from the EC's Acquired Rights Directive. These regulations protect the contracts of employment of both directly employed personnel and the contractor's employees where the service has already been outsourced. An earlier case study discussed how this legislation applied to the transfer of employees – see Chapter 5.

In relation to directly employed personnel, the organisation's obligations are more onerous and will usually involve a consultation period with employees. Where service provider's employees are involved, the (client) organisation will normally only be involved in communicating employee details to tenderers – again, see Chapter 5. However, legal precedent is continually being set in this area, for example the definition of a full-time employee. It is, therefore, advisable and prudent to seek professional advice on the specific implications for each service that is to be outsourced.

Public procurement legislation

In addition to employment legislation, public procurement legislation must be addressed, where relevant. In the UK, the implications of the Public Works, Supply and Services Contract Regulations 1995 must be taken into account. The main principle behind this legislation is to ensure that for service contracts above a specified threshold:

- Specifications are non-discriminatory.
- Firms and individuals are selected objectively for inclusion in tender lists.
- The tendering process is transparent.

These principles have, of course, a wider application to best practice procurement in general. In the EU context, public sector organisations are required by EC public procurement directives to publish tenders for the provision of supplies, services and works over a certain value in the Official Journal of the European Communities (OJEC). The contract value thresholds, above which invitations to tender should appear in the OJEC, are as follows (approximate values depending upon categorisation and exchange rates):

- Supplies and services: €154 014 (roughly £100 000).
- Works: €5 923 624 (roughly £4 000 000).

The above values were correct at January 2004 and are reviewed every two years. An annual periodic indicative notice is required, covering each priority service category on which it is expected that more than €1 000 000 (roughly £680 000) will be spent. Public sector organisations, in particular, should check these limits, and establish whether or not they are required to advertise in the OJEC before inviting tenders. Total contract value, regardless of contract period, is the basis of assessment, not annual cost. Some organisations have tried to circumvent this legislation by reducing the size of contracts to below the threshold by breaking them into smaller parcels. Such practices effectively contravene European law.

Whilst it is possible to generalise on the underlying principles, it is not feasible to provide a comprehensive guide to legislation. Appropriate legal advice should be taken and the position on public procurement procedures verified in order to ensure compliance with the relevant legislation in any place and at any time. This should be part of the ICF – see Chapter 1. Responsibilities should also be clearly split between purchasing and provider personnel when in-house tenders are sought in addition to those from external service providers. This will avoid conflicts of interest that might otherwise arise when subsequently assessing tenders.

Tender documents

Service specifications

A service specification quantifies the acceptable standard of service required by the customer and will generally form a part of the contract with the service provider (see Chapter 8). The preparation of a service specification is a prerequisite for the drafting of a service level agreement – see next section. Specifications ordinarily set out standards covering organisation policy, department requirements, statutory requirements, health and safety standards, and manufacturers' recommendations. A specification may also outline the procedures needed to achieve required technical standards.

Service level agreement (SLA)

The SLA builds on the service specification by amplifying, in practical terms, the obligations of each party. Technical and quality standards will usually be defined in relation to industry standards or manufacturer's recommendations, whereas performance will be related to the specific requirements of stakeholders, that is, frequency of activity and response times to call-outs (see Chapter 8). This agreement need only include, at the tendering stage, a framework setting out the overall performance parameters with detailed procedural issues to be evolved and refined during the life of the contract. Whilst the scope must be made clear, detailed day-to-day operating procedures can only be fine-tuned as knowledge and experience of each service partner is built up over time. SLAs must be kept up-to-date and avoid locking either party into arrangements and practices that are plainly inefficient or, worse, ineffective.

Conditions of contract

Wherever possible, it is recommended that industry standard forms of contracts are used to formalise legal relationships between the client organisation and contractors. Standard forms of contract may be obtained from a number of sources that include:

- The Chartered Institute of Building (CIOB) Standard Form of Facilities Management Contract (second edition, 2001) – used for a client organisation employing a facilities manager. The contract allows for an adjustable annual fee to be paid, together with reimbursable expenses. It is intended primarily for use in the private sector.
- PACE (GC/Works/10) Standard Form of Facilities Management Contract. The form is designed to help in the procurement of facilities management services and can also be used for the appointment of a contractor as a one-stop shop or as a managing agent. It is suitable for use in procuring services on the basis of input or output specifications

and can be used on one or more sites. It is intended primarily for use in the public sector.
- Chartered Institute of Purchasing and Supply (CIPS) – facilities management model agreement for service contracts, cleaning, security and so on.
- JCT (Joint Contracts Tribunal) – building contracts for maintenance and small works (the JCT publishes a range of standard forms and variants of them).

The CIOB contract has helped to formalise the nature of facilities management arrangements. Since its original publication in 1999, it has become a popular form of contract. It outlines and specifies the services to be provided by the facilities manager, and deals with administrative issues – management reporting, personnel, changes etc. – as well as those of a mostly contractual nature, such as obligations, insurances, non-performance and termination. Provision is included for public sector contracts where special conditions apply. The CIOB and PACE (GC/Works/10) forms are likely to be preferable to the CIPS agreement in most cases.

Generally, any amendments required to forms of contract should be clearly stated in the tender documents. Normally, it should not be necessary to amend standard conditions, as to do so might lead to unforeseen events and consequences. If the organisation wishes to amend standard forms, legal advice should be sought.

The purpose of forms of contracts is to provide the formal, legally binding framework within which service specifications and SLAs can operate. As such, they should not attempt to restate the contents of specifications and SLAs. Appendix D contains useful guidance on contractual approaches and terms, whilst Appendix E outlines the possible contents and structure of an SLA. In the case of EastPoint – an organisation referred to in previous chapters – the dividing line between SLAs and the contract is clear: the latter includes all annexes necessary to embody the SLAs so that there is no requirement for separate SLAs or service specifications. The organisation's own contract form, thus, has annexes covering both service specifications and SLAs. In this connection, the latter are intended more as the means for stipulating performance indicators – see Chapter 14.

An important consideration, in terms of contract conditions, is that they should allow for changes to be made as experience of operating a contract grows. Service level agreements (SLAs) should be reviewed and updated periodically. An inflexible contract, unable to accommodate changes, would represent an unworkable arrangement. Contracts should be seen, therefore, not as straitjackets, but as frameworks within which to operate and develop best practice. As a minimum, contracts should contain clauses that allow for changes to be made to the provision of services, so long as they are not so significant as to alter the overall scope and content of the contract. These clauses should also cover the mechanism for adjusting the contract sum in the event of changes – sometimes referred to as variations – being required and sanctioned by the client.

> **Practice Point 6.2   Form your own conclusions.**
>
> **Risk item:** failure to use standard forms of contract for facilities management or inadequate conditions of contract can lead to serious difficulties.
>
> *Key-point: in negotiating contracts with suppliers and service providers, it is essential to ensure that the client's position is properly protected and not compromised. Legal advice should be sought in these matters.*
>
> In one case, an organisation entered into a contract with a service provider only to find later that the terms and conditions were biased in the contractor's favour. The client organisation did not adopt a standard form of contract and, therefore, accepted the contract as drafted by the service provider (the contractor), an established and respected company. A clause in the contract held the client organisation liable for redundancy payments if any of the personnel employed by the contractor had to be dismissed following a decline in the use of certain of the facilities. Subsequently, there was a fall in the use of a particular facility and the organisation had to make substantial payments. An important consideration – in terms of contract conditions – is that they should allow for changes to be made as experience of operating a contract grows. Service level agreements (SLAs) should be reviewed and updated periodically. An inflexible contract – unable to accommodate changes – would represent an unworkable arrangement. Contracts should be seen as frameworks within which to operate and develop best practice. As a minimum, contracts should contain clauses that allow for changes to be made to the provision of services, so long as they are not so significant as to alter the overall scope and content of the contract. These clauses should also cover the mechanism for adjusting the contract sum in the event of changes being required by the client.

Tendering process

Tenderer briefing

Depending on the complexity of the services being tendered, it is often useful to organise a tenderers' briefing during the tender period. This can be either formal or informal so long as the latter is conducted on a consistent basis for all tenderers. The object of this briefing is to:

- Show tendering companies the facilities.
- Describe how they support the core business.
- Identify areas of particular concern or sensitivity.
- Explain the principles of the contract.
- Clarify the requirements of the tender submission.
- Answer any questions that may arise.

In the course of these briefings, it is important that tenderers are advised that lowest price will not be the sole factor in choosing between tenders: quality of service will be taken into account. Care must also be exercised in conducting such briefings in order to avoid collusion between parties or allegations that one party is being treated more favourably than others (see Appendix B).

Tendering period

In the public sector, where the value of services to be tendered exceeds the EC public procurement thresholds (see earlier section), the tender period must comply with the duration set out in the regulations. In any event, it is good practice to allow sufficient time for tenderers to consider fully the documentation and allow them to submit a considered proposal. This should never be less than two weeks from receipt of documents. If it should be found necessary to issue an amendment to the tender documents, this should not be less than two weeks before submission of the tender. One of the greatest failings is to maintain a tender receipt date that squeezes the time given to tenderers in which to prepare a properly considered tender. In the worst case scenario, the client organisation could be left with no tenders or just one that is effectively a cover price. This outcome would be wholly unsatisfactory and be a waste of time and money.

The procedure for the formal submission of tenders is, for public sector organisations, usually highly prescribed. Adherence to the requirements outlined in the 'invitation to tender' should be followed strictly by tendering companies. Failure to comply with just one aspect – no matter how minor it may seem – could lead to the rejection of the tender without it even being opened. Public accountability and the fears of individual officers leave no margin for negotiation in such an eventuality.

Tender assessment

Sufficient time should be allowed for the assessment of tenders. Assessment criteria should be agreed in advance in relation to technical, quality of service and resource requirements and may also be incorporated in the tender documents. These should be applied to each tender submission in order to shortlist companies for interview, requiring them to make a formal presentation. Additionally, inspection of a company's premises and order books could provide valuable insights into its ability to meet the demands of the new contract. A major consideration is whether or not a company is physically able to perform the service for the tender price. Client organisations should enquire as to the credit-worthiness of shortlisted companies and request contact names of existing clients from whom performance references might be obtained.

Clearly, facilities management contracts involve the operation and delivery of services within occupied environments. Consequently, the way in which services are delivered and the manner in which stakeholder communication occurs becomes increasingly relevant. In the authors' experience the choice of the service provider's main representative is a critical component in the identification of an appropriate partner. Effort placed at the interview stage in understanding the strengths, weaknesses and style of the representative and team can provide a valuable insight into the likely relationship to follow. It is recommended that the key representatives are present at interview and that this element is evaluated in its own right.

The concept of least whole-life cost should be used to evaluate tenders alongside risk assessment. Least whole-life cost takes into account the cost of the services over the duration of the contract, including annual price fluctuations, lifecycle cost issues, payback on capital investment and so on. In other words, it is a matter of determining the total cost of each tender, enabling comparison on a like-for-like basis. EastPoint applies a tender assessment mathematical model, based on Monte Carlo simulation, to analyse all standard property, facilities, asset management and engineering contracts. Tender submissions undergo risk assessment of varying depth, covering financial and legal risks as well as the nature of the work itself to determine value. In the future, these two approaches will merge to provide client organisations with whole-life, value-risk assessment.

Practical steps in determining quality and cost

Lowest price is not the sole factor in deciding which tender to accept, although many tenders are accepted on the basis of price alone. Quality should play an equal part in any evaluation if best value is to mean anything. For some contracts it may be difficult to determine the quality of service: rarely can quality or performance be considered in absolute terms. It is possible to take account of quality by judging it against benchmarks established in service specifications or other objective measures.

There are other ways in which quality and cost may be judged. For instance, in the case of professional services, one approach would be to operate a two-envelope tender system. Short-listed consultants are sent model agreements and asked to submit a lump-sum tender, along with their time charges for extra work. The first tender describes the quality of service to be provided; the second gives the price. Two separate panels look at the tenders.

A quality panel of, say, four people is convened to rank the tenders, A, B and C according to the quality that they believe each tenderer represents. The panel applies a percentage adjustment (or weighting) to the services offered by each: it is necessary that all panellists agree. Once the quality panel has finished its deliberations, the price panel opens the envelopes containing the price tenders. The decision is then taken to award the contract to the consultant offering the highest quality at the lowest price, based on a simple calculation.

Contract award, pre-contract meetings, mobilisation and review

A pre-contract meeting should be called once the best tender has been selected and contract has been awarded so as to address the following issues:

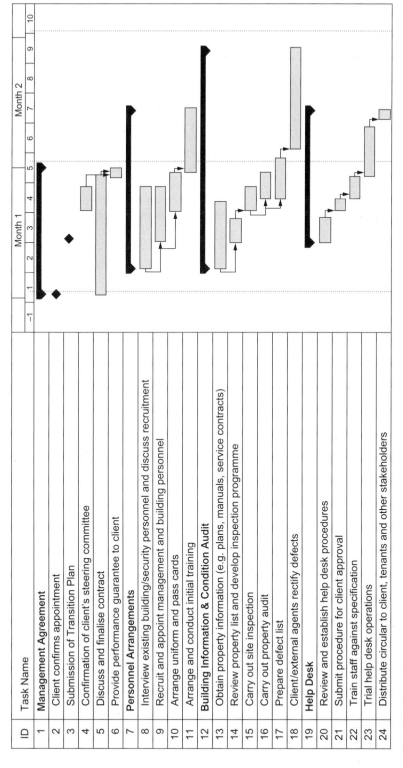

Fig. 6.2 Transition process.

- Service provider's plan for commencement and provision of the service.
- Insurance cover with respect to statutory requirements and specific eventualities.
- Contract administration – payments, meetings and other key events.

The contractor (the service provider) should be given a sufficient mobilisation period to marshal all resources, thus ensuring a seamless continuation of service provision. Where the service(s) affected are to be outsourced for the first time, it is recommended that the service provider visit the organisation to explain to users of the service what is expected of them. During this period, it will be necessary to plan for the regular review of the service provider's performance. The frequency of revisions will depend on the duration and complexity of the contract. Typically, three-monthly reviews would be reasonable, though monthly reviews during the early stages might be more appropriate in order to deal with teething problems.

In cases where the organisation's employees have been transferred to a service provider, special arrangements will be required to deal with the transition. This is illustrated in Figure 6.2.

Ongoing relationships

The relationship between the service provider and the client organisation's representative is crucial to ensuring that the service is provided as expected. Moreover, the client will want to improve the level of performance over time, so sound working relationships are important. Problems that might sour the relationship should be forestalled. For example, the person occupying the role of client representative might also be the person who prepared the unsuccessful in-house tender. Organisations should, therefore, be prepared to make changes to their management, if necessary, to ensure that poor working relationships do not arise as a consequence of earlier decisions – see also Chapters 4 and 5 regarding the acquisition of new skills and the redefinition of roles and responsibilities.

Conclusions

Organisations need to recognise that successful outsourcing of services comes from a process in which policies are clearly defined and procedures are progressive and transparent. Fortunately, there is sufficient advice and published guidance available on how to follow procedures, and detailed aspects of them. Indeed, attention to detail is an essential commodity on the part of client organisations, and this must be matched by those companies tendering for contracts. Thorough preparation and execution takes time and so the organisation embarking on an outsourcing route must plan well ahead and build in adequate time. If followed carefully, procedures that lead to outsourcing can provide a firm basis for the subsequent manage-ment and administration of contracts.

CHECKLIST

This checklist is intended to assist with the review and action planning process.

		Yes	No	Action required
1.	Has the base information in relation to current services, prior to the initiation of the outsourcing process, been properly collated?	☐	☐	☐
2.	Have all stakeholders with an interest in the service to be provided been properly identified and consulted?	☐	☐	☐
3.	Have the services to be outsourced been clearly identified and defined?	☐	☐	☐
4.	Does the organisation grasp the full implications of employment and public procurement legislation?	☐	☐	☐
5.	Do the tender documents include full service specifications, the terms of proposed service level agreements and conditions of contract?	☐	☐	☐
6.	Is the tender process sufficiently rigorous to allow for proper competition?	☐	☐	☐
7.	Are proper tender evaluation procedures in place?	☐	☐	☐
8.	Are arrangements in place to ensure good ongoing relationships between the service provider and the client organisation?	☐	☐	☐

7 Policy and Procedures for In-house Provision

Key issues

The following issues are covered in this chapter.

- Defining the scope of a service is as important to successful in-house provision as it is to outsourced services – there should be no half-measures.

- A poorly defined scope will lead, almost inevitably, to problems in the management of the service with higher supervision costs and a lowering of customer satisfaction: consultation with all stakeholders is essential.

- The organisation must establish the extent of the knowledge and skills that its employees possess.

- Where relevant and appropriate skills are in short supply, retraining and/or recruitment of new personnel will be necessary – again, consultation with stakeholders is essential.

- Customers must be recognised and the relationship between them and the in-house team must be taken seriously and managed professionally.

- Performance monitoring applies equally to in-house and outsourced services.

- A process of continual improvement should be implemented to ensure that productivity and standards of quality and performance are consistently raised.

Introduction

The retention of estates-related and facilities management services might be considered of less interest, even of lower importance, as a topic when compared to outsourcing. In a sector that has grown large on the back of a consistent wave of outsourcing one could be forgiven for seeing in-house provision as having lower economic worth. In fact, nothing could be further from the truth. In most countries, a significant proportion of facilities are competently managed by in-house teams, who consistently deliver customer satisfaction and best value. They have achieved this status by being highly professional and as demanding of their own personnel as others are of external service providers. Some organisations have brought in-house services that were previously outsourced. Our purpose here is not to argue for either in-house or outsourced service provision, since that is entirely a consequence of earlier steps in formulating a strategy, policies and operational plans to deliver best value. The intention is to underline the importance of managing in-house provision to the highest standard. This chapter outlines policy and procedures to be adopted where services are provided in-house. For clarity, the chapter has been set out to follow the process in chronological order. The objective is to ensure that certain critical success factors are met: first, the scope of the services and interfaces with related services must be defined; second, the service level required of the in-house team by all stakeholders must be determined; third, the in-house team must have the capabilities and skills to deliver the service; fourth, the team must treat internal departments as customers; fifth, in-house service provision is provided through a team approach, with each member working towards a common goal; and last, service provision is continually reviewed and improved.

Definition of services

For outsourced services, it is generally recognised that success is dependent upon the clear definition of the services, including their interfaces. In other words, there are 'no cracks to fall down'. This view is also true in the case of in-house service provision, but for different reasons. Where services have been outsourced, definition is required to ensure that all necessary services are provided and that no gaps exist between the interfaces of each service. In-house providers also require clear definition in order to manage their resources effectively. Without obvious delineation of roles and responsibilities, it can be difficult to measure the performance of in-house personnel.

If the customer – taken to be a user department within the client organisation – is unsure as to who is providing which service, it is hard for providers both to achieve and to demonstrate best value. This is also important in the context of avoiding conflicts of interest, because of unclear splits between purchasing and in-house service personnel at the time of preparing tender documents and during the subsequent tendering period.

Identifying stakeholders

As we have now begun to recognise, stakeholders are critical to the success of service provision of any kind. Those affected by the provision of services must be identified, just as they are for outsourced services. It is important for the in-house team to understand the relative influence of the respective stakeholders, as the team will potentially be serving many masters simultaneously. At the same time, it would be wise to avoid embarking upon any path that could conceivably prove divisive and run counter to the organisation's business direction and strategic objectives. The risk of such an outcome is always possible in highly politicised organisations.

In order to ensure the success of the process, each stakeholder's specific requirements must be understood. Whilst it may not always be possible, given the constraints that can be imposed on the in-house team to satisfy everyone, requirements should be ranked according to their business benefit. In this way, an optimal mix can be established, whilst helping to reduce the likelihood of conflict arising from 'political infighting'.

In-house capabilities and skills

The in-house service team must be able to adapt to meet changes in requirements in order to support the core business effectively and provide best value. The ease with which this may be possible will depend upon the skills and capabilities of employees and their willingness to continue in training and development. If necessary, in-house teams may have to recruit new personnel with the necessary skills. Chapter 5 outlined examples of how existing personnel can be motivated and challenged. Retaining and investing in the current workforce should be seen as preferable – and probably less costly and time-consuming – than recruitment.

In technical areas such as maintenance of services installations, many external service providers invest heavily in training to ensure that their personnel are competent and qualified. This is especially so where new legislation and standards come into force and where it is necessary to retain membership of an industry body or association. For a small, in-house team, this may represent a significant time and cost overhead. If the in-house team is to satisfy the organisation's needs this investment must be made.

Departments as customers

The in-house service team probably has the benefit of many years of experience of the organisation, which must not be lost by failing to be responsive to the needs of the customer. Internal departments must be regarded as customers and their needs served accordingly. Furthermore, there should be no difference in the in-house team's attitude towards internal and external customers where the latter could be, for instance, members of the public who are entitled to make some use of the organisation's facilities. A professional approach can and must be adopted and maintained towards all customers. Many organisations have grasped this issue and it has enabled them to provide a focused service that is also responsive.

In-house team approach

It is essential that members of the in-house team recognise that they should operate in the same way as would an external service provider and that they will be judged on a similar basis. Given that the organisation's management may be looking periodically at the market for external service provision, it makes sense for the in-house team to operate in a business-like way so that it can compete fairly if the need arises. Most organisations manage to do this, but the weakness is in maintaining a consistent level over time. One of the biggest threats to the in-house team's success is from complacency, which is easily noticed by customers.

The in-house team should be examined for its efficiency and effectiveness. The constituent personnel must operate as a team if they are to deliver a value-adding service. The starting point for engendering team spirit is through sharing common goals and objectives. In the UK, the government has promoted the establishment of customer charters that set out the type and level of services that can be expected in a number of service sectors. Many private sector organisations do likewise. This kind of SLA has the added benefit of articulating the objectives to be achieved by the team. By sharing common goals and key objectives, and working as a team, additional benefits can result. This will help the in-house team measure up to the organisation's expectations, as well as its own. Care must be exercised, however, in ensuring that customer charters are not seen as some kind of management fad or, worse, as a concoction of imperatives written in superlatives. Such a mistake will easily attract the cynics.

Service provision reviewed and improved

The in-house service provider must be proactive in looking for areas where value can be added. It should not regard service levels as permanently fixed, but as providing the basis for refinement. The provider's expertise can help to assess whether or not the perceived service levels are, in fact, the most appropriate. This is particularly relevant in the case of response times when ordering work. If informed discussion can take place as to real needs as opposed to perceived needs, the service, with its corresponding resource levels, can be designed to meet that need. This value-adding activity can enable the in-house team to differentiate itself from outsourced competitors, and intimate knowledge of the organisation can be used to good effect. That said, knowledge of the organisation is no compensation for a service that does not deliver against customer needs and expectations.

Many support service processes are labour intensive and consist of a high volume of low-value activities. ICT could therefore be of help to the in-house service provider by improving communication and producing appropriate management information. Through the use of low-cost ICT tools, in-house service providers can measure how they are performing against the service level agreed with each identified customer type or group. Thereafter, by means of continual improvement, increases in performance can be compared and reported against a benchmark – see Chapter 14. This activity should extend to a comparison with external service providers both to assess the relative competitiveness of in-house provision and to gain new insights into the business and the disciplines that constitute facilities management.

Conclusions

Many of the stages and issues that an in-house team should consider are comparable to those that apply to outsourced services. The difference lies in the clarity of roles and responsibilities that are usually more obvious in the latter by virtue of a procurement process that has been followed preceding the award of the contract. The in-house team should try to achieve the same position both for the benefit of its customers and its own management needs. This, in turn, will permit more ready measurement of performance. Retaining services in-house has to be the primary goal for the in-house team. It is only likely to reach that goal if it delivers customer satisfaction and best value, and can demonstrate that.

CHECKLIST

This checklist is intended to assist with the review and action planning process.

		Yes	No	Action required
1.	Have all stakeholders in the provision of services been identified and consulted?	☐	☐	☐
2.	Are the services to be provided in-house properly defined?	☐	☐	☐
3.	Are the roles and responsibilities of those providing the services properly defined?	☐	☐	☐
4.	Has the organisation clearly assessed and identified current in-house capabilities and skills and augmented those that might be lacking?	☐	☐	☐
5.	Has the role of departments as customers been recognised?	☐	☐	☐
6.	Is there a clear division between the ICF and in-house service providers?	☐	☐	☐
7.	Are proper arrangements in place for the review and improvement of service provision?	☐	☐	☐

8 Service Specifications, Service Level Agreements and Performance

Key issues

The following key issues are covered in this chapter.

- Stakeholders must be involved from the outset in specifying the kinds of services required and the level of performance that will be acceptable to them, both from in-house and external service providers.

- Service specifications and service level agreements (SLAs) are tools for managing the quality, performance and value of services provided.

- A service specification is a document that quantifies the minimum service that is acceptable if the customer's requirements are to be met. It provides a benchmark against which the level of services delivered to the customer can be assessed.

- An SLA is a commitment by the service provider (in-house or outsourced) to the customer to deliver an agreed level of service. It should specify rewards and penalties, yet retain flexibility so that the customer's changing requirements can be taken into account should circumstances change.

- Service providers should be involved in the process of updating and improving SLAs and service specifications in order to draw upon their experience of actually providing the service.

- Performance monitoring of service providers involves reconciling the level of the service delivered to the customer against agreed standards and targets set out in the service specifications and SLAs.

- Procedures for correcting any discrepancies between service levels require the joint participation of the client organisation and service provider.

- If internal quality targets are to be met, quality-of-service criteria need to be incorporated into contracts with service providers. Contracts should stipulate that payments will depend on the performance of the provider in reaching these targets.

- The organisation should describe its performance requirements in terms of factors that are critical to successful service provision. Key performance indicators (KPIs) can then be used to measure deviations from specifications and SLAs.

Introduction

Service specifications and service level agreements (SLAs) are essential tools in facilities management irrespective of whether services are outsourced or retained in-house. They provide the working guidelines for both client organisations and service providers to focus on the services that should be provided, where, when and in what ways. Since they are intended to bridge the gap between customer requirements and expectations on the one hand and the delivery of a response in the form of services on the other hand, they have a pivotal role in the facilities management process. Moreover, they become the centre of attention when one party feels that the other is failing to meet an obligation. In a positive light, they can provide clarity, certainty and motivation to succeed. They should also be seen as something that is capable of improvement and, by implication, something that is bound to change over time. This chapter reviews the use of service specifications and SLAs arising from the requirements of stakeholders. It identifies the purpose of each and the ways in which they are expected to contribute to the effective management of services provision. These documents provide the organisation with the means to monitor performance and a basis for rewarding excellent results, as well as penalising those who fall short. The issue of quality assurance – including the operation of a quality management system – is discussed and advice offered on the broad approach that should be taken.

Stakeholders' interests

A recurrent theme in this book is that of stakeholder involvement. In this and following sections, we see that the client organisation has a responsibility for engaging stakeholders in the framing of individual service specifications and SLAs. Identified stakeholders should be involved in specifying their requirements and the level of performance that will be acceptable. This means:

- Involving stakeholders, as far as practicable, in defining and detailing their requirements through, for example, the use of questionnaire surveys and by contributing to the drafting of service specifications and SLAs.
- Prioritisation by stakeholders of their requirements.
- Controlling stakeholder input and changes once the specification has been agreed.

The organisation may find that it is defining and detailing its requirements for the first time. In such cases, there is a risk that it might unknowingly specify a higher level of service than was received in the past and that, consequently, tenders may turn out to be higher than forecast. Value management, a technique for ensuring that real needs are addressed, can be used to guard against over-specification, whilst allowing standards to be raised over time. This is a broad philosophy as opposed to a prescriptive means for identifying and eliminating excess cost. The organisation should consider adopting value management principles at a strategic planning level – see Chapter 2 – and then apply value engineering principles to eliminate attributes of service that add cost, but no value. There is ample literature on the interrelated subjects of value management and value engineering – see for example Kelly *et al.* (2002, 2004). The use of value engineering workshops is generally advocated in the literature and is widely practised on building and civil engineering construction projects large and small. What is important is the discipline of questioning the need for, and assumptions embodied in, all attributes of service provision and ensuring that only those adding value, or required to support those that add value, are included. In these ways, stakeholders' interests should be correctly incorporated into service specifications and SLAs.

Rationale for service specifications and SLAs

Service specifications and SLAs are formal documents that together set out:

- Customer expectations of the quality, performance and value of the services to be provided in a clear and unequivocal manner.
- Minimum acceptable standards of the service and the customer's requirements that have to be met.
- Output or performance-oriented measures, concentrating on what is to be provided as opposed to how.
- The agreement between the service provider and the customer for providing a range and target level of services.

In practice, SLAs are often made by parties within an internal market, that is, between the departments or other operational units in an organisation, and act as a type of contract. This type of contract is not necessarily accompanied by a charge for the service. SLAs are also highly applicable to situations where services are outsourced. Here, the SLA supplements the contractual arrangements and is the starting point for developing a partnership relationship. In a previous chapter, we observed that the organisation adopted the practice of including service specifications and SLAs as annexes to the contract. Client organisations are bound to approach this matter differently depending on external factors and the legal advice they receive on the whole question of contracts. What is important here is to emphasise the standing of service specifications and SLAs in binding the parties' intentions together.

What is a service specification?

A service specification is a document that quantifies the minimum acceptable (technical) standard of service required by the customer and will generally form a part of the contract with the service provider. The production of the service specification is a prerequisite in the negotiation and drafting of SLAs and should set out:

- Internal standards – relating to corporate or department policy, as well as those that have been adopted on previous contracts
- External standards – covering conformance to statutory requirements, international standards, health and safety legislation, industry standards and manufacturers' recommendations
- Procedures with which the service provider must comply in order to achieve the required technical standards

Performance and quality targets

The extent of detail in the specification will depend on the importance and complexity of the service or asset item. This is bound to be an area of concern for the organisation. Quality, as we are aware, manifests in many ways. If users (as customers) were asked to write down what quality meant to them in the context of a facility, there would be as many different definitions as there were users. In order to overcome this potential problem, facilities managers need to spend time working closely with customers to elicit their views of what quality means to them. In many instances, it will be possible to substitute the word performance for quality. This is not meant to avoid the issue of defining quality; rather it is a pragmatic and realistic way of focusing on what exactly their customers expect and, therefore, mean by quality. In the context of service provision, quality is something that can be defined, detailed and determined as due performance. For example, the quality of cleaning of, say, offices can be stated in terms of either what the customer will accept as clean or how often the act of cleaning must be performed. Ensuring that worktops are always free from dust is an example of a performance requirement and a target to be achieved. It also says something tangible about the quality of service being provided. The example is simple, but not trivial, as it is illustrative of how we are able to express quality and then communicate it in terms that people not only understand, but are also able to follow through into practice.

What does a service specification contain?

Drafting specifications can be a job in its own right. Fortunately, advice and information on how to write specifications are available from a number of sources and will generally follow accepted practice. Table 8.1 shows the typical format of an example service specification. For some services, trade associations provide guidance to their members and offer model forms of specification. Commonsense dictates that any model will require some adaptation to suit the organisation or contract in hand; in other words, for model read standard.

The approach to specification writing can vary depending on whether or not a prescriptive view is taken or one that is performance-related – the

Table 8.1   Contents of an example service specification.

Section	Contents
Part 1: Terminology	1.1 Definition of terms used
Part 2: Areas/items/services	2.1 Scope of areas/items/services covered by specification
Part 3: External standards	3.1 Statutory requirements 3.2 Manufacturers' recommendations 3.3 Industry-accepted best practice
Part 4: Internal standards	4.1 Corporate/department requirements 4.2 Previously-accepted standards
Part 5: Categorisation of areas/items/services	5.1 Detailed procedures for each category 5.2 Frequency of procedures for each category

former is based on inputs and the latter is based on outputs. In the case of a cleaning contract, for example, the specification could describe the standard of cleanliness to be achieved in terms of the maximum amount of dust or debris that is permitted to remain following cleaning. Below are two extracts from an example service specification for cleaning showing, first, prescriptive specifications and, second, performance requirements.

Practice Point 8.1   Timing can be everything.

Risk item: specifications that are over-prescriptive, concentrating on procedures not outputs

Key-point: specifications need to focus on outputs and not the procedures that are carried out in delivering those outputs.

The times of inspections and maintenance of items at a cargo-handling facility were rigidly set out in a programme in the maintenance contract. On a number of occasions, the contractor was unable to carry out the work on the dates specified, as it would have seriously disrupted the operation of the facility. The programme was developed without taking into account the need for certain items to be kept operational under very busy conditions. A programme that was more flexible in its times would have ensured that the required number of inspections per annum was carried out and the equipment at the facility was adequately maintained.

Example of a service specification – cleaning of open plan offices

Prescriptive specification: daily tasks

1. Empty rubbish containers and bins (clean as required). Collect all rubbish and waste material, place in receptacle provided by the contractor and remove to the nearest designated disposal point.

2. Sweep floors using appropriate antic-static mop sweeper, leaving floors clean and free from visible dirt, dust and smears.
3. Lift primary matting and vacuum beneath.
4. Vacuum all soft floors and carpeted areas (loose or fitted). This is to include all raised areas, stairways etc.
5. Spot clean hard floors.
6. Spot clean tables, desks and chairs.

Prescriptive specification: weekly tasks

1. Damp wipe furniture, fittings and horizontal surfaces.
2. Using high-speed vacuum floor-polishing machines, spray clean hard floor areas with an approved cleaning agent and maintainer, and then use an appropriate brush or pad until floor is cleaned and polished.

Performance-based requirements

1. Ensure that bins and other containers for waste and rubbish are emptied regularly so that they are not allowed to remain full – deposit at the nearest designated disposal point.
2. Do not permit the contents of bins and other containers to pose a threat to health or allow them to detract from the normal enjoyment of space by users.
3. Ensure that all floors are maintained in a clean, enduring and non-slip state, free from debris and other deleterious materials.
4. Do not permit spillage, contaminants or other deleterious materials to remain on floors.
5. Ensure that all work surfaces, fittings and other furnishings remain free from accumulated dust and other debris, and are maintained in a condition that does not detract from the normal enjoyment of space by users.
6. Do not permit spillage, contaminants or other deleterious materials to remain on work surfaces, fittings and other furnishings.

There are obvious differences between the two approaches. The prescriptive specification – because it dictates what shall be done – will ensure that the cleaning of the specified areas and items will take place on a daily and weekly basis come what may. For example, floors will be cleaned and work surfaces wiped over whether or not this work is necessary – at least in theory. In the performance-based approach, the contractor (service provider) is able to schedule cleaning according to need, which arises from patterns of use, access hours, weather etc. More likely than not, the performance-based specification will deliver the quality of service required for less money than the prescriptive approach.

Apart from these differences, there is the issue of flexibility. Prescriptive specifications are, by definition, restrictive and probably incapable of change once the contract is running. The performance-based approach, on the other hand, avoids this problem by setting clear targets which the service provider can use to determine the most appropriate operational response. Detractors of the performance-based approach would argue that the minimum effort will be put into the cleaning and that, at least, with the prescriptive approach one can see the work being performed at specified intervals. However, this line of argument is flawed, because the aim should be to ensure that the workplace is cleaned without inconvenience to users. In this particular sense, cleaning should not interfere with enjoyment of the workplace. When performed at the highest level, with all services being delivered as required, facilities management can be regarded as the 'invisible service'.

What is a service level agreement (SLA)?

An SLA is a statement of intentions existing between the service provider and the customer – the recipient of the service – setting out a specified level of service. The agreement is formalised by producing a document that describes the following:

- Name of each party
- Roles and responsibilities of each party
- Scope of services that are to be provided
- Quality and performance-related targets
- Time-related targets
- Prices and rates – broken down as necessary
- Resources required
- Method of communication and interaction between customer and service provider
- Change procedures

The SLA may be of a general format – applicable to a number of services or facilities – or it may be customer, facility or service specific. In any event, it will incorporate relevant service specifications.

Development of SLAs

The customer will have certain expectations about the level of service that the service provider should deliver. These expectations need to be translated into formal requirements and targets. In the development of these targets, the service provider should be involved and the agreements developed jointly, so that targets are both appropriate and practicable. An example of a target is where the response to a problem, for example the failure of a light fitting or photocopier breakdown, should be within a specified period that is practicable for the service provider and tolerable for the customer. Stakeholders need to specify what their tolerance threshold is for rectifying a range of failures or malfunctions, and they need to be realistic.

Table 8.2   Contents of an example SLA based on a total facilities management service.

Section	Contents
Part 1: Agreement details	1.1 Name of parties to the agreement 1.2 Date agreement signed 1.3 Effective date of agreement 1.4 Period of agreement
Part 2: Scope of services – the service specification	2.1 Management of maintenance of buildings, plant and equipment, external landscaping 2.2 Management of minor building works 2.3 Management of accommodation services 2.4 Management of utilities and telecommunications
Part 3: Delivery times, fees	3.1 Service priority categories and times 3.2 Fees and payment
Part 4: Performance	4.1 Submission of performance reports 4.2 Performance measures
Part 5: Customer/service provider interface	5.1 Communication 5.2 Incentives and penalties 5.3 Customer's rating and feedback 5.4 Procedures for revising SLA

What does an SLA contain?

The SLA can contain details and targets relating to all or some of the items listed earlier. In principle, the document should identify those measures that the customer will use to judge the level of service received from the service provider. These measures will generally fall under the following aspects of the service:

- Quality
- Performance
- Delivery/response time
- Charges for services
- Nature of the interaction with the service provider

The SLA can also set out the procedure for incorporating any changes that occur in these targets. Table 8.2 shows the top-level contents of an example SLA – typical sections of an SLA can be found in Appendix E.

Example contents of an SLA are given below. This illustrates the kind of requirements that might be drafted to deal with the submission of performance reports and the measurement of performance.

Example of a service level agreement (SLA)

(Adapted from original information provided by IBM and Johnson Controls.)

Performance reports

Service performance reports will be completed by the service provider each month on the last working day. Whilst it will be the service provider's duty to complete the reports, the client's appointed representative will furnish the service provider with a master service performance record sheet. These records will register the following items:

1. Maintenance details – incidence of maintenance-induced failures, adherence to agreed planned preventive maintenance (PPM) schedules.
2. Job card – responses and actions within service level.
3. Security – compliance with security procedures, absence of misuses or losses.
4. Cleaning – completion of all specified items.
5. Safety – completion of all recorded action items.
6. Space and facilities planning – space database kept up-to-date, users informed of progress.
7. Reception – procedure for dealing with visitors is followed.
8. Reprographics – photocopiers serviced within four hours.
9. Stationery and printing – orders fulfilled on a timely basis.
10. Fax service – availability of service maintained.

Operations and service assessment

Operations and service assessment will be undertaken adopting the same procedure as for service performance records. This assessment will record the following items:

1. Effective communication – timely reporting and prompt response to requests.
2. Documentation – complete, sufficient, on time and maintained.
3. Additional work – positive attitude, flexibility and proactiveness.
4. Image – general housekeeping and staff appearance.
5. Management and coordination – efficient use of resources and protection of client interests.
6. Process and methods of work – innovative proposals and effective solutions.
7. Supplier relationships – control of supplier performance and quality of supplier performance.
8. Feedback – space utilisation opportunities, with advice on locations.
9. Financial – fully evaluated proposals, with well-structured business cases.

Performance measures

The following performance measures will apply to monthly service performance records:

- Criteria met or exceeded – yes (score 1), no (score 0), for each item.
- Total service performance must be not less than 8 at each monthly assessment.

The following performance measures will apply to operations and services assessment:

- Criteria exceeded, met or failed – exceed (score 2), meet (score 1), fail (score 0), for each item.
- Total service performance must be no less than 9 at each monthly assessment.

The above performance measures will be used to determine overall contract performance for the service provider.

Critical success factors and key performance indicators

In determining the criteria for measuring the performance (or fulfilment) of an SLA, the organisation should consider those factors that are critical to success. Critical success factors (CSFs) are those actions that must be performed well in order for the goals or objectives established by an organisation to be met satisfactorily. Within each CSF will be one or more KPIs. The purpose of KPIs is to enable management to understand, measure and control progress in each of the CSFs. For example, an organisation may have set a goal of providing the highest-quality service that ensures each internal customer receives best value. A CSF in achieving that goal would be 'agreed SLAs'. Here, a KPI might be 'published service level agreements' to show clearly what has to be achieved and then, subsequently, to say what has been achieved.

In another example – an internal perspective on productivity – a CSF would lead to KPIs that highlighted abortive work, backlog and ability (or inability) to perform tasks concurrently. Measures of productivity would include:

- Percentage of total work completed at a given time
- Percentage of activities planned against unplanned
- Percentage of total hours by customer type
- Breakdowns against planned preventive maintenance hours

Where customer perspectives are concerned, a CSF could be quality for which one of the KPIs would be complaints (or the lack of them) that, in turn, would give a measure of the number of complaints over time or, alternatively, a satisfaction rating.

When establishing CSFs and KPIs, it is vital that they correspond to goals and objectives that are aligned to the organisation's business strategy. Without this alignment, successful attainment of service levels may contribute nothing to the success of the core business. It is not just about doing things right, but doing the right things. KPIs are seen as a valuable tool in this regard and have infiltrated all areas of business in the public sector as well as in the private sector. In practice, there will be many CSFs and KPIs that interact and combine to bring about a culture and methods that aim to achieve best practice. Performing at the top end of these measures would bring an organisation to the point of achieving best practice and, with that, best value in the management of its services and facilities.

Practice Point 8.2   ICT helps to spread the workload.

Key-point: monitoring the times, costs and other performance data for a large number of low-value activities can be time-consuming and counterproductive, unless ICT is used.

An organisation had decided that, as part of its performance monitoring of the in-house services team, records should be kept of each and every activity performed. The initial reaction from the in-house team was that they would probably spend as much time filling in forms as doing their jobs, perhaps even more. Although initially reluctant, the team was persuaded to use spreadsheets as part of an office automation suite. The manager set up a template on his spreadsheet that was then used to provide the team with paper forms for recording data, which they then keyed in at the end of the day. After some weeks, the team began experimenting with the spreadsheet's wizard function to help generate some useful graphs. These were used subsequently to present to senior management with the information it had been wanting for some time. Even so, the team felt that it was still spending too much time in logging information and then transferring it to the spreadsheets on the office PCs. Usually, they had to allocate around one hour at the end of each day. After making enquiries with a local computer store, the team acquired several PDAs, which came complete with software and an interface to the office PCs. Within the week, the team had automated the data capture routine and reduced the entire daily ritual to a few minutes.

Performance monitoring

The customer's view of the quality of a service or product is based on tangible and intangible factors, both of which are important. Tangible factors are those that can be objectively measured, such as the time taken to deliver an item, the charge made and the level of operational performance. Intangible factors include those that are more subjective in nature and, therefore, more difficult to measure: for example, the utility of the item to the customer, its adaptability and advantages over other types or merely the courtesy of the service provider's personnel. The difficulty of quantifying some factors should not preclude measurement as they can be as important

Table 8.3   Example performance measures for planned and unplanned maintenance.

Element	Service	Output/measure	Perspective
1	Planned maintenance performance	Tasks planned in period Tasks completed in period Time taken per task Mean time taken per task Resource attendance in period Number of tasks reworked Percentage of tasks reworked of total tasks in period Service delivery resource utlised	by customer by building/location by building/space type by service provider by asset type by asset
2	Unplanned maintenance performance	Number of breakdowns/faults in period Percentage response times met Number of breakdowns/faults completed in period Number of breakdowns/faults outstanding in period Time taken per breakdown Mean time taken per breakdown Number of tasks reworked Percentage tasks reworked of total tasks in period	by customer by building/location by building/space type by service provider by asset type by asset
		Asset availability in period Downtime in period Unplanned stoppages in period Service delivery resource utilised	by customer by building/location by building/space type by service provider by asset type

as those that are easily measured. The organisation should, however, be cautioned against imposing too many or overly demanding performance measurements and excessive monitoring on service providers as this risks becoming counterproductive. A sensible approach is to concentrate on the KPIs. Table 8.3 suggests performance measures that could be used and Table 8.4 a possible scoring scheme.

In practice, the overall performance of a service provider can be determined by monitoring adherence to standards and targets under the following headings:

- Conformance to regulations and standards
- Quality-related and performance-related targets for service delivery
- Expenditure limits
- Time-related targets
- Interaction between customer and service provider

Performance data can be collected in a number of ways. For example, the service provider may complete worksheets and job reports, or feedback from customers might be sought actively in the form of comments on worksheets, complaints and customer surveys. Once the organisation has collected these data they should be used to complete a score-sheet, similar

Table 8.4 Example of unplanned maintenance service scoring scheme (report of faulty lighting on section of floor of main building).

(1) Service criteria[+]	(2) Agreed target level of service (targets in SLA or specification)	(3) Value[+]	(4) Actual level of service delivered	(5) Value	(6) Customer satisfaction	(7) Value
Regulations/standards	Work carried out according to health and safety regulations using certified products	10	Work carried out according to health and safety regulations using certified products	10	Satisfied	10
Performance/quality	Fault to be rectified so that it is prevented from reoccurring. Minimise level of disruption to users.	20	Fault diagnosed and problem rectified. Minor disruption to building users.	18	Concern over disruption to work	12
Delivery time	*Minor lighting fault* Max. response time = 2 hours Max. service time = 4 hours (Total delivery time = 6 hours)	10	Response time = 3 hours Service time = 2 hours (Total delivery time = 5 hours)	8	Concern over delay in response	5
Delivery expenditure	*Minor lighting fault* Total cost = £120.00 to £250.00 (range)	10	Total cost = £200.00	10	Satisfied	10
Customer–service provider interaction	Keep customer informed of status of work and likely completion time	20	Customer informed that fault had been rectified following completion of work	16	No contact between report of fault and completion	14
Overall service delivery	Work to be carried out according to the targets given above	70	Work carried out satisfactorily, within agreed cost; however, not within agreed response time	62	Work and cost satisfactory, delivery time and contact unsatisfactory	51

[+] = Each activity is assigned a weighted agreed target level of service value. Actual level of service delivered and customer satisfaction values are determined relative to this base value.

to that presented in Table 8.4, at regular intervals. This should be undertaken for a sample of the services delivered by each service provider based on KPIs. These will be given in the SLA and contract and will provide a basis for measuring performance in a way that involves both the service provider and the customer. On the score-sheet in Table 8.4, column 4 (actual level of service delivered) contains the service provider's measurement of the service or product, based on data and information held by the service provider's organisation. These measures will relate to response times to fault reports, customer surveys, charges made for services and measures of quality levels. Customer satisfaction relates to the customer's view of the level of service delivered, based on records held by the organisation. Reasons for any discrepancies between the three values in Table 8.4 then need to be established and corrective action taken as necessary. This will entail the active involvement of the client organisation and the service provider.

Practice Point 8.3   A fair return.

Risk item: absence of, or poor arrangements for, providing incentives for improved performance.

Key-point: performance-related systems that aim to raise the standard of service delivery should be based on a fair distribution of rewards and penalties.

An organisation intended to introduce a performance measurement system in its contract with a security contractor as a means for improving the level of service it received. During early discussions with the service provider, the organisation proposed that incentives in the form of bonus payments were awarded for improved performance and penalties imposed for substandard performance. However, in later discussions, the organisation revised the system so that good performance was recognised, though not accompanied by financial rewards, whilst financial penalties for poor performance were retained. At that point the security contractor withdrew from the discussions, claiming that there was no real incentive for workers to raise their performance beyond the minimum specified.

The service provider's level of service delivery will be, to a greater or lesser extent, affected by the quality system that the client organisation has in place. The satisfactory performance of the service provider will be more assured if the quality system is geared to the levels of service performance established in the SLAs. In other words, the ways in which quality and service performance are measured, in accordance with the SLAs, should reflect those prescribed in the client organisation's quality system.

Updating service specifications and SLAs

Service specifications should not be regarded as fixed statements of service requirements, but as a basis for continual improvement as circumstances and customer requirements change. Experience will reveal how better results and improved value for money can be achieved by a change in specification. Service providers should be involved in the process of updating and improving service specifications and SLAs in order to draw upon their experience of providing the service. If necessary, visits to other facilities might be necessary to provide insights into how improvements are possible. These actions will ensure that the organisation is able to determine if the specified service was obtained and so draw lessons for the future. At all times, it is essential that the requirements set out in the service specifications and SLAs should be incorporated into the contract with service providers.

Quality system

If the client organisation is to receive a satisfactory level of service, not only should it have a quality system in place, it must also require the same of its service providers. In fact, service providers' quality systems should form an integral part of their service provision. To add value, service providers have to apply the principles of quality assurance in order to enhance service provision through a reduction in errors and reworking, and as an effective means for handling customer complaints (non-conformance), action and feedback. A quality assured approach can save money. The assessment of a tenderer's quality system should therefore be one of the criteria used by the client organisation in its assessment of tenders.

A common misconception is that a formal quality system is administratively burdensome, costly and, therefore, unnecessary. If a quality system were to be seen as simply generating paper or adding a layer of administration then it has been misunderstood or misapplied. Formal recognition through accreditation under ISO 9000/9001: 2000 is important in underscoring the organisation's commitment to achieving total customer satisfaction and that it is prepared to open its system to external scrutiny. By means of a third party audit – in addition to periodic internal audits – the organisation is more likely to meet this commitment and, furthermore, be able to demonstrate it visibly.

The approach advocated in this book is sufficient to provide a basis for a quality system, embracing the entire facilities management function within an organisation. A quality system normally consists of a policy statement and a quality manual with procedures. The policy statement is the organisation's explicit commitment to a quality-assured process embodying its services. The quality manual provides a detailed interpretation of the way in which each of the quality standards is to be met within the context of the operations of the business. The procedures, not surprisingly, explain the detailed steps that must be followed in order to comply with the quality system. For a system to be effective, it needs to be applied as work is being done. Thus, for example, logs and reviews should not be completed retrospectively. Contract documents should incorporate quality-of-service criteria and stipulate that payments will depend on the provider meeting these criteria. These contractual provisions should ensure the quality of services or products of service providers. The issue of penalties and incentives relating to performance standards should be considered following performance reviews.

Conclusions

Service specifications are an integral part of the facilities management process and combine with SLAs to define the quality and/or performance required from a service. Both are fundamental to the business of effective facilities management, irrespective of whether or not the service is outsourced or retained in-house. Time spent in preparing accurate service specifications and SLAs that reflect customer (and other stakeholder) interests will be repaid amply in the future since contracts will be easier to manage and less prone to misinterpretation. A quality system should be adopted by the organisation as a necessary part of its facilities management and used to support the work of managers and service providers alike. This will ensure, as an absolute minimum, that a consistent set of standards is applied as a basis for seeking continual improvement.

CHECKLIST

This checklist is intended to assist with the review and action planning process.

	Yes	No	Action required
1. Have identified stakeholders been involved in specifying their requirements as to the level of performance that will be acceptable?	☐	☐	☐
2. Have service specifications and service level agreements been prepared?	☐	☐	☐
3. Have the critical success factors and key performance indicators for the provision of services been identified?	☐	☐	☐
4. Are proper arrangements in place for performance monitoring of service provision?	☐	☐	☐
5. Does the facilities management strategy provide for the updating of service specifications and service level agreements?	☐	☐	☐
6. Is a quality system in place in the client organisation?	☐	☐	☐
7. Is the existence of a quality system on the part of tenderers adopted as a criterion for the assessment of tenders?	☐	☐	☐

9 Employment, Health and Safety Considerations

Key issues

The following issues are covered in this chapter.

- Compliance with employment, health and safety legislation applies to everybody in the workplace. It includes shared parts of buildings and the grounds in which the organisation's buildings are set.

- A competent person must be appointed to the organisation or act as a consultant to assist in implementing and complying with health and safety legislation, whether services are retained in-house or outsourced.

- A general policy statement must be produced by the organisation and this must be communicated to all stakeholders.

- An organisation and administration management method for implementing the policy must be produced and its effectiveness measured.

- A growing body of legislation affecting workers and the workplace is appearing – client organisations must not only be aware of their responsibilities, they also need to ensure that their service providers comply too.

- Policies, detailed safety rules and safe working practices to ensure compliance with health and safety legislation must be devised, implemented and reviewed regularly.

- Not all health and safety issues have a legislative dimension – a growing area of concern is that of stress at work. Today, the courts are sympathetic to the plight of workers who succumb to stress-related illnesses.

Introduction

Employment today is framed by a large body of legislation designed primarily to protect the rights, health and safety of employees. The point is that it is morally unacceptable for people to be exposed to unnecessary and avoidable risks and hazards at work. Moreover, the nature of work should not be such that it leads to a reduction in the quality of life. The onus is on organisations – irrespective of type or size – to comply with legislation for the protection of employees. Where services are outsourced, the client organisation cannot escape responsibility, even if it believes that certain legislation does not apply directly to it. Steps must be taken to ensure that the organisation is fully compliant. Far from being a minefield – a word sometimes used alongside 'begrudging acceptance' – employment, health and safety legislation can be used positively to help define working arrangements including those relating to facilities management. Looked at from this end of the telescope – so to speak – it is likely to be easier to comply with the requirements than attempt to work around them. In a practical sense, the facility manager is likely to become a key figure in translating the intentions of the legislation into policies and procedures for the workplace. This chapter discusses issues that can help the organisation ensure it provides a safe and healthy place for internal and external users. It reviews the legislation and describes the characteristics of a well-managed health and safety regime. The review is set in a UK context, although its principles are paralleled elsewhere, not least in other EU member states and countries whose legal system is similar to that of the UK. Checklists are included to indicate the scope of matters for which attention is required. Whilst every care has been exercised in identifying relevant legislation, it should not be regarded as a complete guide to employment, health and safety law. The organisation should verify the extent to which any legislation applies to it.

Relevant legislation

In the UK the principal legislation is that contained in the Health and Safety at Work Act 1974. Where organisations have industrial workshops, additional legislation applies, for instance the Noise at Work Regulations 1989; and where building works are carried out on the premises, the Construction (Design and Management) Regulations 1994 (CDM) will also apply. Current legislation will be progressively tightened. CDM therefore marks only the beginning of a major push at reducing accidents and the hazards that lead to them. Organisations must recognise that safety management is a significant item on the agenda for operating a facility of any description.

General policy

The organisation must have a general policy on health and safety. The requirements of this general policy are:

- To provide and maintain as far as is practicable, a healthy and safe place of work.

- To take responsibility for compliance with relevant legislation including, in the UK (in alphabetical order):
  - Construction (Design and Management) Regulations 1994
  - Construction (Health, Safety and Welfare) Regulations 1996
  - Control of Substances Hazardous to Health Regulations 1988 (amended 1994, 1996 and 1997)

- o Disability Discrimination Act 1995
- o Electricity at Work Regulations 1989
- o Employment Relations Act 2004
- o Fire Precautions Act 1971
- o Health and Safety (Display Screen Equipment) Regulations 1992
- o Health and Safety (First Aid) Regulations 1981
- o Health and Safety (Safety Signs and Signals) Regulations 1996
- o Health and Safety at Work Act 1974
- o Manual Handling Operations Regulations 1992
- o Noise at Work Regulations 1989
- o Personal Protective Equipment (PPE) Regulations 1992
- o Provision and Use of Work Equipment Regulations (PUWER) 1992
- o Reporting of Injuries, Diseases and Dangerous Occurrences Regulations 1995
- o The Management of Health and Safety at Work Regulations 1992
- o The Working Time (Amendment) Regulations 2003
- o Workplace (Health, Safety and Welfare) Regulations 1992

Organisations need to be aware that their responsibilities for health and safety extend beyond their employees to the extent that no activity should pose risks to visitors or persons outside the premises. The organisation has responsibility for anybody and anyone who is affected by the action of an employee, and the organisation's policy statement and risk assessments must reflect this. It is necessary to appoint a person who can be judged to be competent in implementing and ensuring that the organisation complies with health and safety legislation. Employers must have access to a 'competent person' (who could be an employee, service provider or other contractor, even a consultant) and must ensure that he or she has adequate training, time and resources to discharge his or her duties under health and safety legislation.

Organisation and administration

It is necessary to identify responsibilities as imposed by legislation at all levels of management and supervision, and not just for those employees who are directly involved in the day-to-day management of facilities; for example, the purchasing manager and members of senior management will have roles to play. Care should be taken to apportion responsibility in line with authority, with resources to cover the administration procedures for dealing with accidents and contingency plans for handling power cuts, bomb alerts, flood and fire. Safety representatives from all user bodies should always be involved.

Proper consideration should be given to provide information about substances, plant and machinery to employees and to updating this information. Additionally, training in health and safety responsibilities for all employees should be provided.

Workers' rights

There is a plethora of legislation stemming from the European parliament that is enacted in each of the EU member states. Of these, The Working Time (Amendment) Regulations 2003 affords workers rights and protection regarding, as the name suggests, time spent at work. The basic rights and protection that the regulations provide – and which were current at the date of publication of this book – are:

- A limit of an average of 48 hours a week which a worker can be required to work (though workers can choose to work more if they want to)
- A limit of an average of 8 hours work in 24 which night workers can be required to work
- A right for night workers to receive free health assessments
- A right to 11 hours rest a day
- A right to a day off each week
- A right to an in-work rest break if the working day is longer than 6 hours
- A right to 4 weeks paid leave per year

These Regulations have proven particularly contentious amongst employers and employees alike and it is possible that some modification will occur – though is difficult to predict what exactly this will be. It is important, therefore, to check the current situation before either offering contracts of employment or renewing existing arrangements. Where services are outsourced, the organisation needs to ensure that service providers do not break the law. If they do, the client organisation may find itself culpable.

There is also the matter of minimum wages – another enactment from the European parliament – which is covered in the UK by the Employment Relations Act 2004. Client organisations need to be aware of the current national minimum wage and impending changes as they might apply to their own departments and to service providers under contract to them. Legislation aside, client organisations cannot turn a blind eye to what they suspect to be worker abuses of any kind. Apart from the illegality of what may be happening there is also the issue of morality and the motivation of others who may be affected by malpractice. A European Commission proposal for a Directive on (temporary) agency work is under discussion, at the date of publication of this book, and is bound to add to the weight of legislation faced by employers in the coming years.

Disability discrimination

Organisations must take account of the special problems faced by disabled persons and others with special needs, and should make certain that appropriate measures are taken to ensure their health and safety in the workplace. This may involve adaptation of existing means of access to, and escape from, buildings. Organisations should seek professional advice on how their buildings and other facilities comply with relevant legislation.

In the UK, the Disability Discrimination Act 1995 (DDA) recognises the many kinds of disability that affect people. In any society, the proportion of the population with some kind of disability is significant. The DDA takes into account the needs of people with disability affecting, in particular, mobility, sight and hearing. Although widely understood in terms of intent and requirements, the DDA has been overlooked by many UK-based employers – notably those employing 15 people or less who until recently were largely unaffected by its scope. With effect from 1 October 2004, these organisations were also required to make 'reasonable adjustments' to their businesses: for instance, providing access for physically handicapped people and taking other steps to ensure that no one is excluded for reason of a disability. Although many organisations of this size are unlikely to have their own formal facilities management arrangements, most of the principles that apply to larger organisations will also apply to them. Full enactment of the legislation has removed any distinction or excuse for not making adjustments to businesses. The requirements extend beyond building-related alterations to include changes in customer information to ensure that, for example, people who are visually impaired are not disadvantaged. The intention of this and other legislation is to ensure all-inclusiveness. In other words, no one should be excluded from buildings, transportation or any other facility because of a disability.

Safety rules and practice

Organisations will need to assess the risks to the health and safety of employees and anyone else affected by the activities of the organisation (for example, employees, customers, visitors and the general public) and devise means of implementing preventive and protective measures. Assessment must cover planning, organisation, control, monitoring and reviews. There is a close link between risk assessment and arrangements specified in the policy statement.

With a policy and a management system in place, organisations must monitor and review arrangements to achieve progressive improvement in health and safety. Improvement will be enhanced through the development of policies, approaches to implementation and techniques of risk control.

The following checklists will enable organisations to monitor their adherence to, and progress against, health and safety legislation.

Organisation

- Are policy, management and organisation, safety rules and procedures in place?
- Are these details available to all employees and other building users?

- Have arrangements been made for consultation with employees and other user bodies?

Noticeboards

- Is the safety policy clearly displayed?
- Is the health and safety law poster displayed?
- Is a copy of the employer's liability insurance certificate displayed?
- Are the names of trained first-aiders displayed?
- Are emergency procedures displayed?

Accident reporting

- Is an accident book held on the premises?
- Are employees and other building users aware of the location of the accident book?
- Are internal accident report forms held?
- Is the Health and Safety Executive (HSE) leaflet, *Everyone's Guide to RIDDOR*, available?

Training

- Have all those with health and safety responsibilities received specific health and safety training?
- Have all employees attended a general health and safety awareness course?
- Are records maintained of training undertaken?
- Are there employees who have received specialist training, for example NEBOSH national general certificate in occupational health and safety?

First aid

- Is a current list of first-aid personnel and their locations displayed on each notice board?
- How many first-aid personnel are there and how are they spread throughout the buildings?
- Does each first-aider have an adequate first-aid box?
- Who keeps top-up supplies for first-aid boxes?
- Who is responsible for inspecting all first-aid boxes for their contents, visibility and availability?
- Who organises first-aid training?
- Which organisation supplies first-aid training?
- Are records of first-aid training adequate and up to date?
- Are treatment record sheets available by each first-aid box or located with the accident book?

Fire precautions

- Is there a fire certificate for the buildings?
- Who has delegated responsibility for fire precautions?
- How often are evacuation drills carried out?
- Are full records of these drills kept, including building clearance times?
- How often are fire alarms tested and are full records of these tests maintained?
- How often are smoke and heat detectors tested?
- Is this in accordance with manufacturers' recommendations or fire certificate?
- Are full records of these tests maintained?
- How often are fixed hose-reel and sprinkler systems (if applicable) tested?
- Are full records of these tests maintained?
- Do the drills and tests comply with the conditions of the fire certificate?
- Are records kept of visits from the fire officer?
- Is there a service contract for the maintenance of fire extinguishers and other fire control equipment?
- Are there adequate fire extinguishers of the correct type?
- Is there at least one fire warden for each floor?
- What training, practice or regular meetings are arranged for fire wardens?
- How often are the offices inspected in relation to fire precautions?
- Is there a procedure for notifying the fire authority of alterations to buildings?

Statutory risk assessments

- Have assessments been carried out for all display screen equipment workstations?
- Is there a valid risk assessment for the premises?
- Have all hazardous substances been assessed under the Control of Substances Hazardous to Health Regulations 1988 (COSHH)?
- Have any other assessments been carried out, for example, lifting of loads and personal protective equipment (PPE)? – see also points below
- Are the control measures specified in the risk assessments being adhered to?

Inspections and audits

- How often does the facilities manager or other person with delegated responsibility inspect the offices for physical hazards?
- When was the last inspection carried out?
- When was the last audit of procedures carried out and by whom?

Work equipment

- Who is responsible for arranging annual lift/elevator inspections, where applicable?
- Are the premises' electrical installation and all portable electrical appliances and equipment tested by a competent person, as required by the Electricity at Work Regulations 1989, with the results of those tests and any necessary remedial action properly recorded?
- Are there procedures for inspecting and maintaining all work equipment?
- Is the use of potentially dangerous work equipment restricted to authorised persons and are those persons properly trained?

Personal protective equipment (PPE)

- Have assessments been carried out to determine the requirements of employees?
- Have records of these assessments been kept?
- Is all necessary PPE available?
- Are records kept of PPE issued?
- Have employees been trained in the use and maintenance requirements of PPE, if applicable?
- Has adequate storage for PPE been provided?

Off site

- Have risks associated with visiting other sites or working outside been assessed?
- Is a procedure for lone working defined and in use?
- Are employees aware of these procedures and have they been trained in them?

Employing contractors (service providers)

- Are contractors used for window cleaning, maintenance, electrical installation and so on?
- Is there a 'contractors on site' policy document that all contractors must read and then sign as evidence of their awareness of their duties and obligations?
- Does each contractor carrying out work on the premises before they are engaged complete a health and safety questionnaire?
- Who vets these questionnaires and on what basis is it decided that a contractor is competent to carry out the work?
- What information is given to contractors on emergency procedures, safety rules and access?
- Who is responsible for ensuring compliance with CDM?

Notices

- Are all necessary compliance and safety signs in place?

Stress, employees and the organisation

Whilst organisations might strive for more from fewer workers, the reality is that people are capable of giving only so much before serious (and sometimes irreversible) damage sets in. At best, this limits organisational effectiveness; at worst, it can lead to conflict, sickness and even litigation. In fact, there is strong evidence to link 'organisational ill health' with employee sickness, absences, high labour turnover and low productivity. Moreover, stress, which can be directly related to job and organisational problems, is thought responsible for 60–80% of all workplace accidents. Work-related stress is now a common reason for absenteeism. The collective cost of stress to organisations in terms of absenteeism, reduced productivity, potential compensation claims and so on is colossal. Stress-related absences are ten times more costly than all other industrial relations disputes put together. Factors within the workplace causing stress include:

- Unsatisfactory working conditions – poor quality internal environment (air quality, light/daylight and temperature), physical location or individual posture.
- Mental and physical overload from excessive work-related demands – long working hours, lack of breaks, working weekends and curtailed or cancelled holidays.
- Role ambiguity and inconsistency in management style – poor senior management (leadership) that causes confusion and discord.
- Responsibility for other personnel – assuming a position for which one is ill-equipped or unsuited.
- Unsatisfactory working and personal relationships – conflict or tensions between individuals or groups.
- Under-promotion or over-promotion – failing to reward or, conversely, moving personnel to new positions where they are unable to cope.
- Poor organisational structure/culture – ineptitude in managing the social infrastructure to the extent that personnel become disillusioned, downbeat and distrustful.

Things are likely to get worse, as reorganisations, relocations of personnel, redesign of jobs, and reallocations of roles and responsibilities make changes to the normal way of doing business in the coming years.

The hidden costs of stress caused by not adequately creating an environment that enhances the well-being of employees are manifest in a lack of added value to the organisation's products or services and the costs of rectifying under-performance. Study of work stress has tended to concentrate upon ways in which the individual can cope with or adapt to stress. Instead, effort should concentrate on how the work environment can alleviate stress. The effort of coping with stress absorbs energy that could otherwise be invested in more productive and satisfying work activities. Williams (2002) discusses the effects of stress on performance and productivity and how to recognise it, manage it and prevent it.

A preoccupation of many managers is how to measure performance, especially in an office environment where production line principles do not apply. This may appear to be a legitimate goal and is one area where the use of ICT has led to electronic monitoring. This has the capacity to provide fairer compensation for performance through more accurate and timely feedback. The links between performance and reward are such that this should be beneficial to productivity. However, negative effects of such monitoring, in terms of worker stress and health problems, can actually mean a decline in productivity. The stress that stems from performance measurement and monitoring would seem to be associated with lack of control, loss of trust, and an increased administrative workload involved in operating such procedures. Placing emphasis on monitoring employee performance closely can therefore create more problems than it solves.

One workers' union has been reported as dealing with 7 000 stress-related claims at one time. Transferring employees to more challenging jobs may be how some organisations approach the management of their personnel. That view may not, however, be shared by employees. Moreover, it may bring them into a working environment that damages their health, forcing them into premature retirement and a poor quality of life.

Today, courts are more likely than ever to take a sympathetic view of an employee whose quality of life has been ruined by an inconsiderate or unprincipled employer. In fact, as far back as 1999, a former council employee was awarded over £67 000 compensation for stress at work. This was the first time that an employer had accepted liability for personal injury caused by stress and also the first time that the courts awarded damages for work-related stress. This particular award – other cases have been settled out of court – covers loss of future earnings and the cost of prescription medication. The plaintiff worked for Birmingham City Council for 16 years before being forced to retire on grounds of ill health. She began her career as a junior clerk in the housing department and progressed to become a senior technician. In 1993, she was promoted to housing officer, a job that involved dealing face-to-face with tenants. The plaintiff asked for training for this new job, which brought her into direct contact with the public for the first time. Training was promised, but never materialised. Not long afterwards, she began to show symptoms of stress, which descended into clinical depression and ultimately forced her to retire. The judge found in favour of the plaintiff and awarded costs against the city council in addition to the compensation for loss of future earnings.

Conclusions

Providing a safe and healthy place of work and business for employees and customers not only involves compliance with statutory requirements but also safeguards the people using the organisation's buildings and facilities. These commonsense requirements are generally well defined within the law and so ought to be obvious to competent practitioners. Even so, new legislation continues to appear – much of it initiated in the European parliament and/or by its executive, the European Commission. Rights of workers now extend into areas affecting working time and all-inclusiveness. For client organisations, there is the additional requirement to ensure that where outsourcing has taken place (or is about to), service providers are not in breach of the legislation. As important is the need to avoid arrangements that become divisive and counterproductive. Another area of concern is the now recognised and growing incidence of stress, which is classed as a major industrial disease. Facilities managers should be alert to hidden dangers in the workplace. Guidance in this and other important areas of health and safety cannot be exhaustive and so the organisation must take its own steps to ensure compliance. All organisations are advised to ensure they comply with the relevant requirements by seeking professional advice.

CHECKLIST

This checklist is intended to assist with the review and action planning process.

	Yes	No	Action required
1. Are the organisation and its advisers aware of relevant legislation in relation to the management and occupation of premises with particular emphasis on health and safety issues?	□	□	□
2. Have the organisation's requirements for implementing health and safety legislation been properly identified and arrangements made for their proper organisation and administration?	□	□	□
3. Has a proper assessment of the risk to health and safety for employees and all others affected by the activities of the organisation been completed?	□	□	□
4. Have the means of implementing appropriate measures been devised?	□	□	□
5. Have responsibilities for health and safety matters been identified and placed?	□	□	□
6. Are the premises able to accommodate people with disabilities of different kinds, i.e. mobility, sight and hearing?	□	□	□
7. Are the organisation and its advisers aware of the factors that can lead to stress-related illnesses and are they making sufficient efforts to eliminate them?	□	□	□

10 Workplace Productivity

Key issues

The following issues are covered in this chapter.

- Productivity in the workplace is a focus of attention for most organisations. The balance between the demands of work and the well-being of the individual is paramount if productivity is to be maintained or enhanced.

- A key factor in realising productivity gains through ICT is that the organisation must be structured to take advantage of the technology and to optimise the contribution of those who use it.

- There are essentially two ways in which the work environment can impact on productivity – enabling it or hindering it.

- Environmental factors affecting productivity include air quality, noise control, thermal comfort, privacy, lighting and spatial comfort. Not all of these are entirely negative in their impact.

- Factors related to sick building syndrome are exacerbated in the high-tech workplace.

- Environmental characteristics that influence work at the individual level include architectural properties – size of office, number of walls, ergonomic factors, heating and light.

- The issue of control is one that is continually referred to in a variety of contexts. The use of individual environmental control systems can increase productivity.

- Realising that people engage in different activities, and how they do so, then matching the space and facilities to the activity is a critical element of an integrated workplace strategy.

Introduction

The last 10–15 years have seen renewed interest in understanding the factors that impact upon productivity in the workplace – generally taken in the context of the office environment. There is now substantial literature on the subject, and a range of issues so diverse that it is difficult to summarise succinctly; however, many themes and issues recur, not least the difficulty of measuring the actual impact of various factors on worker productivity. Nonetheless, evidence does exist of factors that are acknowledged as contributing positively to worker productivity, though arguably fewer than exist in relation to detrimental or negative impacts. Design issues feature strongly in this chapter and some insights are provided as to the kinds of working environment that could bring about useful contributions towards raising productivity. Findings from studies in a variety of specialist fields concerning workplace efficiency tend to be stronger on assumptions about how work should be structured and what will be the future trends than on practical advice as to how these might be addressed. A commonly propagated view, as to the impact of a combination of measures and improvements in areas affecting productivity, is that a substantial gain may be possible – perhaps to the extent of 50%. The basis of this view is examined. Understanding how productivity is affected by various actions is covered under four headings: work itself, the organisation, communication and working environment.

Measuring productivity

There is a growing body of literature on factors affecting productivity in the workplace, with a particular bias towards those factors which impact on decisions regarding the use of space – for a broad treatment of the subject see, for example, Clements-Croome (2000). Most of the factors affecting productivity are consistently identified in literature covering specific and general workplace issues, even where there is sometimes an admission that the particular claim is unsupported by empirical evidence. In some cases it is not possible to amass such evidence, due to difficulties in measurement. In fact, one overriding consideration is the agreement that productivity in the office – as opposed to the factory – environment is extremely difficult to measure. This should not, however, be allowed to be an obstacle to attempts at identifying factors affecting productivity because of another issue which is subject to widespread agreement: the possible gains from a combination of improvements in all suggested areas affecting productivity could be substantial, perhaps to the extent of 50%.

Particular difficulties in isolating and measuring the relationship between productivity and the physical setting do not imply that the latter is minor. It is generally agreed that 'any programme to increase the productivity and effectiveness of office-based work should employ the design, management, and quality of the work environment to maximum advantage' (Aronoff and Kaplan, 1995). The environment is, however, only one aspect: workers experience the office as a whole, including the physical, psychological and management setting, with each aspect affecting the others. For this reason, the remainder of this chapter is split into sections covering productivity factors relating to:

- Work itself
- The organisation
- Communication
- Working environment

Most emphasis will be given to working environment, where the issues raised in the previous sections will be seen to impact. This is achieved by reviewing findings in a variety of specialist fields impacting on workplace efficiency and considering professionals in the facilities management sector. Unfortunately, the literature tends to be stronger on assumptions about how work is now structured and, therefore, suggestive of future trends than on practical advice as to how these might be addressed.

Work itself

In today's business environment employees are not simply under pressure to 'work smarter, not harder' but to do both. A more apt saying is 'lean and mean'. Idle time is pushed out as the means for work intensification are sought, not always with a view to quality rather than quantity, the latter still being easier to measure (Thompson and Warhurst, 1998).

There is general agreement that the nature of work has undergone significant changes in the last few decades. Major changes include a shift of the workforce from a concentration on production to service industries. The vast majority of workers are now employed in offices: as many as 80% are now white-collar workers. This remarkable shift immediately highlights a disquieting point: production industries have been able both to achieve and to measure substantial productivity improvements whereas performance levels in office work, as far as it is possible to measure them, have lagged significantly, in spite of substantial investment in ICT. Given the current high percentage of white-collar workers, this is a disturbing state of affairs and indicates the pressing need to achieve greater productivity. This also explains the growing interest in organisational effectiveness, which becomes of national economic interest when it is shown that the country concerned lags in international competitiveness.

The work that is now concentrated in the office sector has also changed. It is generally agreed that the workplace of today is likely to be a high-demand environment, subject to fast and continual change, increasing demands and fewer resources. With moves towards downsizing, restructuring and re-engineering, and initiatives such as total quality management, and an atmosphere of perpetual change, prompted by changes in consumer demands and increasing personnel and accommodation costs, jobs have tended to become less individual and isolated and more multi-activity and integrated. It is already becoming clear that an increasing number of people will also be expected to pursue multiple careers. Advances in ICT have facilitated such changes and many routine tasks have been taken over by computer-based systems. These moves have been paralleled by advanced manufacturing technologies in the factory environment, in both cases increasing the psychological or cognitive demands of modern work. There is a move away from non-interactive routine work towards both more collaborative and more highly autonomous styles of working. Much routine work is becoming automated or exported to lower cost economies. The large number of outsourced call centres and other technical functions to low wage countries is clear evidence of this trend.

In some cases, greater job diversity has been achieved, in other cases simply greater workload and responsibility taken on by a diminishing workforce, resulting in longer hours and/or more intensive work. The technology, which has enabled such advances, has also supported advances in monitoring some aspects of performance, thus increasing the pressure to perform, which in turn adds to stress.

It is often argued and generally assumed by many analysts that the majority of work now done in offices is 'knowledge work' and consequently it is the productivity of the knowledge worker that must be maximised. Creative knowledge work demands a combination of highly concentrated individual work alongside interactive teamwork. Knowledge workers tend to pursue their own interests and see their own value. If their needs can be accommodated within the workplace they can boost productivity within a more collegial form of management, which involves the sharing of information, delegation and the encouragement of upward and horizontal communication. Coordination is now based on collaboration between technical and professional groups, which retain authority over their own work. This is part of the flattening of hierarchical structures and also of the move towards teamworking focused on problem solving and continual improvement in a culture of trust and empowerment.

Worker morale is of obvious importance to productivity. This has previously been linked to issues such as security, routine and stability in job tasks. While this remains true to a large extent, future demands of workers from their work are more likely to focus on independence and creativity. Added to this is the increasing flexibility of working patterns and practices that many organisations are now offering their employees. The following are options open to some workers, often in combination:

- Homeworking or telecommuting
- Flexible working hours
- Out-of-office working – use of satellite centres and the concept of the virtual office

The options have been enabled by technological change, which involves not just a change in the way a job is done, but also a major social transformation in the nature and/or location of the workplace. This flexibility is seen as being mutually beneficial to individuals and their organisations.

There is considerable evidence in various areas of the positive impact of control on the job satisfaction and general well being of the individual. Conversely, lack of control is detrimental. Given the links seen between satisfaction, well-being and productivity, discussed below, it can be agreed that this type of flexibility will be beneficial all round. Moreover, there is evidence to suggest that working away from the office leads to higher levels of productivity, subject to the nature of the work, the individual and the alternative environment. It is also most beneficial if conceived as part of an integrated workplace strategy.

There is assumed to be a link between personal satisfaction with one's workplace and the effectiveness of the individual and the organisation. The validity of the satisfaction/productivity model is backed up by research, which suggests a relationship between employee satisfaction and the factors of absenteeism and turnover, although the relationship to productivity, while consistent, is not as strong as might by expected. A third variable, rewards, seems to determine the relationship. Good performance may lead to rewards, which in turn can lead to satisfaction; however, this way of looking at it would then say that satisfaction, rather than causing performance, is actually caused by it.

There are two types of reward: extrinsic (pay, promotion, status, security) and intrinsic (personal satisfaction). For this reason, it is more important for the organisation to look at the match between satisfaction and performance rather than addressing satisfaction in itself. The match seems to depend on the perceived equitable distribution of rewards. This may have an impact on issues of space quality and allocation. Reward is not usually linked to professional achievement, but to managerial hierarchies, on the basis of which enclosed, high-quality spaces are allocated as visible status symbols as opposed to being allocated according to quality of performance as a means for rewarding productive workers.

There is a need to focus on the environment in relation to the ease of task performance, rather than in relation to a given job. Ease in accomplishing work affects productivity directly, but also appears to affect motivation and, therefore, performance through its influence on intrinsic rewards. Moreover, 'task performance and work satisfaction are optimised when job demands are high enough for the work to be challenging and interesting, but not so high as to be overwhelming' (Aronoff and Kaplan, 1995). Although factors related to job satisfaction may not be the same as those related to job performance, both impact on productivity and are, therefore, of consequence for the organisation.

In exchange for the removal of restrictions, workers are now required to demonstrate their added value and to do whatever is necessary to achieve the organisation's goals. We can now look at the impact of the organisation on productivity and how this has changed in recent years, as part of changes in the nature and pattern of work.

The organisation

The virtual organisation is now a reality, but not commonplace. Many changes have been taking place that make the forward-looking organisation of the present highly differentiated from the traditional organisation. European organisations in particular have experienced a wave of domestic and cross-border mergers, acquisitions and strategic alliances, as well as restructuring from privatisation or in response to increasing market competition. Reorganisation has an immediate productivity impact in terms of time involved in recruiting or reassigning staff, moving staff and/or furniture, re-establishing and resuming work. The traditional hierarchical pyramid has been squashed to accommodate more horizontal communication and empowerment. The move to flatter and leaner organisational structures has increased the workload and demands on the individual employee. An atmosphere of uncertainty and a need for continual adaptation to new working practices and managerial styles and work cultures, combined with concerns over job security in the move towards short-term contracts, have led to increasing degrees of job-related stress. Chapter 9 discussed factors giving rise to stress amongst workers.

At the beginning of this chapter, we commented on the difficulty of measuring performance in the office environment. The pervasiveness of ICT has led, *inter alia*, to electronic monitoring which has the capacity to provide fairer compensation for performance through more accurate and timely feedback. The links between performance and reward are such that this should be beneficial to productivity. However, negative effects of such monitoring, in terms of worker stress and health decline, can mean a reduction in productivity. Stress from performance measurement and monitoring would seem to be associated with lack of control, loss of trust, and an increased administrative workload involved in operating such procedures. The continuing emphasis placed on closely monitored employee performance, linked to reward and advancement, rests uncomfortably alongside empowerment and participative management, especially if employees are not consulted on targets or the selection of performance criteria.

Focus on the employee as a resource, particularly the soft approach, sees the potential that can be realised in the workforce through training and development, and through cultivating employee commitment to the organisation. This last emphasis will require the physical work environment to be more supportive of the human resources strategies adopted by the organisation. This is particularly evident in the case of flexibility, where the built environment must be able to support the demands for individual and organisational flexibility in order to respond to changes in the marketplace.

Communication

The drive to achieve more efficient realisation of office assets and to promote productivity becomes more feasible with ICT and, in particular, networking. The impact of advances in ICT should be self-evident. However, the effect on productivity is less so, at least in the office environment. Whereas technology has facilitated remarkable increases in productivity in manufacturing, it has had little impact in the office sector and has not provided immediate payback on the high costs of its implementation. Unlike the manufacturing sector, where automation rapidly increases production, technology in the office is likely to increase productivity only to the extent to which users integrate it into their way of working. A key factor in realising productivity gains is that the organisation must be structured to take advantage of the technology and to optimise the contribution of those who use it. The greatest productivity gains are only likely to be achieved when ICT has been used to restructure workflows so that inefficiency and waste are driven out.

ICT has been responsible for some important changes, such as removing the functional and spatial division between headquarters, back office and customer face-to-face offices, leading to greater flexibility in work patterns. Adjacency planning has become less constrained by the demands of physical workflow, with emphasis now given to clustering work activities that require similar background environments, services and equipment. Value can be added to office use by improving productivity through the more effective application of ICT and greater flexibility in its use. For example, the organisation can choose to manage work in a variety of settings, on multiple sites and even across time zones – the location of call centres overseas is but one example.

With up to 80% of office workers reckoned to be knowledge workers, typically spending around 70% of their time on communication activities, they need a mixture of periods of quiet concentration to allow for creative or complex thought and collaborative work. The group element enhances individual capabilities and it is therefore critical for their success that they are able to communicate and collaborate as necessary. Moreover, people can learn from each other in informal situations, by working alongside people with whom they do not normally share space. Many organisations now plan adjacencies to take advantage of unanticipated opportunities created by social interaction.

Work environment

There are essentially two ways in which the office environment can impact on productivity: through enabling it or through hindering it. The ways in which the environment adversely affects worker satisfaction and performance are fairly well known and empirically established. Less is known of, or certain about, the ways in which the environment can positively impact on productivity, other than in removing the factors that adversely affect it.

The many issues known or believed to affect production include, but are not restricted to:

- Prevention of diseases and accidents, resulting in reduced costs
- Reduction of sick leave and lower personnel turnover
- Improvement of communication – consent on the topic of working conditions

- Commitment of workers and improvement of industrial relations
- Enhancement of quality
- Improvement of productivity and efficiency
- Better position in the labour market – more attractive jobs

Seven aspects of the work environment have been identified from the perspective of users:

1. Indoor air quality
2. Noise control
3. Thermal comfort
4. Privacy
5. Lighting comfort
6. Spatial comfort
7. Building noise control

In the above context, the physical environment for office work is believed to account for a variation of some 5–15% in employee productivity (Rostron, 1997). These aspects or factors are now discussed. In this connection, it is important to bear in mind the complexity of the factors and the difficulty of uncovering the root cause of most problems affecting workers. In a book of this kind, we can only hope to provide a summary.

Environmental factors having an impact on productivity

Indoor air quality is one of the major areas of dissatisfaction amongst workers. It is an umbrella term for a variety of factors that include ventilation, pollutants and moisture. Stale air is a common complaint and arises from inefficient ventilation. Natural means of ventilation can often alleviate problems caused by a low rate of mechanical (i.e. forced) air changes; however, the subject is complex and cannot be discussed comprehensively here. Indoor pollution sources that release gases or particles into the air are a significant cause of indoor air quality problems. Inadequate ventilation can increase indoor pollutant levels by not bringing in enough outdoor air to dilute emissions from indoor sources and by not carrying indoor air pollutants to the outside. High temperature and moisture can also increase concentrations of some pollutants. In fact, moisture is a widespread problem often linked with mould growth, resulting from spores that drift through indoor and outdoor air continually. When mould spores land on a damp spot indoors, they may begin growing and digest whatever they are growing on. The way to control indoor mould growth is to control moisture.

Noise and vibration at high levels can be both physiologically and psychologically harmful; they can obstruct communication and mentally disturb the worker, resulting in job performance impairment and/or accidents. When noise distraction is a problem, people rate it as a serious hindrance to productivity, although they do not claim the absence of noise to be an important benefit. Even so, some level of background noise is, in fact, thought to be beneficial to concentration. Noise at inappropriate levels increases mistakes and slows work rates. People also tend to use more simplistic problem-solving methods. Thus, as noise distraction becomes more troublesome, people not only work less effectively they think differently, leading to a quality cost as well as a productivity cost. Noise causes breaks in concentration, making it harder to address tasks that require sustained concentration and reducing the ability to make creative leaps. It also interferes with the ability to differentiate relevant issues from those that are unimportant.

Thermal comfort tends to receive the highest number of complaints in most user surveys. Overly cool conditions make people restless, impairing concentration and increasing error rates, particularly for demanding mental tasks. Being too warm can cause weariness, sleepiness, a reduction in performance and a tendency to make mistakes. Fluctuations in temperature can be even more troublesome.

The biological effect of light is significant not only on visual task performance, but also in controlling physiological and psychological functioning of the human body. As with many other factors, the ultimate effect of light and lighting on human well-being is determined in part by individual perception and satisfaction.

Aesthetic choices in office design affect human behaviour and job performance, influencing workers' perceptions of the work environment, how quickly they tire and how tolerant they are of physical stressors. Considerations regarding interior design must therefore take into account the idiosyncrasies of the human visual system. Extremes of contrast are, in particular, visually fatiguing. However, people with certain kinds of visual impairment may benefit from contrasting colour schemes that pick out important objects. White light switches on a white background may not be easily found, for example, even if the designer has located the switches where they are expected to be.

Sick building syndrome

Factors related to sick building syndrome (SBS) are exacerbated in the high-tech workplace. Offices with more than two symptoms per person of SBS are likely to show general productivity losses. The reported effects of SBS may combine with other job-related factors to produce an overall sense of dissatisfaction. This means that the concentration of research and business efforts and expense on maintenance and cleaning may be misplaced in the search for improved productivity. Moreover, psychosocial problems may actually lead to susceptibility to symptoms through increased stress in working environments.

Minimising the constraints placed on employees at their workstations will increase social and economic productivity. The more choice people have, the happier and more productive they become. The reason why many people under-perform is because their behaviour and degrees of freedom are systematically reduced by decisions over which they themselves have no control – decisions usually taken higher up the organisation.

Environmental characteristics that influence work at the individual level include architectural properties – for example size of office, number of walls, ergonomic factors, heating and light – and architectural attributes, that is, people's perceptions of architectural properties. The very design of workplaces might be creating ill-health. In fact, health and stress problems are greater in high-demand, low-control environments than in high-demand, high-control environments.

The issue of control is one that is continually referred to in a variety of contexts. It surfaces in connection with the work itself and within the organisation and is a major factor concerning productivity in the context of the working environment. Control of one's working environment includes temperature, lighting and ventilation, as well as choice and configuration of furniture. The use of individual environmental control systems can increase productivity by up to 7%. However, the modern office often acts against this, with top-down (or external management) control over functions such as heating and ventilation.

Design implications

An investigation into the influence of the working environment on self-reported productivity found that most respondents considered that the office had a direct influence on their well-being and productivity. They felt that productivity in particular would rise by 10% if environmental conditions were improved. Generally, an improved fit between the physical setting and the work process, both at the individual and the organisational level, should improve performance directly, but also indirectly contribute to future successful job performance by enhancing the intrinsic rewards of the job – performance leads to satisfaction leads to performance.

The design of workspace must address not only employees' lower order needs, such as safety and physical comfort, but also higher order needs such as self-esteem. Once environmental needs are satisfied, the individual becomes dominated by the unsatisfied needs and environmental conditions cease to be important to the individual's current concerns. Instead, issues such as amenity, view, décor, space provision and furniture standard come to the fore in the context of status and self-fulfilment.

Whether a better workplace improves individual performance or more productive workers gravitate to organisations with better work environments is not entirely clear. Yet, there are measurable productivity benefits to be gained by improving the physical working environment. Problems may however arise as much from the perception of space, such as open-plan layouts, as from the reality, including its perceived inferiority to enclosed spaces occupied by managers. Consequently, interventions that alter such perceptions might be a productive approach.

Whilst open-plan settings are intended to offer greater flexibility, it is often the case that this flexibility is not utilised, as the upheaval involved is itself considered counterproductive. Minimising the disruption to productivity caused by constant reshuffles can be achieved through such planning measures as the 'universal footprint' or the fixed service spine. The former limits the number of different office sizes to facilitate movement of staff, the latter mixes rigidity and flexibility, enabling quick reconfigurations to facilitate different types of activity with minimum disruption. Within the universal footprint, as in other schemes, furniture may also be standardised but with individuals able to choose a personalised combination from a standard range of components. This results in a degree of equity, essential to employee satisfaction, as well as direct productivity benefits in matching the tools to the task and the individual. Worker preference for private spaces even for routine tasks and the level of worker satisfaction achieved by this may be more important to productivity than the benefits of social contact provided in less private spaces. A moderately arousing setting benefits monotonous or dull tasks, while a non-arousing setting benefits more complex ones.

Realising that people engage in different activities, and how they do so, and matching the space and facilities to the activity is a critical element of the new workplace. There are reports of improvements in productivity following reorganisation, which took place with user involvement. Organisations can maximise the productivity of their workforce through such a choice of settings that allows individuals and teams to select the one most suited to their task needs at any given time. Allocated workspace cannot be optimal for all activities, all of the time.

Unconventional working arrangements

One approach to revising space utilisation is to abandon designated spaces or workstations in favour of shared facilities, within schemes such as 'hot-desking' and 'hotelling'. This is not always the best way to increase the productive use of office space, in spite of the obvious cost savings. More can be achieved by zoning space, so that, for example, special 'touch down' places, accessible to everyone, are set aside for concentrated, group or specialist work. This can offset some of the problems associated with open-plan offices. In order to maximise the productivity benefits of the non-territorial office, the initiative has to be business-driven rather than cost-driven. The former will involve a fundamental rethinking of organisational structure, performance measurement and business processes.

The productivity increases offered by telecommuting and other new work arrangements can only be maximised if the right sort of space is provided in the office for the times when workers are there. If the office cannot offer appropriate support then productivity gains may be negated. Appropriate support may involve turning the traditional concept of the office inside out. The primary function of the central office space might become support of communication and interaction. Areas for individual, concentrative work would become the support space for the more team-oriented interactive spaces. A system of loosely coupled settings linked physically by the movement of employees and the electronic movement of information could maximise productivity in an organisation with this approach to work. The need for an integrated workplace strategy to accommodate and support new modes of work is paramount.

One large office may appear an efficient option in terms of running costs but there is evidence that decentralisation and the fragmentation of the organisation into several smaller centres is beneficial to job satisfaction and organisational well-being. Hindrances to communication include screening, too little space provided at individual workstations so that impromptu group interactions cannot take place there, and little or no other provision for meetings. Designs that actively support teamwork, collaboration and chance interaction may be highly beneficial to productivity within an organisation which values that approach.

These ideas have come together in the total workplace concept, guided by three principles: breaking down barriers to encourage functional diversity and mixing people who would not normally mix, increasing stimulating and beneficial exposure to differences and diversity; access to the physical resources necessary for effective work, with environmental equity; and varying the optimal setting for accomplishing work according to variations in an individual's work over time. This also encourages spatial mobility between office locations and increases the potential for chance interactions.

Design features that can contribute to this scheme include suitably located activity magnet areas, such as places for breaks designed to create the right kind of behavioural force fields, shared services and information centres to place the employee's contribution in the wider organisational context and promote contributions to company thinking and development. This concept of the total workplace takes a dual approach to effecting productivity: it accommodates the worker to the greatest extent in some respects, while encouraging mobility and interaction through not making every facility as accessible as possible. Other steps could include dedicated project-team rooms, saving time spent on assembling and disassembling material and facilities before and after each meeting. A combination of such spaces with private workstations to accommodate concentrated individual work, plus the clustering of services, may also bring about higher performance from these potentially productive groups.

Conclusions

Proper understanding of worker satisfaction and performance in the office environment requires examination of a complex set of interacting subsystems, including physical environmental factors, job characteristics, organisational factors, socio-cultural characteristics and past experience of workers. More detailed operational definitions of the variables being investigated (such as noise, space, health, privacy, satisfaction and productivity) must be developed. This has not prevented a considerable amount of literature developing on these topics as the root problem that must be addressed and becomes ever more urgent as does the need to justify investments in the office environment. Improving one aspect, such as the physical setting, while ignoring others may send conflicting messages. Moreover, the work environment can only operate productively if all aspects are considered as part of an integrated workplace strategy. The high-performance workplace is much talked and written about, but is barely evident. There are so many factors contributing to productivity that proving a cause and effect relationship is bound to be problematic. Decisions on the quality of the office workplace demand informed judgement. Whilst it remains elusive to be able to predict reliably the returns on facility investments of the kind outlined, the evidence that a better work environment promotes better performance is more than superficially compelling. The overriding message is to strike the right balance between maximising communication and space for quiet reflective work; between group, team and project work, and confidential or individual work; and between group areas and individual access to daylight, aspect and ventilation.

CHECKLIST

This checklist is intended to assist with the review and action planning process.

	Yes	No	Action required
1. Has the organisation undertaken any formal measurement of productivity in the workplace?	☐	☐	☐
2. Is the organisation aware of the factors that can lead to dissatisfaction with the workplace?	☐	☐	☐
3. Is the organisation continually monitoring the quality of the internal environment?	☐	☐	☐
4. Are workers' concerns about the work environment taken seriously and incidents properly investigated?	☐	☐	☐
5. Have steps been taken to minimise negative impacts upon worker well-being?	☐	☐	☐
6. Has the organisation taken steps to maximise beneficial aspects of the workplace?	☐	☐	☐
7. Has the organisation adopted a flexible policy in relation to the workplace, e.g. working hours, off-site locations and non-traditional office layouts?	☐	☐	☐

11 Facilities Management Service Providers

Key issues

The following issues are covered in this chapter.

- There are four types of service provider arrangements in the marketplace: managing agent, managing contractor, managed budget and total facilities management – there are variations on them too.

- The degree of flexibility of service provision enjoyed by the client organisation will vary with each type and is a factor that has to be taken into account.

- All types of service provision attract costs in managing and administering contracts.

- The organisation needs to weigh the risks and costs of the different types of service provision and to have based this on reliable data from the marketplace and information from service providers.

- The employment of a total facilities management company – effectively providing a single point of responsibility – whilst attractive, will not relieve the organisation from managing the contract and the interface between the contractor and customers. There are bound to be costs in connection with the management of even a single appointment.

- Novel solutions and their providers have entered the marketplace and include support of a temporary or long-term nature based on fully serviced workspace, which is available in many countries and regions therein.

Introduction

Selecting a particular type of service provider is in the same bracket as deciding whether or not to outsource – for some, the answer may appear obvious, but this might not be so. In a similar manner to that adopted for approaching the question of outsourcing, the organisation should look closely at the types of provision available and make an objective decision. For simplicity, the four main types of service provider range from additional support for the client organisation to full support in providing anything the organisation might want. There will be variations in these types according to particular circumstances, but they are, otherwise, the most common. Each of the types attracts its own supporters and detractors, and there is distortion in the marketplace as to what is being offered. However, the real issues are those concerning risk for the client organisation, both financially and in damage that could be done by, for example, a careless service provider or subcontractor, and the management and administration required to support the subsequent service contracts. Whilst these are clearly important considerations, pursuit of these points are peripheral to the main substance of this chapter and, indeed, this book. In any event, the organisation should maintain awareness of the state of the market for facilities management, although any market testing should be done with sensitivity – see earlier discussion in Chapter 3 – as part of its ICF. Whatever type of service provision is ultimately selected, the client organisation must do so on the dual criteria of likely customer satisfaction and best value.

Preliminary approach

The opening assumption is that the organisation will have determined which services to outsource and will have done so by taking account of the market for facilities management – see Chapter 3. Earlier actions will have established whether or not the market is capable of delivering what is required by the organisation. An important consideration should be the bundling of individual services in a way that will provide best value. There are two aspects to consider. First, client organisations will have worked out how best to arrange their outsourcing to ensure that best value is likely to be achieved. Second, service providers will take a commercial view on what is profitable for them. Bundling of services can prove to be an attraction for service providers; likewise, carving up the totality of facilities management into very small contracts may not. It is also useful to recognise that arrangements, which may involve a lot of subcontracting and, possibly, sub-subcontracting, can confer a financial disadvantage because cost is added at each point in the supply chain without necessarily adding value. Preliminary enquiries will, however, help to establish the most advantageous approach to the bundling of services, as well as militating the likelihood of redundancy occurring in the supply chain. This can be achieved by considering various combinations of services for which indicative quotations can then be sought – although the points in Chapter 3 regarding market testing should be noted.

The organisation will also need to consider the attributes of service provision that are important to them so that they are able to identify the most suitable service provider – again, see Chapter 3. Qualitative criteria can be used to help in weighing different attributes of service and provide a basis for subsequently judging the suitability of service providers before an invitation to tender and, thereafter, in assessing tenders.

The organisation's representatives should be appraised of the financial standing of any service provider before entering into a contract with them – see Chapter 6. Credit references should be sought in addition to performance references from existing clients. Failure of a service provider, large or small, will have implications for the client organisation. Whilst it is never possible to eliminate the likelihood of this happening, its occurrence can be minimised by taking up references with reliable sources.

Types of service provision

Service provision ranges from an agent, acting largely in a consultancy capacity, to a contracting company providing a complete portfolio of services. The decision as to which is the most appropriate will depend on requirements – identified earlier in the process – as well as the risk tolerance (or aversion) of the client organisation. Important in this regard is to appreciate that the marketplace is continuously evolving the nature of facilities management services as firms compete for their share of business by devising novel ways of delivering customer satisfaction and best value.

Essentially, four types of service can be distinguished. They range from the use of an external organisation or individual who manages the client organisation's own employees, through the appointment of a contractor to manage some or all service providers, to an arrangement where all facilities are managed by an external entity offering a single point of responsibility. Figure 11.1 shows the four main types in terms of their contractual and management (communication) links.

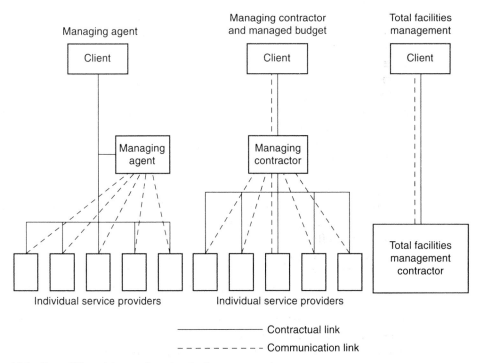

Fig. 11.1   Four different types of contractual arrangement.

Managing agent

This arrangement is adopted when the organisation has determined that it does not wish to hand over control of its facilities to a contractor, yet does not have the skill or expertise with which to manage them efficiently and effectively. By bringing in an external organisation to manage the facilities, the organisation is essentially appointing a client representative. This person – almost invariably the appointment will specify an individual – will act almost as if he or she were part of the permanent establishment of the client organisation. The client representative (managing agent) will perform better and more reliably if performance criteria are laid down, in fact, as would apply to an in-house manager. Under this arrangement, contracts with service providers will be with the client organisation.

There are distinct and, perhaps, obvious advantages in adopting this arrangement. Both the agent and the various service providers (contractors) can be selected on the basis of competitive tendering. Moreover, the appointment (or re-appointment) of the agent should not affect contracts with service providers or vice versa. Dissatisfaction with a given contractor would not place other contracts at risk; indeed, it could positively assist in those cases where poor performance has had a knock-on effect.

The managing agent approach offers considerable flexibility for the client organisation to find and then hold on to the combination of contracts that suits it best. There is no reason why services should not be part in-house and part outsourced. The managing agent role attracts particular significance since the client organisation would be using the agent to contribute expertise and exercise judgement when deciding between in-house and outsourced service provision. There are, however, potential disadvantages for organisations that adopt this approach. For example, it is possible that gaps might occur between the scope of the various contracts, including that of the managing agent. Even so, managing agents can be made responsible for ensuring that the scope of service contracts is such that gaps do not occur.

From a risk perspective, the organisation is moderately exposed. It may have to accept the possibility of introducing an uncertain combination of risk factors by its own selection of contractors (including the managing agent) on an individual or piecemeal basis. The reasoning here is that a number of contractors coming together for the first time will place extra demands on the managing agent. Sound relationships between different contractors are needed if services are to be provided properly and facilities are to operate efficiently. These relationships may take some time to develop. A conscious effort will therefore be required on the part of the managing agent to integrate the work of the different contractors in such a way that they become moulded into a single, efficient team.

Some words of caution are necessary. The client organisation may find that administration costs increase as the number of separate contracts rises. Allowance must be made for these when evaluating outsourcing as an option – see Chapter 3. Risks can be mitigated and administration reduced by appointing the managing agent first and requiring that he or she establishes the suitability of service providers. In deciding to embark on this route, the organisation should allocate adequate resources to planning and implementation.

Case study – Facilities management in the public sector

This case study describes a facilities management consultant engaged in a managing agent role in the public sector. In addition to illustrating general and specific issues in facilities management, the case study illustrates the importance of a well-developed informed client function (ICF) and of managing relationships between facilities managers and their various customers. The requirement for compulsory tendering led a UK government department to outsource all non-core business and to bring in a facilities management expert to help define and manage the services, which the department would itself procure and contract. This followed an earlier decision to rationalise the department's property portfolio, reducing it to six occupied buildings in central London, thereby forming part of a complete overhaul of property and facilities management within the department. Initially, the facilities management of two buildings was outsourced, with the remaining four buildings subject to market testing a year later. As a result of this two-stage process, two different facilities management consultants became involved, creating an unusual situation, which will be discussed below. The case study focuses mainly on the management of the group of four buildings, forming the basis of the second tendering exercise.

As a result of these two initiatives, many personnel were lost from the facilities management function, such as it was, and a new structure was imposed constituting an ICF. The client had previously given little attention and even less prestige to the facilities management function, which had been resourced mostly by lower-grade civil servants. As neither management nor personnel viewed the existing roles as career positions, there was a high turnover. With the new regime, more high-ranked officers were involved, with specific responsibility for specialist areas, including procurement. There were also two liaison officers, each acting as the first point of contact for one of the managing agents. Once these positions had been established, the personnel affected tended to remain, providing a degree of continuity and consistency previously lacking in the facilities management function.

The flagship building, approximately 150 000 sq ft (14 000 m²) in size, was in central London. It accommodated the ministers, top civil servants and various departmental divisions within the ministry. The building was also occupied by equivalent ministers and civil servants attached to another ministry, for which facilities services were provided by the host. The remaining three buildings were 150 000 sq ft, (14 000 m²), 100 000 sq ft (9 000 m²) and 60 000 sq ft (5 500 m²) in size respectively, all accommodating further departmental divisions as well as an affiliated government agency.

A straightforward tender document was advertised on the basis of an open competition as required by law. The services to be managed were wide-ranging, as shown below. With the client's ICF now well established, the requirements as stated in the tender document were clear. However, it was necessary for the consultants tendering to be 'intelligent' in interpreting and understanding the full range of services required and the associated personnel and other costs. An organisation unused to providing facilities management services – perhaps operating out of a building surveying or quantity surveying firm – might be unable to appreciate the full implication of all items and thus provide a tender based on a partial understanding of the work involved. For this reason the development of the ICF prior to tendering this key function is doubly critical; first, so that clarity can be achieved in tender documents and, second, so that clients can be intelligent in their choice of consultant.

The consultant already managing the first two buildings tendered unsuccessfully for the remaining four. A second consultant was awarded the contract to provide facilities management on a managing agent basis. The initial contract was for a period of three-and-a-quarter years, after the three-month mobilisation period. The consultant would then be required to re-tender in open competition.

Under this managing agent arrangement the client remained a contract principal with the service provider and procured all service contracts. The facilities management consultant's role was to manage facilities service contracts on the client's behalf. These contracts were:

- Security
- Cleaning
- Mechanical and electrical engineering services maintenance
- Catering
- Post and messenger services
- Inter-building minibus
- Furniture supply
- Stationery 'just-in-time' supply
- Air, train and taxi travel

In opting for a managing agent arrangement, the client fulfilled its need to retain overall control. It was also aware that it would have to carry and manage the risk. Part of the careful establishment of the ICF was to ensure that it was in the best position to do so. While the client procured all the services, the managing agent helped with the analysis of requirements, the development of specifications and the assessment of tenders, as a facilities management expert.

The contract allowed the managing agent substantial licence in the approach to managing the facilities. The combination of the well-developed ICF and the facilities management expertise of the managing agent meant that this caused few problems. Service contracts were more specific, but did not have clear input and output specifications and only basic descriptions of the work to be performed under each contract. This approach, and the reluctance on the part of the client to provide adequate prior information and familiarisation with the buildings, led to problems for the managing agent from the tender stage onwards. These restrictions prevented tenderers from providing client-specific specifications. The standard specifications submitted had then to be customised later on an 'exchange' basis. Items that the contractor claimed not to have included, but which were specifically required by the client, were 'traded' for tasks incorporated in the standard specification, for which the client had no need or priority.

In the three-month mobilisation period, the managing agent recruited personnel necessary for its role, while the buildings were still run by civil servants. When established, the facilities management team of 11 people comprised a facilities manager, a deputy with building surveying skills, a building manager in each building and a mechanical and electrical (M&E) engineer to manage the M&E contractor and also project work. Personnel were supported by a central team providing a helpdesk, financial planning and reporting, purchasing space planning, project management, performance measurement and review, as described below.

Helpdesk

A three-person helpdesk team took responsibility for handling calls from the two departments occupying the buildings, which housed 2 000 people. Initially, the helpdesk was a manual system, with instructions and required completion date issued by fax to contractors and job completion information handled similarly. The client required every helpdesk instruction received to be followed up on completion by the issue of a job satisfaction sheet to the person initiating the helpdesk call. Satisfaction levels were recorded and analysed for inclusion in the managing agent's monthly report.

The set-up was perceived by the managing agent to be overly bureaucratic, but was insisted upon by the client. Although placing a high value on feedback, the client was not prepared to resource the helpdesk to the extent of providing appropriate ICT, as requested by the consultant. In the absence of special application software, the consultant used part of a standard software system to support the recording and analysis of helpdesk data.

Financial planning and reporting

The facilities management consultant was responsible for formulating annual budgets for each building and tracking expenditure against a variety of expense heads. All financial processes complied with the client's financial procedures and government-imposed timetables. In order to ensure compatibility with the client's financial systems, the consultant was given access to the client's finance package and was able to extract data for post-processing on spreadsheets.

Purchasing

The helpdesk team was also responsible for purchasing a wide range of services and supplies from the contractors on site and other service providers and suppliers. The team's duties covered obtaining quotations where necessary, order placing, delivery recording and invoice reconciliation. The client provided purchasing software and training in its use. For audit purposes, none of the consultant's personnel were authorised to carry out more than one action in the supply chain process.

Space planning

Building managers were assigned responsibility for the management of space in their buildings, covering minor to major moves, from receipt of a move request to completion. To assist the building managers, a space planner would produce layout drawings using CAD software. Space usage by cost centre was recorded in a CAFM database. The client selected the software and also provided full training in its use for the consultant's personnel. Building managers also specified and purchased furniture and chairs from a call-off contract.

Project management

The consultant was required to manage both minor and major M&E and fabric maintenance projects ranging in cost from a few thousand to a million pounds. Projects included the installation of fan coil units throughout one building, new fire alarm and public address systems, energy management data collection systems, major refurbishment and redecoration. Contracts for substantial projects were generally arranged separately from the main facilities management contract.

The day-to-day management of facilities was left to the managing agent, with the client adopting a 'hands-off' approach other than for exceptional circumstances and other critical actions. Each month, the facilities management consultant would prepare a report covering expenditure against budget, project work, contractors' performance, health and safety record, accidents and new initiatives. There was constant monitoring and measurement of performance, although the consultant's fixed monthly fee did not depend on it. Rates for various types of service provision were agreed upon. The consultant had responsibility for purchasing, but this was via the client's own arrangement and out of a specific budget.

Performance measurement

In order to monitor the performance of the primary service providers (main contractors), the consultant devised a performance measurement system. Each month, building managers and on-site contract managers would meet to review the month and plan future actions. This meeting would include an assessment of the previous month's performance based on helpdesk information and the building manager's own assessment of other issues. Although neither the facilities management contract nor the service contracts allowed for penalties for poor performance, failing contractors would reflect poorly on the managing agent, which might be critical at the point of re-tendering. Although this did not prove to be a serious issue, there was the potential for a conflict of interests. High expectations and the drive to raise and maintain standards, on the part of building managers, inevitably led them to register criticism when contractors under-performed; however, these criticisms could suggest too easily that the managing agent was not performing well. Although there were fixed measures against which service provider performance could be judged, there remained a degree of interpretation and the opportunity for inconsistency in the assessment.

Review

There were several aspects of this particular arrangement, which were relatively unusual, but which illustrate issues that both client organisations and consultants need to consider and to manage. First, as explained above, two consultants were involved, each doing much the same tasks in different buildings. Each had his or her own approach and style, as well as overall organisational objectives. These did not necessarily cause conflict between the two managing agents, but were an extra factor for the ICF to manage. The two consultants reported to different heads within the government department; thus, the responsibility for managing this rested with the client.

Some services had of necessity to be managed by cooperation between the two facilities management consultants. The contract manager had to report to and deal with representatives of two different companies with two different management styles. Moreover, contractors, who sometimes had difficulty in coping even with the idea of facilities managers, found dealing with two different managers in relation to one service problematic. This was exacerbated by one consultant, who aimed for more of a TFM approach and, therefore, had somewhat different objectives in guiding the management of service providers. Moreover, the different approaches of the two consultants highlighted the need for awareness of a further, more typical, division. There were effectively two customers: the ICF and personnel using the building and requesting services. One consultant focused attention on the former based on a perception that – particularly within the public sector – budgets were of prime importance. This perception extended to the need to 'look after' the ICF, providing sufficient contact, reassurance and moral support. Although this consultant became aware of a weakness in the area of customer care, in the meantime its contract manager was receiving the full support of senior personnel from the consultancy, who retained contact with the ICF. The other consultant focused attention on those actually requesting and using the services, being responsive to their needs at the expense of directly supporting the ICF. The contract manager was largely left to get on with the task without either interference or obvious support from senior personnel within the consultancy. In retrospect it is clear that it is essential to manage both areas, to balance the political with the practical and for both parties to manage relationships in order to get the most out of them.

During the contract period, one consultant, in competition with the other, won extra business with the client, covering the management of some of its minor buildings at other locations. This work constituted a separate contract, but at the point of re-tendering it was included in a consolidated facilities management package for which a single consultant was appointed, as part of the client's developing awareness of its optimal facilities management requirements.

Managing contractor

Under this arrangement there is one contract between the client organisation and the appointed contractor (primary service provider). Subcontractors (secondary service providers) will be under contract to the managing contractor and so will not have a contractual relationship with the client organisation. This means that the organisation has a single point of contact with the contractor on all matters pertaining to service provision. Thus, if a service falls below the required performance for work carried out by a subcontractor, the organisation need only direct its complaint to the managing contractor. However, as the chain of command is longer, delays in receiving prompt action may occur. Although the subcontractors are contracted to the managing contractor, the organisation should protect its position by reserving the right to approve the selection of subcontractors.

Since there is a single point of contact, there should be a sizeable reduction in paperwork and fewer payments. Gaps in service provision should be eliminated because the managing contractor is required to ensure that they simply do not occur. By using a managing contractor to undertake some or all of the work, with the support of subcontractors, the organisation is able to mitigate much financial risk. The managing contractor is generally paid a fee usually expressed as a percentage of the value of the expenditure managed, and this can, of course, be related to performance. The organisation is, despite the limitation of being in just one contract, able to see where its money is being spent because open-book accounting is usually adopted in which the client organisation has access to the contractor's premises, books and records, including invoices from subcontractors.

The right to access is necessary as the managing contractor may insist on larger trade discounts than are acceptable, or may demand some other preferential terms that are not consistent with best practice. In these cases, the managing contractor's approach may result in poor performance by the subcontractor and, therefore, poor service to the organisation. Open-book accounting also ensures that there are few misunderstandings as to the cost of services. Under this arrangement it will, however, be more difficult to make changes to a contract, once it is formalised, than would be the case under the managing agent arrangement, unless the changes are provided for in advance in some way.

Managed budget

The managing agent model, whilst still valid for many organisations, does not fit with the culture of some, notably those that have invested in enterprise-wide management (ICT) systems and that wish to reduce the number of transactions. The major objection is the requirement to establish purchase ledger accounts for service providers (suppliers), although a managing agent handles all but the payment process.

In order to overcome this objection the managed budget model was developed in which a managing contractor takes responsibility for the payment of all suppliers and provides a consolidated invoice at the end of each month. A management fee is agreed, which is larger than that found in the managing agent model, since turnover from specialist subcontractors goes through the managing contractor's accounts. The management fee is based on a combination of the resources as deployed and the value of budgeted expenditure – all subcontract invoices and contract-specific employee costs are processed without any mark up. Usually, the managing contractor places an element of the management fee at risk, subject to the attainment of pre-agreed service levels. For discretionary expenditure, such as stationery and couriers, a simple handling charge can be added to the invoice.

Contractually, the managed budget approach is similar to the managing contractor model. However, important differences lie in the apportionment of risk and in an improved relationship between the client organisation and managing contractor. Through the removal of a supply chain 'mark-up', and remuneration based upon a management fee, the kind of friction that might otherwise build up between the two parties is alleviated. The benefit of the managing agent model in providing access to professional advice, with management working alongside the client, results in little or no conflict of interest. There is also the further advantage of fewer transactions to be processed, thereby reducing administration for the client organisation.

Total facilities management

Under this arrangement, the client organisation is able to pass the full responsibility for managing its facilities to a single organisation for a fixed price. This does, however, require the organisation to provide the contractor (service provider) with sufficient scope to be able to manage the various services efficiently. While total facilities management might appear to provide an ideal solution, because it provides a single purchasing point for the organisation, the reality can be that the contractor actually subcontracts all or most of the work. Since there is just one contract – that between the organisation and the total facilities management contractor – there is the chance that terms and conditions between the contractor and subcontractor do not mirror those of the main contract. Difficulties can arise because terms and conditions that are embodied in the contract between the client organisation and the contractor may allow for situations that are not subsequently recognised in the contract with the subcontractor or vice versa.

The total facilities management contractor may be better able to offer a more complete and competitive solution to an organisation's needs than in the case of the managing agent or managing contractor. Relationships built up over years between the contractor and (specialist) subcontractors may mean that efficient working relationships are established from the start. Total facilities management can provide a sound solution, but only if the organisation is prepared to spend time in identifying the right basis for such an arrangement and then in selecting the best contractor.

In practice, things can go wrong. Reasons include the contractor's relationship with subcontractors. For example, as with the managing contractor arrangement, the total facilities management contractor may insist on larger trade discounts than are acceptable or some other preferential terms that are not consistent with best practice. Also, during the currency of a contract, the contractor may decide to change subcontractors. These decisions are not always made to improve performance; they may arise because the contractor is seeking to increase margins through the employment of a cheaper subcontractor. As with any change, newly appointed subcontractors – for whatever reason they are employed – will undergo a learning process. In this case, the client organisation should ensure that the procedure for assigning or subcontracting is open to inspection and that they have the right, under the contract, to prior approval before such assignment or subcontracting. Open-book accounting should also be in place.

In terms of risk, the organisation is only moderately exposed and can derive a good deal of comfort from knowing that there is a single point of contact and less administration. Value for money may not be quite as good as in the managing agent approach, although the additional cost of organising and managing many more individual contracts in that approach must be taken into consideration.

Totally serviced workplace

Increasingly, the marketplace is offering novel solutions for organisations wishing either to outsource all or part of their facilities management, or to support new business development. Common amongst these solutions is what is termed the totally serviced workplace. The idea is that an organisation looking for a temporary solution to an accommodation problem can rent fully serviced office space for as little as one month up to a few years. In some cases, the serviced workplace may be intended as a permanent solution or at least one that does not have a specified time horizon. For organisations looking to expand their business internationally, the availability – at short notice – of this kind of solution can be very attractive, albeit obtained at a premium.

In one case, a major telecommunications company has secured several thousands of workplaces for its international operations. Moreover, it has an arrangement that is simplified to the point of its paying a lump sum fee based on the number of workplaces multiplied by the unit rate per month. Reducing transaction costs for the organisation is another benefit from the arrangement, alongside low risk exposure and a high level of flexibility. Of course, the client organisation in this case has to be absolutely certain of the financial standing of the service provider and the status of the underpinning property title.

Evolution in the nature of service providers

In the early 1990s the UK government – following the demise of its Property Services Agency (PSA) – awarded a number of contracts for property management on the basis of a managing agent contract. The scope of these contracts was narrow, but it allowed various government departments to employ professional consultants to advise them on the most appropriate ways of managing their estates. During what was a time of transition, the approach proved beneficial and expenditure plans for the estates were developed, providing a commercially sound basis for future strategies. In the private sector, the basis of the contractual relationship was what was termed a total facilities contract (TFM) with a single organisation providing the range of services required. The popularity of TFM spread and other public sector contracts were awarded on this basis. More contractors moved into the marketplace from different disciplines, seeing the potential to increase their margins and enter into long-term agreements.

Over the last five years, the criteria by which client organisations have valued the benefit from their facilities management contracts have changed. It is no longer enough to use the one service provider, one invoice approach as the basis of a strategic decision, neither is it 'base cost' as many clients have subsequently found. The TFM model has proved to be inflexible, lacking in visibility and requiring a high level of policing. In many cases, because the types of organisation involved in this work originate from a particular service delivery background, they will seek to 'self-deliver', with the emphasis placed on the number of operatives on site to achieve their return. Consequently, the focus is on task management and not the strategic management of the client's portfolio or relationships. Typically, contracting organisations have sought to make a return on the supply chain they lead, usually expressed as a percentage of the value of the subcontracted element. An argument supporting this can be developed where the main contractor is bearing risk or adding something unique to the process. However, the desire to improve overall margins results in the

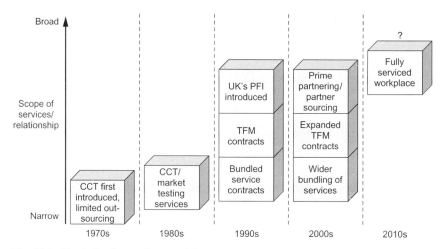

Fig. 11.2   Evolution in service provision.

addition of a traditionally accepted mark-up to this element, irrespective of risk or value added. Market pressures, as described earlier, have driven the questioning of such contractual arrangements and the conflicts of interest that arise through the application of a percentage based mark-up. Client organisations are looking to achieve a partnership-based relationship where returns are agreed in advance and both parties work together to innovate and reduce cost.

The trend depicted in Fig. 11.2 shows evolution towards serviced workplaces. The number of serviced office providers has increased in the marketplace and can provide greater levels of flexibility using a 'menu of prices' geared to levels of service provision. However, for major occupiers this does not need to be externally provided. It can be delivered internally where there is a desire to change and as long as financial controls are also put in place. Where a serviced environment is priced appropriately and re-charged it can provide business units with real information that can enhance decision-making. Evidence suggests that the old habits of liberal space usage are quickly reformed when the true cost is revealed. Space is a valuable and significant component of the facilities cost equation and this is where the greatest opportunities for cost reduction often lie. Even so, the opportunity to tap this potentially rich seam is dependent upon the appetite of the organisation to change as well as having the resources for this purpose. Implementing a successful flexible working arrangement requires information which under a typical TFM relationship is in the hands of the service provider not the client. Facilities management service providers can provide expertise in these areas, but the key to this lies in the level of management expertise deployed on the contract and in the congruence of its objectives with those of the client organisation. Traditional arrangements have inhibited this congruence, with commercial imperatives often driving the service provider in another direction.

Determining the best approach

The choice of which approach works best for the client organisation will depend on many factors. If the procedures outlined in Chapter 3 have been followed, the organisation should be able to see which approach is best and proceed with confidence. Competition in selecting the best value option has to be the criterion applied to all situations. Whether the organisation chooses to manage all service contracts itself – perhaps through an appointed managing agent – or passes the responsibility to a third party, there will be risks and cost involved. The organisation must decide which risks it is prepared to take and at what cost, and which risks to pass to someone else for what may well be a higher sum. Flexibility is a factor that has to be taken into account, along with the attendant cost and risk.

The selected approach should be one that will provide best value for the organisation and its customers. Total facilities management has obvious attractions, but it will not relieve the organisation from managing the contract and the interface between the contractor and its customers. In deciding between the approaches, the organisation must consider carefully how to ensure that customer needs are fully addressed. The best value solution should not be one that compromises on customer satisfaction.

Finally, the client organisation must always take into account the track-record of any contractor, subcontractor or agent it may be considering, together with an understanding of the particular expertise the contractor or agent can offer.

Conclusions

There are basically four ways of procuring facilities management services from the marketplace. The first involves the employment of a managing agent under contract to the organisation, acting as the client's representative. The second is the appointment of a managing contractor. This differs from the managing agent in that the contractor takes responsibility for engaging and managing the various services contracts for a fee. The third – managed budget – is a variation on the former two approaches and hands the burden of multiple transactions to a managing contractor. The last is where a single point of responsibility is established, with one contractor providing all services. The best approach for the client organisation will be the one that is most closely aligned to its needs as previously defined, as well as the one that delivers best value. If the ground is thoroughly prepared beforehand, the choice of option will be obvious and uncomplicated. Attention can then turn to the selection of the best service providers. If it is not straightforward then some shortcoming in the steps leading up to selection is probably to blame and the organisation may have to re-examine its earlier decisions and assumptions.

CHECKLIST

This checklist is intended to assist with the review and action planning process.

	Yes	No	Action required
1. Does the organisation understand the types of service provision available and, in particular, the distinctions between the roles of the managing agent, managing contractor, managed budget and a total facilities management approach?	☐	☐	☐
2. Is the organisation clear about its own role in managing each type of service provider?	☐	☐	☐
3. Is the organisation aware of the current market for services and how this might impact on its selection or approach?	☐	☐	☐
4. Has the organisation followed an appropriate procedure to identify which approach would best suit its current requirements?	☐	☐	☐
5. Has the organisation understood where the balance of risks lies for the type of service provision selected?	☐	☐	☐
6. Has the organisation taken all the necessary steps to verify the capabilities and financial standing of the service providers it intends to select?	☐	☐	☐
7. Has the organisation checked the position regarding the use of subcontractors by the (proposed) contractor (or service provider)?	☐	☐	☐

12 Managing Service Provider and Supplier Relationships

Key issues

The following issues are covered in this chapter.

- All service providers and suppliers have to be managed – the nature of the relationship between the client organisation and providers/suppliers is where it varies.

- Buying a service without concern for the ensuing relationship might be to ignore a useful source of skill and expertise – competent service providers and suppliers have much to offer if the conditions are conducive to their offering expertise.

- Cooperative relationships with service providers and suppliers can provide greater certainty of provision without being non-competitive or compromising on quality or performance.

- Partnering is the most common form of cooperative relationship for managing service providers and suppliers – it is not, however, an answer for all needs and situations.

- For public sector organisations, partnering should be seen as an entirely acceptable alternative to competitive tendering provided it too has a competitive element.

- Cooperative relationships imply working toward goals that have to be shared by the client organisation and service provider (or supplier) alike.

- Continual improvement is a necessary part of the culture of cooperative relationships and one that must include measurable targets in all arrangements including partnering.

Introduction

As a reflection on how the world has changed and, in particular, how relationships in commerce and industry have developed, we might be tempted to say that a chapter devoted to managing relationships would have been unnecessary some years back. Service providers (contractors) were awarded contracts on the basis of competitive tenders and instructed to perform. Fortunately, business culture has changed and with it the simple realisation that a successful contract outcome depends on the willing – as opposed to enforced – cooperation of service providers. This chapter considers how the client organisation can get the best from its service providers and suppliers. Rather than seeing them as simply a source that can be tapped as and when required, the organisation can use them to help produce greater economy and higher levels of customer satisfaction through less waste and a generally more efficient process – see also introductory comments in Chapter 1 on establishing and maintaining good relationships. There are many ways of bringing about a culture of cooperation and formalising it in workable procedures and practices. Over the past decade, partnering has emerged as, arguably, the most distinct type of cooperative arrangement. Introduced originally in some quarters as a means for fighting adversarial behaviour, it has developed rapidly to become a sophisticated technique for delivering customer satisfaction and best value; moreover, it lays the foundation for a process of continual improvement – see also Chapter 14.

Service providers and suppliers

There is an obvious distinction between the provider of a service – taken to include the supply of labour and equipment, as well as materials – and the supply of goods or materials alone. However, in this chapter the term 'supplier' is taken to mean service providers too – the term is all-embracing and is in keeping with current practice that sees supplier management as a critical success factor for organisations of all kinds.

Suppliers have traditionally been regarded simply as someone or somebody paid to provide. Where a supplier is responsible for something that can be provided easily by many others, such as cleaning, there may seem little need to bother about a relationship beyond that of a straightforward commercial arrangement. However, this ignores the possibility that the supplier's knowledge about products and processes could be used to reduce waste and raise productivity. Clearly, where the supplier is of economic significance to the organisation, it makes sense to explore ways in which unnecessary cost might be eliminated. Having a close working relationship with the supplier can achieve this goal, yet does not necessarily risk being non-competitive.

The term 'supplier' therefore needs to be broadened to embody any person or organisation external to the client organisation who can contribute to its success or failure. A contract cleaning company is a clear example, but so is an architectural practice working on a refurbishment programme. Each has a relationship with the client organisation and this has to be managed to ensure the success of the contract.

Types of relationship

When considering the nature of the relationship that an organisation should have with its suppliers, it is important not to focus on contractual

Table 12.1   Partnering compared with a traditional contracting arrangement.

Partnering	Traditional contracting
Innovative, not well-developed	Established, well-developed
Ability to negotiate on price	Difficult to negotiate on price
Close interaction between parties	Arm's-length relationship
Quality improvement possible	Quality likely to be minimum specified
Proactive contractor response	Reactive contractor response
Disputes less likely	Disputes common
Long-term benefits	Short-term gains

arrangements until a sensible basis for working with a supplier has been found. Contractual arrangements should not override how a given product or service should be provided. Relationships with suppliers can be improved by incorporating incentives for levels of performance that exceed agreed targets and by making use of the expertise that many suppliers undoubtedly have. Successful relationships will come from treating suppliers as partners even where there is a contract based on traditional price competition in which different terminology prevails.

Partnering is a practice that has become popular across the breadth of the real estate and construction sector, including therefore facilities management. Some see it, erroneously, as the means by which they can avoid tendering competitively for a service. The aim is to build a business relationship that is founded on trust. It is not a way of working around financial constraints. Partnering aligns the objectives of the customer and supplier in an attempt to maximise the benefits to both. For the client organisation, there can be savings from not having to tender repeatedly; for the supplier it can mean regular work from a customer whose requirements are better understood than they would otherwise be. Business arranged in this way can bring about significant savings over the medium to long-term. A comparison of partnering with a traditional contracting arrangement is given in Table 12.1.

The essence of partnering is that the client organisation decides to work with a select number of firms or individuals who will share the work in a prescribed area. This is easy to achieve for a regular and large procurer of new buildings, for example. For other types of organisation, the opportunities to partner are more limited, although they do exist in the sense of sharing with someone or somebody who will provide a real gain for the client organisation. Partnering could exist in transportation services and vehicle maintenance or where related organisations collaborate on the bulk purchasing of utilities supplies to form a procurement consortium. Such arrangements create an economy of scale that can provide smaller organisations with better value for money than under an arrangement where they attempt to negotiate on their own. An additional benefit from this kind of collaboration is that expertise and risks are also shared.

Practice Point 12.1   A clean sweep.

Key-point: A partnering arrangement can allow organisations to benefit from the expertise of service providers to everyone's benefit.

An organisation had long held the view that cleaning was a generally straight-forward activity for which there was an accepted approach. This tended to mean that the contractor's supervisor would requisition supplies of cleaning agents and other consumables as and when required from a local supplier. On the operations front, there was a daily pattern which, though not perfect, was accepted as the way things were done. For some time, the facilities manager had been wondering how she could reduce what appeared to be a wasteful and, therefore, expensive approach. The time was fast approaching when the organisation was due to test the market for a range of services, including clean-ing. The facilities manager took the initiative to talk to a couple of local service providers who were working on various office developments on the nearby science park. After a short time, it became apparent that the organisation was probably paying far too much for its cleaning – it was buying in expensive and perhaps unnecessary agents and consumables and the frequency and timing of a large amount of cleaning was unnecessary. In the event, the facilities manager asked all three service providers to consider bidding for the cleaning contract on the basis that the successful contractor would be asked to enter into a partnering arrangement. Whilst a contract would still be in place, there would be flexibility to explore ways of improving quality and performance and reducing cost. Two of the three accepted the invitation.

What kind of relationship is needed?

Few services or supplies are of exactly the same degree of importance. Failure in certain of them could prove disastrous – for instance, a failure to test electrical appliances – whilst other types of failure might be tolerated or at least a means found to minimise their impact. It is therefore important for organisations to recognise where the kinds of suppliers with whom they are dealing lie within the matrix in Fig. 12.1. Locating suppliers in the correct position within the matrix focuses attention on the kind of relation-ship that has to be managed (Gadde, 1996). Procedures will then need to reflect the different emphases that are required of the relationship. In this way, it should be possible for client organisations to achieve higher levels of service from suppliers.

Understanding the kinds of relationship that are possible is only the beginning. The organisation will need to adopt appropriate controls and incentives that may well differ between sets of relationships. It should be possible for the organisation to devise relationships with individual suppliers that are more closely aligned with the needs of both parties. For example, the relationship demanded of a cleaning contract might embody incentives for ensuring that areas are cleaned in ways and at times that provide maximum flexibility for building users. The extent of the

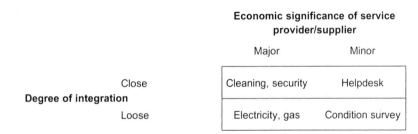

Fig. 12.1   Locating service providers and suppliers according to their relationship.

requirements might be so complicated that without a close working relationship – perhaps founded as a partnering arrangement – the quality of service expected might be unattainable. Extensive dialogue and discussion may be needed before a deep understanding can be reached.

In another example – that of the helpdesk – a well-managed service for responding to enquiries and complaints could yield worthwhile savings for the organisation. For instance, helpdesk employees who are well versed in technical procedures and competent in some aspects of problem solving could obviate the need for further action, by providing timely advice on how to deal with problems concerning heating, ventilation or other aspects of engineering services. Savings from the avoidance of calling out service operatives could amply repay the cost of providing the helpdesk. However, helpdesk personnel would need to be specially trained to perform in this way; consequently, the organisation may then have to pay more for their services. Establishing a close working relationship with the service provider – or assessing the capabilities of prospective providers – would seem sensible. In terms of controls, the service provider could be rewarded for reductions in the costs of calling out service engineers and, if the situation arose, penalised for failing to deal promptly and sensibly with enquiries – see Chapter 13 for further comment on providing incentives.

In other areas, for example, the supply of a utility such as electricity, there may be little point in attempting to bring about a closer working relationship other than in arranging consortium purchases. Generally, the greater the involvement or interaction of the client organisation with the supplier, the more indirect costs there will be.

Contractual arrangements and partnering

Contracts generally serve two main purposes: they identify the service to be provided in terms of scope, quality or performance, cost and timing, and they apportion risk. Partnering arrangements are, however, concerned mainly with the way in which the work will be carried out. In this way, partnering should theoretically be achievable with any method of procuring services. However, while no procurement route can compensate for an adversarial approach, some approaches may be more readily adapted to certain aspects of partnering such as gain-sharing – see next section.

Certain kinds of partnering relationship have no contract at all and it has been claimed that a formally binding contract can inhibit the partnering process. In most cases, however, a standard form of contract is used, even when partners declare business objectives that appear contrary to the principles of partnering. This view is to be expected as partnering is still somewhat new to many client organisations and a contract is seen as a form of safety net.

While contracts can embrace some aspects of a partnering approach, such as gain-sharing, others such as ideas of cooperation and goodwill may be less easily expressed within them. Other issues concern the accommodation of long-term partnering arrangements in workable contractual terms. For instance, contracts to undertake future work may be rendered void because of uncertainty, since it is not possible to pre-determine the value of future work and many factors can come into play even over a short period. However, this does not preclude non-binding framework agreements – those covering a number of contracts over a specified period – that stipulate terms on which the parties intend to contract and the type and extent of the services and/or work envisioned.

Partnering charters can be used to outline the client organisation's philosophy, commitments and the goals of the arrangement. For some organisations, partnering charters are regarded as vital support for its contracts. Partnering charters can also be used to indicate ways of overcoming problems, establish roles and responsibilities, and define clear lines of communication. That said, the relationship between a partnering charter and the contract may appear unclear. Put simply, the contract defines the rights and duties of the parties and to some extent covers the process implicit in delivering the specified service. However, a partnering charter does not sit on top of the contract, but is complementary to it and vice versa.

EastPoint has adopted the use of partnering charters, notably in its approach to cooperative development with strategic partners. Embodied in one such example are the following commitments:

- Establish clear benefits, objectives and milestones.
- Share documentation of process development and manuals to increase efficiency.
- Maintain confidentiality and intellectual property rights on all matters.
- Establish a long-term relationship based on a successful outcome for both parties.
- Reduce administration costs and raise productivity.

These commitments are followed through by mutually accepted goals, including:

- Trust by way of transparent systems.
- Maintain open-mindedness and receptiveness to change.
- Integrate ideas, systems and people and benefits by sharing.
- Maintain clear communication through effective discussion and openness.
- Achieve continual improvement through flexibility, reviews and innovation.

Gain-sharing

Some partnering arrangements include gain-sharing. This is where cost savings arising from performance improvements are shared between the parties. This can provide an effective incentive for performance that exceeds a given level – see also Chapter 13. In practice, gain-sharing arrangements can be straightforward, with the client organisation and service providers dividing any savings above a target price on an equal basis with the providers liable for 100% of any loss. They can also be more sophisticated, with partners exposed to levels of risk and reward according to their degree of influence on service delivery. Whatever means is devised, a commitment to open-book accounting is necessary if efficiency gains are to be encouraged. There must be no incentive or opportunity for the parties to achieve a higher return through adversarial behaviour or by 'hiding behind the contract'.

Continual improvement

The adoption of some means for measuring the performance of a partnering arrangement is critical to ensuring that its objectives are met. This generally involves the client organisation and service provider outlining the improvements over traditional approaches that the arrangement intends to pursue, together with measures of success in achieving these objectives. In the case of longer-term partnering relationships, targets for performance improvement can be incorporated into the partnering arrangements. With appropriate monitoring and feedback, continual improvement – felt to be central to the whole idea of partnering – can be achieved (Bennett and Jayes, 1998). Some features of continual improvement are easy to identify and address, but others may require more of a change in the culture of the organisation.

While longer-term partnering relationships can evolve targets and maintain an acceptable level of competition between different service providers or suppliers, it may be more difficult to establish performance targets for single contracts of a limited duration. In such cases, benchmarking against similar projects may be useful in identifying possible improvements – see Chapter 14. The initial service provider selection process and subsequent negotiations are therefore crucial in helping to identify performance criteria.

Conclusions

The relationship with a supplier does not end once the contract has been placed. That is just the beginning and it will take hard work to manage the relationship successfully into the future. Ways can always be found to add incentives for both sides to ensure the satisfactory performance of a service or supply. Setting targets as part of a programme of continual improvement is possible. These can be based on gain-sharing to provide an added incentive – see also Chapter 13. In any event, engaging the skill of the supplier in the process – as opposed to traditional arrangements that actively exclude it – can lead to better ways of delivering customer satisfaction at lower cost. Partnering or other forms of cooperative relationship can be entirely appropriate for an organisation in its search for best value. However, partnering is not a panacea and its selection must be based on a well-founded case. Nonetheless, it can be a perfectly acceptable arrangement even in the public sector, where there is rightful concern about the probity of contractual arrangements. Partnering can succeed so long as there is a competitive element to it; the latter does not invalidate the approach, rather it improves the prospects for delivering best value.

CHECKLIST

This checklist is intended to assist with the review and action planning process.

	Yes	No	Action required
1. Has the organisation identified its key suppliers?	☐	☐	☐
2. Does the organisation understand the economic significance of each of its service providers and suppliers?	☐	☐	☐
3. Has the organisation differentiated between the type of relationships that are possible and are these sensitive to the nature of the service/supply and customer needs?	☐	☐	☐
4. Has the organisation considered instances where partnering, or some other cooperative arrangement, might be preferable to traditional, competitive tendering?	☐	☐	☐
5. If the organisation is in the public sector, has it examined the arguments for and against partnering and has it therefore come to a decision based on fact and objectivity?	☐	☐	☐
6. Are appropriate strategies in place for managing relationships with suppliers?	☐	☐	☐
7. Is the organisation benefiting from consortium arrangements for the supply of utilities, or has it at least examined the economic case for them?	☐	☐	☐

13 Contract Management and Financial Control

Key issues

The following issues are covered in this chapter.

- Organisations need to develop the ICF if they are to manage contracts and control finances – this applies irrespective of whether or not services are outsourced.

- Procedures should be transparent and follow accepted accounting standards.

- Actions must be performed according to the contract and at intervals dictated therein – this is not only to ensure compliance with the contract but to ensure prompt payment to service providers and suppliers to avoid cashflow problems.

- Service providers should receive reimbursement or attract penalties appropriate to their performance against the service specification and SLA.

- In-house service providers should be assessed against the same criteria as external providers. Any changes that are required should be controlled in accordance with the principles of the original contract.

- Contract costs should be monitored against both the budget and tender price on a basis that is appropriate to their duration and size.

- The level or extent of contract review should be appropriate to the value and complexity of the contract. For most services, this period should be 12 months unless otherwise agreed as part of a specific public-private partnership arrangement – see Chapter 15.

Introduction

In keeping with previous chapters, the subjects of contract management and financial control flow largely in chronological order within the overall facilities management process. If earlier procedures have been followed carefully, the management of contracts should be – in the sense of their administration – relatively straightforward. Sufficient precedents exist for contract administration, largely in the context of monitoring, control and, where necessary, corrective action. Contract management and financial monitoring are, however, aspects of facilities management that can represent a significant resource issue for client organisations, not least because they are ongoing commitments. As such, they will always involve a minimum level of resource whether services are outsourced or retained in-house. In these respects, the role of the ICF – see Chapter 1 – is one that should develop over time as working knowledge accrues of how contractors perform – mostly service providers in this context. For the purpose of this work, contract management and financial monitoring include contractual approach and terms, payments, cost monitoring, performance monitoring, change control, contract administration and review. Together they offer a sufficiently broad treatment of this stage in the process to enable the client organisation to put effective controls in place. Even so, there may well be additional procedures – most likely linked to the organisation's own accounting provisions – that will necessitate further development of some functions.

Contractual approach and terms

The guiding principle is that in all cases, payment must be dependent upon performance. Contracts should define, therefore, how payments are to be adjusted when performance deviates from what is acceptable. Given that facilities management is about the provision of services, rather than tangible products, it is important to see reimbursement as something that should vary according to the performance of the service provider. This will mean that the client organisation has to define the level of poor service delivery at which reduced payments are no longer a sufficient redress and the client can terminate the contract. In this connection, contracts may need to contain a clause stating that, if the client organisation does terminate the contract, the service provider can go to arbitration or some other cheaper and quicker alternative dispute resolution method. Appendix D outlines how contracts should be approached and what terms should apply.

Payments

The client organisation will need to be aware of the implications of cash-flow both for itself and service providers. Whilst the organisation might be expected to have up-to-date financial information and so be appraised of its cashflow position, service providers may not be so well supported. It is likely to prove beneficial, therefore, for service providers to submit a cashflow forecast for their service provision before the contract comes into effect and to keep this up-to-date. This tends to be less of an issue in general facilities management contracts; however, forecasts or allowances for reactive works and discretionary expenditure items can be useful. Taking these issues into account will mean that both the client organisation and service providers will know what their likely pattern of payments will

WESTERN LEISURE COMPLEX		**Month:** 6
Contract: Mechanical & Electrical Maintenance	**Service provider:** Emeny (Contractors) Ltd.	**Ref:** ..PPM01 . . . .
Covering period:		**Payment no:** 6
Annual contract sum: £449,000.00		
Gross values to date: • Planned contract services • Changes to planned services • Unplanned/reactive services	£176,000.00 £ 22,000.00 £112,000.00	
Sub-total		£310,000.00
Less previous		£236,000.00
Payment due:		£ 74,000.00
VAT @ 17.5%		£ 12,950.00
Total amount due:		£ 86,950.00
Authorised by:	**Date:**	
. . . . Supervising Officer		

Fig. 13.1   Monthly payment form.

be. This will also help in measuring actual performance against forecast performance. Regular payments to service providers are essential to ensure that they do not fail financially. It is dangerous to assume that a large service provider will always have funds flowing in from other contracts. Sometimes too many clients think the same, resulting in the failure of the service provider.

The structure and format of payment documentation should be clear and simple; an example is shown in Fig. 13.1. The advantage of the format is that as the gross value of services is recalculated each month any over-payment in a previous month will be automatically taken into account without the need for credit notes. In addition, the value of planned contract services and any changes in them are clearly identified.

Cost monitoring

A report should be completed by the client organisation in order to ensure that contract costs are monitored and controlled systematically. An example format is shown in Fig. 13.2. This should incorporate all monthly payments to service providers, as referred to above, as well as the anticipated final account. The use of an accounting system – or failing that spreadsheets or a database management system – can easily improve the efficiency of this process and is a highly recommended practice.

WESTERN LEISURE COMPLEX

Month: 6

(A) Service or service element	(B) Annual contract sum	(C) Changes	(D) Anticipated outturn account (B + C)	(E) Gross value of service to date	(F) Comments
Planned preventive maintenance	449,000	22,000	471,000	176,000	PPM programme behind schedule
Unplanned/reactive services	–	112,000	112,000	112,000	High level of reactive repairs
Total	449,000	134,000	583,000	288,000	

Fig. 13.2   Cost control report form.

The complexity and value of the particular service contract should determine the frequency and detail of the report. Some contracts may need a one-line item; whereas, for example, expenditure under a mechanical and electrical engineering maintenance contract may be broken down into the following elements:

- Planned preventive maintenance
- Unplanned/reactive services
- Special equipment maintenance
- Performance-related payments

Performance monitoring

In order to ensure the continued performance of the service provider against the service specification and SLA, a performance score-sheet should be completed regularly by the organisation so as to arrive at an agreed rating for each provider. An example format for a performance score-sheet is provided in Fig. 13.3.

The above performance rating can be applied to a performance-related payment table that would reward the service provider for exceeding the specification – if the organisation has previously agreed that enhanced performance is to be sought – and penalise the service provider for not meeting the specification's minimum requirements. The level of detail in the table must be commensurate with the size and complexity of the service provided. However, the golden rule is to concentrate on KPIs – those that can be determined and analysed cost effectively.

WESTERN LEISURE COMPLEX			**Month: 6**
Item	**Service criteria**	**Priority weighting**	**Monthly rating**	**Score (weighting × monthly rating)**
01	Planned Preventive Maintenance Regime	5	2	10
02	Response Times to Breakdowns	5	0	0
	Total score			10
	Performance rating % **(Actual total/maximum × 100)**			50%

In this simple example, the scoring is based upon the following:
  0 = service does not meet specification
  1 = service meets specification
  2 = service exceeds specification
A more detailed scoring system can, however, be employed where a specific measurement system has been agreed.

Fig. 13.3 Performance score-sheet.

The importance of maintaining continuity of service is one aspect of performance that may require special attention, particularly in the case of mechanical and electrical services. Persistent non-functioning of such services could have dire consequences for the client organisation. Financial penalties to cover the losses that might be faced by a serious failure have to be carefully considered. However, it is important to set these in the context of the value of contracts. For instance, it would be unreasonable to expect a service provider to accept a level of penalty that was so onerous that any failure would discount all payment.

Change control

The client organisation must be able to control changes if it is to be fully in charge of managing its facilities. It is suggested that the organisation:

- Approves all changes before they are implemented.
- Before approval, identifies all possible risks together with the impact of the proposed change – see Chapters 1 and 5.
- Only allows a designated member of management, or nominated representative, to grant authorisation to proceed with a change.

In any event, changes should be avoided unless the consequences are agreed beforehand. Where they are necessary, their cost should be based on tendered prices and rates. Where this is not possible, it should be clear that the contract administrator will value the additional works at market rates. The evaluation of changes should always be consistent with the conditions of contract.

Contract administration

Diligent contract administration is essential if the organisation is to achieve continual improvement in the management of its facilities. Successful contract administration includes the following key practices:

- Roles and responsibilities should be clearly defined and allocated, with responsibility for the supervision of service delivery vested in the ICF.
- Every contract (and therefore contractor) should have its own contract manager.
- A helpdesk (or central coordination point) should be set up to manage the interface between customers and service providers, regardless of whether the service providers are in-house or outsourced.
- An open-book agreement can be put in place under which the client organisation will have the right to inspect the service provider's accounts for the contract.
- Frequent meetings should be held with service providers to discuss performance in the early days of the contract, in order to deal with teething problems – as the contract progresses, the need for such meetings should diminish.

Contract review

In the case of outsourced service provision, contract review is necessary in order to establish if the decision to outsource is still valid in terms of the organisation's facilities management strategy, current market conditions and the performance of the service provider. The necessity for reviews will have been built into the SLA and formalised in the contract, although here we are concerned primarily with an internal review. The frequency of contract reviews will depend on the size and complexity of the contract – as reflected by the nature and scope of service provision – with more frequent reviews likely during the initial period. The following matters must, however, be addressed in each case:

- Comparison of tendered costs against actual costs.
- Current performance rating.
- Ideas for improving and/or providing better value for money and increased customer satisfaction.
- Prompt highlighting and discussion of contentious issues, thereby avoiding escalation and further dispute.

Practice Point 13.1   Passing the buck.

Key-point: the need for roles and responsibilities to be clearly defined – within the client organisation and the service provider – is highlighted by the following arrangement.

A contracted facilities management company was impeded in its ability to deliver a timely, best value service due to overlapping roles within the client organisation. Although a contract manager had been appointed to act as the client representative and was the single point of contact, the contractor's facilities manager regularly had to consult a number of in-house managers in the client organisation before a decision could be made. On one occasion, the repair of an item of mechanical plant was delayed because the manager had to approach three managers before finally receiving authorisation for the works to go ahead.

Conclusions

All contracts must be managed. This requirement applies both to formal contracts with external contractors and to informal contracts (SLAs) with in-house service providers. The principles and procedures must be appropriate to the contracts being managed and provide a realistic level of flexibility. Whatever approach is taken, valuable resources will be consumed in managing the contracts and in ensuring that the correct financial controls are exercised. Important in this latter connection is that due account should be taken of the organisation's wider accounting practices, especially in the public sector where controls to guard against irregularity are in place.

For these reasons, it is inappropriate to prescribe a single approach here; rather, best practice dictates that customer-related and financial measures should be considered. It is possible to derive hundreds of performance measures for services, but only KPIs should be captured. To do otherwise would divert valuable resources away from where they are needed most and prove a distraction to an otherwise competent service provider.

CHECKLIST

This checklist is intended to assist with the review and action planning process.

		Yes	No	Action required
1.	Is the organisation satisfied that its facilities management service contracts properly define the level of payments that should be made and how they should be adjusted when the contractor's performance deviates from that defined as acceptable?	☐	☐	☐
2.	Has the organisation considered the cashflow implications both for itself and service providers in relation to its management of contracts?	☐	☐	☐
3.	Is the organisation providing resources at an appropriate level to support its contract management and financial control?	☐	☐	☐
4.	Are appropriate cost monitoring and control arrangements in place?	☐	☐	☐
5.	Are arrangements in place to enable the continued assessment of the performance of service providers against service specifications and SLAs?	☐	☐	☐
6.	Are adequate controls in place in relation to the agreement of any changes to the service specification and SLAs?	☐	☐	☐
7.	Is the organisation satisfied with its contract administration and audit arrangements?	☐	☐	☐

14 Benchmarking Best Practice

Key issues

The following issues are covered in this chapter.

- Benchmarking is one tool of many that can assist managers in their pursuit of improvement, but it is also one that is widely understood and applied.

- Benchmarking is an external focus on internal activities and is aimed at supporting the drive towards best practice through objective comparisons and insights gained as a result of studying best-in-class organisations.

- For benchmarking to work successfully, it has to be stakeholder-driven, forward looking, participative and focused on quality or performance.

- Benchmarking can work well between organisations that might otherwise regard themselves as competitors.

- The organisation needs to recognise that the gains from benchmarking with other comparable organisations far outweigh the perceived disadvantages.

- Goods or products can be compared objectively, along with the processes that create them. Facilities management offers no such simplicity and relies on policies and procedures that may not be well defined and/or are poorly documented in comparison.

- Benchmarking methods are relatively easy to understand and apply – in the specific case of facilities management there are simple and accessible ways of undertaking benchmarking.

Introduction

More than a decade has passed since benchmarking came to the fore in a wave of new management thinking, conventions and tools designed to improve the fortunes of business organisations. Views differ on the success achieved by the new wave, with some dismissing it simply as a fad. This is both true and false. Business process re-engineering is a case in point, having been promoted by many as an all-or-nothing solution to an organisation's ills. Aping the mantra of management gurus is bound to have its dangers. For each organisation that failed to respond to its treatment, there have been hundreds that have benefited from a critical review of what they had been doing – often with little or no change – for years. No convention or tool can be good for all organisations in all situations. More importantly, new tools do not necessarily lose their effectiveness because of the passage of time; some are simply the victim of new fads. For many people and organisations – clients, consultants and service providers alike – benchmarking has a value. That is not the same as saying it is the only tool or the one that can give all the answers. However, in the right hands, it can be as powerful as it is simple: benchmarking is not rocket science. The primary purpose of this chapter is to show why benchmarking should be an appropriate tool for facilities management, how it can be applied and how it relates to best practice. Knowing how an organisation is performing is vital. Without such knowledge, it is difficult to measure the effects of any improvement. Benchmarking is about establishing the norms for performance in terms of financial, organisational, innovation and change management and customer focus. People tend to have notions of what things might cost, how long they might take and what they should expect. Benchmarking is chiefly concerned with formalising these notions. In making organisations look out from themselves, the exercise also directs energy towards serving the organisation's best business interests and away from internal conflict.

Pursuing continual improvement

Benchmarking is a tool for supporting a process of continual improvement. Its objective is to identify current performance in relation to best practice in areas of concern to the organisation. In this context, it is about measuring performance in the underlying processes of facilities management. This means, for example, establishing how much the organisation is paying for its services and supplies. Typical in these respects are the costs of energy – electricity and gas – and other utilities (for example, water, sewerage and telecommunications), as well as domestic services like cleaning and security.

The organisation needs to appreciate that benchmarking should not be used simply to compare costs of services but, where appropriate, to measure the effectiveness of the process that leads to those costs and a given performance. As was shown in Chapter 2, the facilities management strategy and its resultant plan will outline the means for measuring whether or not business needs have been met and cost optimised. If the optimal cost level is to be measured, the organisation must be able to compare the costs of different methods of delivering the required performance. Benchmarking can also be used to measure the effectiveness of in-house practices against external practices in related organisations or industrial sectors and against an organisation identified as achieving best practice in the area under scrutiny.

Benchmarking provides management with a tool for making decisions about policies and procedures in regard to how services should be procured, i.e. whether they should be outsourced or retained in-house. It is neither complicated nor expensive to apply, and may be a relatively easy route to establishing and then recording key performance indicators (KPIs). Since many organisations lack basic information on their own estates-related and facilities services, benchmarking can provide the necessary focus to enable such information to be gathered objectively and relatively painlessly. In these cases, cost or price and quality or performance of service should become the primary targets for study if the organisation is to be sure of achieving best value and have a basis for seeking continual improvement.

Organisations that have raised the profile of facilities management, perhaps as the outcome of re-engineering their business processes, and given it the clear mandate of adding value, need to know whether or not their objective is being achieved. Benchmarking can supply the answers not once, but at intervals as the organisation pursues improvement. Continual comparisons with organisations recognised as achieving best practice allow the organisation to recognise and close the gap between its own performance and that of the best practitioner.

Benchmarking practices

The origins of formalised benchmarking are well documented (Leibfried and McNair, 1994): it is 'an external focus on internal activities, functions or operations in order to achieve continuous improvement'. The main purpose is to measure quality of service and the processes that support it, against the organisation's goals and aspirations and best-in-class organisations in other sectors. In these cases, it is likely that the best practitioner is better, because what it does is different.

A benchmarking study begins with an analysis of existing activities and practices within the organisation. These processes have to be properly understood and measurable before comparison can take place with another organisation – if you cannot measure it, you cannot improve it.[3] Usually, benchmarking is a one-on-one activity; that is, it is used by one organisation to help identify improvements in its own processes by exchanging information – often in a workshop – with another. The activity is normally a collaboration of mutual benefit, however strange it might seem to look so closely at one's competitors and vice versa. Competitors can provide not only the challenge, but also the insights into how performance can be improved and costs reduced.

In partnering arrangements – especially those where an organisation is going to share business amongst a few select suppliers – the necessity of benchmarking becomes all the more apparent. Continual improvement is an integral part of any partnering relationship, without which there can be no purpose served – see Chapter 12. By comparing a partner's performance against other service providers, it is possible to provide the

---

[3] Attributed to Lord Kelvin (1824–1907).

stimulus for improvement. This can effectively replace the stimulus provided by the competitive tendering of each new contract. Concerns that a
partner might have about feeling exposed are unlikely to arise, since all
partners are aware from the outset about the arrangements to be adopted
and have signified their acceptance of them by entering into a partnering
agreement.

Measuring performance

Performance measurement is at the centre of good facilities management.
Benchmarking begins by identifying perceived critical success factors (CSFs),
typically the strategies, roles and processes existing within the organisation.
Preliminary questions are:

- Who is involved in delivering the service?
- Why are they involved?
- What are they doing?
- Why are they doing it?
- Is what they are doing adding value?

The last question recognises the need to add value to the services provided to the customer.

In offering an approach to benchmarking there is bound to be the
danger of appearing too prescriptive. The organisation should apply the
approach outlined below having regard to any practical issue that might
be an obstacle. Authors will differ on their prescription for benchmarking.
Here, we identify eight steps in a benchmarking exercise:

1. Identify the subject of the exercise
2. Decide what to measure
3. Identify who to benchmark within sector and outside
4. Collect information and data
5. Analyse findings and determine gap
6. Set goals for improvement
7. Implement new order
8. Monitor the process for improvement

Step 1 – identify the subject of the exercise

- Agree on the objective(s) of the exercise
- Decide on who to involve internally
- Define the process (core business or otherwise)
- Identify the scope
- Set the limits for the exercise
- Agree on the process
- Produce a map or model of the process

Step 2 – decide what to measure

- Examine the elements of the process
- Establish measures of performance
- Verify that measures match objective(s)

Step 3 – identify who to benchmark within sector and outside

- Identify main competitors and 'rising stars'
- Agree on those to benchmark
- Identify out-of-sector comparisons
- Identify best-in-class outside own sector

Step 4 – collect information and data

- Draft a checklist or questionnaire
- Pilot the questionnaire
- Conduct structured interview(s)

Step 5 – analyse findings and determine gap

- Score answers/responses and weight them, as necessary
- Analyse qualitative responses
- Summarise findings
- Measure gap between one's own performance and others

Step 6 – set goals for improvement

- Identify goals for performance improvement
- Establish criteria for judging performance
- Draft action plan with milestones for improvement

Step 7 – implement new order

- Draft new procedures
- Communicate procedures to all stakeholders
- Train those affected by the new order
- Implement new process(es)

Step 8 – monitor the process for improvement

- Conduct regular review meetings
- Observe progress of best-in-class comparison
- Determine if any corrective actions are required
- Document changes and communicate them to all stakeholders

Benchmarking facilities management

Many organisations now routinely collect data and engage in their own benchmarking of the costs of energy, water, maintenance, cleaning, security etc. Some organisations also participate in benchmarking clubs involving similar organisations and in arrangements with very different kinds of organisation. Commercial enterprises have been set up to bring together organisations seeking to benchmark; some universities have even become involved in benchmarking within key sectors. The success of some initiatives is however unclear. The organisation should look very closely, therefore, at the costs of getting involved against the likely benefits.

Facilities management as a recognised discipline is not only relatively new, but also has great potential for reducing cost and increasing service levels in the long term. Mechanisms for benchmarking can and should be built into newly defined facilities management operations, whether services are retained in-house or outsourced. One example of benchmarking the overall approach to facilities management that an organisation takes is described below. It is based on a validated model of best practice facilities management and has been tested with a large number of organisations across different sectors.

The Micro-Scan*fm* diagnostic tool enables senior managers to review, discuss and modify its facilities management in the light of responses to a detailed questionnaire, which is held and analysed by computer. Micro-Scan*fm* provides an opportunity to understand and assess the scope for business improvement and to highlight the potential gain. It does this against four separate perspectives.

1. *Customer* – how do the users and occupiers of the facility see us?
2. *Financial* – how is the function managed to achieve best value?
3. *Operational* – how efficient and effective is the delivery of estates-related and facilities services?
4. *Innovation* – how does the facilities management function continue to improve and assist the core business in creating value?

The overall approach is consistent with that of the perspectives adopted in *The Balanced Scorecard* (Kaplan and Norton, 1996). Areas of potential improvement are identified easily and can be monitored over time to gauge the extent of improvement achieved. *The Balanced Scorecard* relies upon the minimum amount of information that is necessary in order to obtain a balanced view of the organisation's performance. Micro-Scan*fm* adopts the same approach through 80 questions, the answers to which can then be compared across respondents and organisations. Thus, it is possible to compare understanding, attitude and actions within a single organisation as well as across many.

The baseline (or benchmark) against which scores are calibrated is that of best practice. This is established from industry sources and is reviewed periodically so that recalibration of the tool can be undertaken as required.

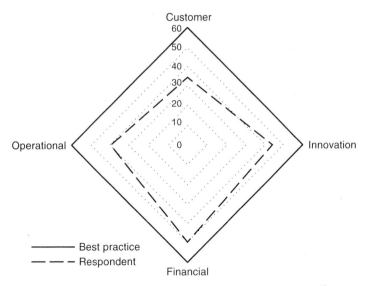

Fig. 14.1   Comparing one organisation with best practice.

In this connection, it is important to appreciate that understanding develops over time and so today's best practice will not necessarily be tomorrow's best practice. The diagrammatic presentation of the scores resulting from an individual analysis is shown in Fig. 14.1. This reveals at a glance where an organisation (or respondent) needs to direct attention. Likewise, it can confirm that current initiatives are measuring up to the pursuit of best practice.

The four perspectives have shown themselves to be purposeful and aligned to both the facilities management strategy of organisations and their strategic business objectives. The idea that one can have strong financial controls and yet be less concerned about, say, customers, is easily highlighted. Balance across all four perspectives, as shown by best practice organisations, can be the only sensible path to follow. In this respect, it is not a matter of having the right answers, but more a case of knowing where improvement lies and how this might enable the organisation to close the gap on best practice. Examples of the many issues that stand behind the four perspectives are information technology, human resources management, education and training, and customer satisfaction. Typical questions used in dialogue with users are given in Table 14.1.

Micro-Scan*fm* has been constructed so that each element in its dialogue with a user – typically a facilities manager – relates to a CSF. Quantitative analysis of a more detailed series of questions could be added to enable actual performance to be measured against best practice. However, the aim is not to provide measures of performance, but to guide facilities managers and their organisations to understand better how they are thinking and behaving now. Developing that understanding is the cornerstone of the Micro-Scan*fm* tool.

Table 14.1   Example dialogue taken from Micro-Scan*fm*.

1. We allocate our budgets based on a priority of needs.
2. We measure improvement by achieving lower costs this year than last.
3. We conduct tendering competitions for all services and supplies over a specified minimum contract value.
4. We require our in-house services costs to be compared against the costs of buying in the same services.
5. Our service contracts are procured on an annual basis.
6. We form cooperative relationships with our major suppliers and service providers.
7. We seek the advice of external consultants in areas where we do not have the expertise ourselves.
8. We manage our services effectively by leaving them with the same provider.
9. We retain in-house as many of our services as possible.
10. We assess the cost effectiveness of all services whether in-house or bought in.
11. We are more concerned about value for money than cost or quality alone.
12. We have indicators for measuring the cost effectiveness of all services and supplies.
13. We compare the costs of our services and supplies with those of organisations similar to ourselves.
14. We compare the costs of our services and supplies with those of the best organisation irrespective of their business sector.
15. We undertake skills audits to determine our management needs in regard to facilities and services.
16. We have explicit procedures for buying in services and supplies.
17. We produce service level agreements for services and supplies.
18. We measure the performance of our service providers whether in-house or outsourced.
19. We have up-to-date specifications for our services whether provided in-house or outsourced.
20. Our data on the costs and performance of services are held centrally and are readily accessible.
21. Our data on the costs and performance of services are held electronically.
22. We apply service level agreements to assist in measuring the performance of services provided in-house.
23. We are able to show what our space utilisation is.   . . . *and so on*

Against each of these questions, respondents are required to indicate the frequency or extent of their actions according to the following:

Always	Frequently	Occasionally	Seldom	Never

Other kinds of benchmarking

Openness in relationships between the client organisation and service providers, whether as part of a formal partnering arrangement or not, is essential to the successful operation of facilities management. The role of ICT in facilitating the efficient transfer of information cannot be underestimated in this respect. Information management is essential to achieve margins and therefore to create client satisfaction. As such, it is a major tool in the strategic management of facilities. For this reason, research has been under-taken to identify the level of ICT use in support of facilities management. The ICT use and performance of ten organisations, in relation to facilities management, was charted against the industry norm and an international organisation whose achievements were accepted as representing current best practice. The selection of an acceptable example of best practice for comparison is one of the most difficult aspects of benchmarking, and those conducting the benchmarking exercise should look as widely as possible to find an organisation suitable for valid comparison.

The research in this instance looked at the application of ICT in relation to the following six areas of facilities management:

- Strategy, policy and procedures
- Strategic management
- Building and engineering services management
- Environmental management
- Domestic services
- Administration and service support

Anonymity of the organisations was maintained in the published results, although each participating organisation was shown how its own performance related to those of others in the exercise. Descriptive informa-tion regarding current use of ICT and future plans was also volunteered by participants and made available in the final report for general benefit. Figure 14.2 shows a typical chart generated from the study as used to pro-vide feedback to the participating organisations.

The findings show how the benchmarking exercise, despite having meas-ured organisations against their competitors, can be of mutual benefit to all participants without threatening commercial sensitivity or competitiveness.

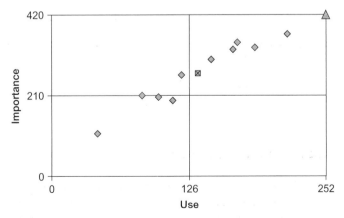

Fig. 14.2 Comparing the performance of organisations within sector against best-in-class out of sector. The graph shows the positions of benchmarked organisations (use against importance) relative to best-in-class (top right) and the sector average denoted by ⊠.

Moreover, as the process is directed at technical and general managerial processes, commercially sensitive information is unlikely to be exposed.

Other methods of providing objective comparison of performance have been devised and are widely implemented. Their supporters claim considerable success and this is not in question. What is important is that the organisation understands its processes implicitly – in this context those of facilities management – and is able to apply tools that lead to answers consistent with its declared business strategy. For some organisations, benchmarking is able to provide a simple and direct solution, but for others more developed tools and techniques, such as *Six Sigma*, are deployed (Pande et al., 2000). *Six Sigma* is used to help companies improve customer satisfaction, profitability and competitiveness through a focus on the customer by the disciplined use of facts, data and statistical analysis – the term itself refers to a statistically derived performance target. The whole approach is more demanding and more rigorous than that of the benchmarking methodology outlined above. In the right hands, *Six Sigma* can deliver benefits for the client organisation.

Case study – Diageo plc

Diageo plc is the world's leading premium drinks business with headquarters in the UK. Over the past 10 years the organisation has achieved strong growth in both turnover and profitability. It is highly regarded among financial institutions and has become the benchmark company for its sector.

This dramatic growth has been achieved through a combination of increased market share from its own range of brands – for example Guinness, Pimm's, Johnnie Walker, Smirnoff and Gordon's – and also the addition of new products through company acquisition. However, the consequence of this has been an unprecedented amount of change throughout the business with many challenging demands being placed on support functions.

The objective for each of Diageo's acquisitions has been to grow the revenue base of the products involved, through increased sales and clever marketing to expand the number of market segments for which a particular product has appeal. Significant growth has been achieved in turnover, which has dwarfed the corresponding increase in the cost of support functions. Consequently, these functions have escaped any significant attention.

The organisation is now faced with major challenges in continuing to grow at the same rate, with market share proving harder to increase and the lack of attractive targets to acquire at a reasonable price. The focus more recently has been on targeting waste reduction and increasing efficiency and through these two elements to reduce its cost base.

Facilities management is gaining greater visibility and although not represented by a single function, the different regions within Europe are collaborating and sharing knowledge with greater frequency. Initiatives in the South East of England in particular have created an outsourced management model which in turn has generated significant savings in the order of 20%. However, such savings must be sustainable and continued effort is required to drive out any inefficiency.

Diageo has recognised that significant differences still remain between the various geographical regions within Europe. This was highlighted through a benchmarking study, which compared both cost and quality of service provision. Large disparities exist between sites in terms of service levels and, ultimately, cost. The key to achieving cost effectiveness is to ensure that the services offered are appropriate and fit for purpose. However, within the real estate portfolio, differences exist between the use of sites, ranging from breweries to distilleries to commercial offices. The challenge for Diageo is to obtain a degree of homogeneity, whilst recognising that the sites themselves will always have their differences.

After careful consideration, a unique approach was developed that would allow a degree of diversity whilst still applying a consistent approach to service levels. If the facilities management function could come up with a framework and achieve consistency, yet retain a degree of flexibility, Diageo was confident of further efficiency. The approach was to develop a set of guiding principles for services that could be agreed with the principal stakeholders. These principles would in effect be a set of rules by which the level of each service could be set. Local differences to these rules would be permissible, but had to be justified by the business case.

A steering group chaired by the Facilities Director for the South East of England was set up with representation from Scotland and Ireland. The group received its mandate from the Board with further direction from a group of sponsors from within the human resources function to whom facilities management reported.

The steering group decided that whatever approach was taken it had to be inclusive. Diageo commissioned the services of a facilities management consultant to assist and considered how best to go about this challenge. The group, aided by the consultant, developed a process to review each service and then to pilot one of the simpler services. The process had four key elements:

- Rationale
- Cost drivers
- Comparators
- New service definition

The rationale sought to challenge historical custom and practice by considering the service in the light of Diageo's core values. It sought to ask 'why is the service provided or needed?', 'who does it benefit?' and 'how does this service drive value for the business? The link to Diageo's core values was important as custom and practice had allowed incremental rises in service levels with corresponding cost increases. Any change downwards would be difficult to implement and to get senior management 'buy-in' unless a disconnection with core values could be demonstrated.

Once the rationale was proven, it then became important to understand what the primary drivers of the service were. By gaining an understanding of these drivers, Diageo could analyse the service and thereby enable the later brokering of service levels. Examples of such drivers included, in the case of security, the extent and level of technology used, the number of guarding hours required, pay rates and adoption of *The Working Time Directive*. Each service has unique drivers, as well as generic drivers applicable to the majority of services.

Understanding the cost base provided valuable information; however, a geographically dispersed portfolio meant that it was also necessary to understand the current situation site-by-site. The primary purpose here was to identify notable differences for further measurement. This provided an internal means of benchmarking which was then supplemented by an understanding of other organisations, ideally within Diageo's sector, but also out of sector where world-class organisations could be identified.

The last activity within the process was to consider the service in the context of a new facility. If this service were to be specified for the first time how would it be defined and what typically would be included? The steering group piloted this new approach for the provision of a health and fitness service. It proved workable and immediately identified the disparities from site-to-site and the level of service provided by others. The next step was to set up this initiative as a specific project. This was managed by the consultant with support from the steering group and ownership of the service by nominated facilities managers in each geographic region. The first workshop proved to be difficult to complete. Whilst the facilities managers were motivated to work through it and input significant effort, they found initially that the process was hard to grasp.

Further examples were developed and two subsequent workshops proved successful, with the output of a service standard framework endorsed by the project sponsors. Diageo has benefited from this project and is now in a position to continue this work reconciling the cost of service provision against 'fit for purpose' service levels.

Conclusions

There are many tools at the disposal of managers and organisations that are pursuing improvement. Each will have its proponents and detractors. Benchmarking is not a new invention and so has the benefit of being tried, tested and refined. Other methods that have been touted as the route to improved organisational performance are associated with it. Benchmarking should be taken on its own merits and for what it is – a relatively simple tool to apply so long as the user understands the process that is to be measured. There is no one form that benchmarking can take and it is neither exclusively quantitative nor qualitative; it can be both. Benchmarking has a place in providing management with a tool for continual improvement, especially when formal market testing is inappropriate. It provides a simple, but effective, means for measuring performance and cost, leading to a better understanding of best value. It can be applied easily and can produce immediate benefits as soon as the results are available. Several examples of successful benchmarking are now in the public domain and it is likely that more will appear in the future. With this in mind, it will pay most organisations to consider active participation in benchmarking clubs or associations, or even to mount their own benchmarking initiatives and exercises.

CHECKLIST

This checklist is intended to assist with the review and action planning process.

		Yes	No	Action required
1.	Is the organisation aware of benchmarking as a tool for helping to effect improvement in a (business) process?	☐	☐	☐
2.	Has the organisation evaluated or adopted other, objective methods for assessing and comparing performance as an alternative to straightforward benchmarking?	☐	☐	☐
3.	Does the organisation appreciate the importance of benchmarking as a means for measuring its effectiveness in achieving best value in its facilities management?	☐	☐	☐
4.	Has the organisation made arrangements for the benchmarking of its facilities management performance in terms of the quality of services delivered?	☐	☐	☐
5.	Are appropriate arrangements for measuring performance in place?	☐	☐	☐
6.	Has the organisation considered cooperating with other organisations or joining or forming benchmarking clubs to help assess relative performance in key areas?	☐	☐	☐

15 Public-Private Partnerships

Key issues

The following issues are covered in this chapter.

- A public-private partnership (PPP) is an arrangement that brings together a public sector need with the skill and expertise of private sector actors to deliver a solution.

- The Private Finance Initiative (PFI) is the UK government's mechanism for PPPs.

- The PFI represents an opportunity for public sector organisations to procure services, or the buildings and infrastructure to provide those services, whilst leaving the risks of asset and infrastructure ownership and maintenance to the private sector.

- Facilities management is an essential part of any major PPP/PFI project proposal and a key to its successful outcome – this may also apply to smaller schemes.

- Consideration can be given to incorporating facilities management for separate or additional sites within proposed capital schemes. This should, however, be subject to an initial feasibility study to determine potential efficiency gains.

- Although private investment arrangements continue the policy of out-sourcing facilities management services, the former can have wider implications.

- Best value considerations must apply at each stage – it is essential to demonstrate that best value is likely to be achieved and to define the means for measuring it.

- Properly defined output specifications are required so that it is clear what is to be provided.

- A common form of PPP/PFI project is that of a design, build, finance and operate (DBFO) scheme that is likely to extend for up to 30 years.

- Although there are many potential benefits, the relative newness of such projects means that their long-term implications may not yet be fully apparent.

Introduction

Public-private partnerships (PPPs) are not a recent phenomenon. They first appeared hundreds of years ago and many governments around the world have long established the practice of sharing the risks of major projects for public benefit with the private sector. This chapter considers how organisations can ensure that opportunities for private investment and partnership can be fully and effectively considered in plans to develop or improve the quality of their facilities. The Private Finance Initiative (PFI) launched back in 1992 is the main mechanism for this within the public sector in the UK. However, PFI principles also have application in projects within the private sector, as well as outside the UK as a type of PPP. Important here is to stress that the PFI is a particular type of PPP – not the other way around. The aim of the chapter is to show the relationship between facilities management and private investment and partnership, specifically within the context of new capital schemes. Private finance arrangements offer a chance to challenge traditional practice, yet also have the potential for problems that must be recognised and properly addressed. When first introduced, the greatest interest in this kind of project was found amongst consultant architects, consultant engineers and construction companies, each seeing an opportunity to create work. A more developed understanding today recognises the pivotal role that facilities management and, therefore, service providers play. Ensuring that the design of the proposed facility – the creation of the asset upon which the proposed service will operate – will not cause financial problems requires expertise of the kind that, possibly, service providers are best able to provide. Even so, caution is advised, as all PPP projects stretch out into the distance. 30 years can be a long time over which to sustain a loss instead of a profit.

Public-private partnerships (PPPs)

Interest in PPPs – the PFI in the UK – has been rising steadily over the past decade to the point where it has become a sector in its own right, supported by a market in secondary financing. This new market provides the means to re-finance a project once the asset is in use, enabling the equity partners to trade their shareholding and exit cleanly. This is especially important for construction companies whose business planning horizons would not normally extend beyond a few years. PPP are concerned with the delivery of services, which in most cases happens over a long period, perhaps 20–30 years. The characteristics and extent of services are dependent upon the authority of the public sector body involved and how a given service fits into its business plan, i.e. core or non-core activities. Regardless of the object of the PPP, the public sector body is withdrawing from activities that formerly have been carried out within its own organisation. It has, therefore, a strong interest in ensuring satisfactory quality and performance in the outcome. The risks and responsibility for delivering and managing the product or system during operation are, to a large extent, transferred from the client organisation to a private sector actor. Thus, attention is turned from the perceived needs of the client to the provision of customer-related services. This creates a different situation for actors in the construction sector to those traditionally experienced where, in the main, they have been largely content with short-term commitments, investments and returns.

The definition of a PPP – as broad as it is – together with the wide perception of partnerships has given rise to a large number of arrangements that could be legitimately termed PPPs. To make matters more confusing, the term PPP is also used in a narrower sense in attempts to describe the characteristics of specific projects. Thus, in order to provide a description of how PPP applies to the real estate and construction sector, it is necessary to break down the term into more manageable categories.

A PPP is essentially a method for procuring capital projects, to enable enhanced service delivery, but where capital expenditure in the present is converted to an expenditure commitment in the future. An external company will usually design, build and operate the facility, by sponsoring a project and holding an equity stake in it. The financial interest that the sponsor holds in the project helps to ensure efficiency. In this sense, in particular, it is easy to see how the principles of a PPP are transferable to other types of organisation.

Several broad types of partnership can be differentiated. They are, however, general and there will be projects/arrangements that can overlap two or more categories. These categories of partnership are presented in short below.

1. Public sector assets are sold to the private sector in the belief that private sector finance and management can increase the value of the asset and thereby give the taxpayer better value for money.
2. Shares in state-owned businesses are sold to the private sector, which can retain either a minority or majority stake of the business. This could be done with or without the use of legislation or regulations in order for the public sector to retain control of the business. The main objective of this kind of PPP is to improve the overall achievement of the business by bringing in private sector finance, managerial and marketing skills.
3. The public sector uses private finance and managerial and marketing skills so as to exploit the potential of public assets, both physical and intellectual, that cannot easily be sold or in which the state wishes to retain ownership.
4. Arrangements where the public sector contributes to the funding of private sector projects/establishments that are considered to be of public benefit, but which are not capable of fully funding themselves on the capital markets.
5. Arrangements where the public and private sectors under joint management combine their assets, finance and expertise in order to pursue common long-term goals and shared profit.

6. The public sector contracts services, with defined outputs, from the private sector including the construction and maintenance of the required facilities and/or infrastructure.

The UK government's PFI includes projects that lie within all six categories presented above and accordingly some projects will not feature estate or construction work. For a robust description of the PFI see *Public Private Partnerships: The Government's Approach* (The Stationery Office, 2000).

Procurement and contractual approach

In order to describe the particular project's contractual arrangement, terms other than PPP are used. Generally, the various kinds of contract are given three or four letter abbreviations, most of which are not so easily differentiated. Indeed, some of them are confusingly alike. It is more important, therefore, to understand the main characteristics of projects than it is to be able to match a specific project directly to a contract abbreviation. Nonetheless, most of them are presented below.

- BOOT – Build, Own, Operate and Transfer
- BOR – Build, Operate and Renewal of Concession
- BOT – Build, Operate and Transfer
- BRT – Build, Rent and Transfer
- BTO – Build, Transfer and Operate
- DBFO – Design, Build, Finance and Operate
- DCMF – Design, Construct, Manage and Finance
- MOT – Modernise, Operate and Transfer
- MOOT – Modernise, Own, Operate and Transfer
- ROT – Rehabilitate, Own and Transfer

A short description is given below for the two most common: BOT and DBFO.

- BOT – Build, Operate and Transfer is by far the most widespread and it is not uncommon for literature to use the term to represent all types of PPP project. BOT and BOOT are often used interchangeably, although there is a marked difference between them. These types of project are characterised by the major part of the payment for the private sector coming directly from customers in the form of user fees of one kind or another.
- DBFO – Design, Build, Finance and Operate, and to a certain extent DCMF, are the most common for projects where private sector revenues come exclusively, or to a large extent, from a public sector body.

Generic PPP project set-up

A PPP brings together a large number of stakeholders, each with its own agenda, priorities and goals. This plethora of overlapping – and potentially

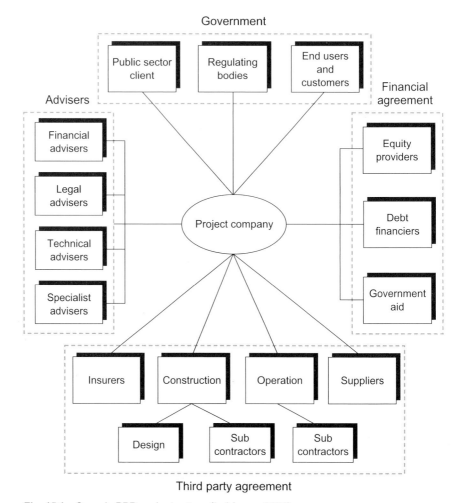

Government

Fig. 15.1   Generic PPP project set-up (Leiringer, 2003).

conflicting – interests ensures that any PPP will abound with contracts and agreements. The exact nature of these and their interrelationships are, of course, specific to the project in hand, but there are some common features. A generic project set-up is presented in Fig. 15.1. The rest of this section deals with the main actors and their roles in a generic PPP project as presented by Leiringer (2003).

The public sector client

It is a government's responsibility to provide essential services for society. To help in this task, the government typically sets up a wide range of institutions. The exact division and legislative empowerment of these public sector bodies vary from country to country. The following could, however, be considered generic:

- Governmental departments
- Governmental agencies
- Local authorities
- Municipalities
- County councils
- Single purpose agencies

One of these actors will become the public sector client in the project. It is this body that contracts with the private sector for the delivery of a service over a specified period and it is not uncommon that the public sector client creates a client's representative organisation whose primary task is to monitor the project.

Regulating bodies

Depending on the nature of the service that is contracted, the project will – apart from the particular sponsoring public sector client – also come under the jurisdiction of one or several other public sector bodies. These could be anything from governmental departments or agencies to local authorities or single purpose agencies. The size and statutory powers of the public sector bodies involved that claim regulatory jurisdiction vary widely. Each has its own standards and regulations and, in certain cases, the relationships between the bodies are quite complex.

Customers/end users

There would be no need for – and, in fact, no interest in – a project if there were no demand for the service that it could provide. Of importance here is the relationship between use of, and payment for, the service. A distinction is made between paying customers and indirectly paying users. If users pay for the service they are called customers. If the service is paid for by other means such as through taxes, the users are deemed end-users of the service.

The project company

The company – known as the concessionaire – is the legal entity that tenders for, develops and supplies the required service(s). The precise form of this entity will depend on the circumstances at hand, taking into account fiscal, accounting and legal issues as well as the physical nature of the required construct and service. In some cases, the project company could be an existing company that takes on the project by itself – on the balance sheet – or a subsidiary of a larger company established to undertake PPP projects. However, it is far more usual that it takes the form of a special purpose vehicle (SPV), established either in the form of a consortium or as a joint venture for undertaking the project. Arrangements exist to make it possible for companies of different sizes, financial strength and objectives to participate in the SPV. Participation is grounded in the added value of the skills that a company brings to the consortium/joint venture and the members are dependent on the nature, size, scope and complexity of the project. Projects that involve more than a modest amount of construction will most commonly have a construction company as a shareholder, with the same being true for the operational phase and for the operators.

Equity providers

The equity providers in a project own that project. Equity is the lowest ranking form of capital in the project and the claims of the equity investors are therefore subordinate to those of the project's debt financiers. Hence, the equity providers bear the greatest risk of loss if the project is unsuccessful. This risk is balanced by a greater return than that of the debt lenders – they stand to gain the most if the project performs better than expected. The principal equity investors are the members of the project company, although several other parties might contribute. Equity providers can be divided into three groups:

1. Long-term providers – the organisations responsible for construction and operation, major suppliers of technology and some specialist investment funds and banks.
2. Retail or institutional providers – these tend to be institutions such as superannuation funds, life insurance companies and fund managers without controlling interests in the business.
3. Quasi-equity providers – these are mainly risk capital funds and institutional investors that do not have a controlling stake in the project company.

Debt financiers

Debt finance is, as mentioned above, senior to equity. It also distinguishes itself from equity in the sense that it is secured against the assets of the project. Accordingly, the return expected by the debt financiers is lower than that of the equity providers. The debt financiers have no controlling stake in the project company, but they have considerable leverage in issues concerning project execution. A project usually has a mixture of short and long-term loans. Once the project is operating, a syndicate of commercial banks generally provides the long-term debt. The short-term loans – they are sometimes referred to as bridging loans – are used to finance the construction phase. Several different kinds of financial institutions are capable of providing short-term finance.

Bonds

There is also the possibility of obtaining finance by raising bonds. Bond-holders generally do not have any interaction with the project company after the bond has been issued and do not exercise any control over the execution of the project.

Government aid

Government aid is by no means normal in PPP projects and it can take a wide variety of forms. Usually though, it consists of the provision of equity or additional debt financing and various forms of guarantees. In addition to host governments, institutions like the World Bank, European Investment Bank (EIB), European Bank for Reconstruction and Development (EBRD) and various development finance institutions provide aid.

Design and construction contractors

The construction contractor will normally be signed to design and build the asset. Depending on the size and scope of the project it could either be a single construction company that takes on the work by itself – with or without the additional hiring of designers – or a consortium of design and construction companies. Either way it is usual that responsibilities are passed on to a variety of subcontractors. It is common that the main contractor has a stake in the project company.

Operators

If the contracted service includes the operation of the asset then this would normally be contracted out to a specialist operator. In these cases, it is usual that the operator would be part of the project company. Operation is normally divided into soft and hard services and it is not unusual that the operator has one or more subcontractors. In the case that the service provided is of a maintenance character, it would be likely that the construction contractor takes on the role of the operator – or else a major, dedicated service provider.

Suppliers

The role of supplier is very much dependent on the required service and the characteristics of the built asset. Strategic suppliers and suppliers of major components and/or large technology owners usually take a part in the project company.

Insurers

Insurance is sought to cover as many commercial risks as possible. It is often the case that all or a significant part of the insurance cover is reinsured with other insurers. These can be either local/domestic or international and a mix of them is usually preferred.

Legal advisers

Due to the complex nature of the projects and the large number of agreements that have to be agreed and later interpreted, the need for legal advice is crucial. Both public and private sector parties use specialist legal advisers.

Financial advisers

Financial advisers are retained by the public sector client as well as by the project company and will also have expertise in risk management.

Technical advisers

Technical advisers are used by the public sector client as well as by the project company, irrespective of whether or not the construction contractor has a stake in the company. The financiers in the project may also retain technical advisers in order to oversee the design and any changes during the project life.

Specialist advisers

The competences of specialist advisers vary from project to project and could include, for example, transportation engineers, behavioural scientists and clinicians.

Main types of service provided

In PPP projects one of the most significant problems will be caused by the different interfaces between the public and private sector actors. These interfaces will vary according to the authority vested in the public sector actor and this will, in turn, influence the nature of the contracted service. Four broad groups of PPP projects each with rather distinct operating characteristics can be identified, where the operator provides:

1. A facility for a single client, most probably a public sector body
2. Services directly to the customers (public or private)
3. Several different, but interrelated, services to a single client
4. Several different, interrelated services to a variety of customers

Payment mechanisms

The choice of payment mechanism is a key factor that will inevitably affect the project set-up. There are three typical approaches in which the private sector collects revenues depending on the service that is provided and who is considered to be the customer. Whichever form is used, its influence on the management of the project is highly significant.

- Revenue streams are collected from customers, e.g. users of a sports centre or toll road.
- Revenues are collected from the client organisation, e.g. a road with shadow tolls.
- Revenue is provided by a combination of the above.

There is a marked difference between a toll road where all revenue is collected from the end-users and a prison, where the revenue could be collected according to the availability of cells and the quality of service provided.

Facilities management and private sector participation

In terms of new capital schemes, a PPP (or PFI) project offers public sector bodies the opportunity to procure the design, construction, finance and operation of their new facilities from one provider and to transfer the attendant risks. This enables the client organisation to concentrate on its core activities. Facilities are, therefore, designed with proper consideration for their management by a party with a vested interest in the long-term success of the project.

In any new capital proposal, especially those involving private sector investment or partnership, due consideration must be given at the feasibility stage to the extent of potential facilities management provision. Facilities management will need to be provided on a best value basis and the means for demonstrating this has to be included in any study.

In all cases, it will be necessary to assess whether or not facilities management is appropriate for inclusion and, if so, in what ways. This can cover those situations in which the bundling of services for other buildings or sites might make the proposal more attractive because of economies of scale. Equally, it may be that facilities management is not suitable for inclusion and so should be left out, perhaps because of implications for the organisation's overall facilities management provision. Additionally, the organisation may consider other variations to service provision, such as partial facilities management involving selected services only. Whatever is decided, the organisation will need to demonstrate that it has considered the relevance of facilities management to a proposed new capital scheme and the options available for its delivery. A sound articulation of the case for and against, as appropriate, should be provided.

The organisation will need to consider the mode by which facilities management should be supplied. This refers to the choice between in-house service provision and outsourcing. The same assessment criteria as apply routinely to determining which of these paths to follow also apply to assessing capital scheme proposals for private sector investment and partnership. It is vital to assess risk transfer, including the risks of in-house service provision.

This kind of private investment arrangement continues the policy of outsourcing support services for facilities management, although it differs from outsourcing in that the private sector is involved as a provider of a capital asset as well as a provider of services. It also has accounting implications that can be beneficial to the client organisation.

Output specifications

Earlier chapters – notably Chapters 8 and 12 – have proposed procedures for specifying service requirements. In any capital scheme proposal likely to include private sector investors or developers, it is essential to advance consideration of facilities management to the point where all of the issues and likely actions have been examined. The thoroughness that should apply to specifying service requirements without direct private sector participation should apply to the same extent to those schemes with it. The organisation may find this easiest to achieve when contemplating an entirely new scheme unencumbered by past arrangements.

Relevance and benefits of private investment and partnership

The benefits of private investment and partnership to facilities management within the public sector can be summarised as follows:

- All types of organisation have the potential to simplify their procurement of capital schemes and subsequent operations.
- The client organisation can transfer responsibility and risk to a single provider and concentrate on its core business.
- Consideration of the operation of new facilities can be built in at the design stage – the input of reliable lifecycle cost data into the design is at the heart of successful arrangements.
- A long-term focus can be built into the project, thus avoiding the dangers and costs of short-term, reactive facilities management.
- Since the operational period will far exceed the design and construction periods, facilities management receives higher priority as its importance to the successful and efficient operation of the organisation's core business is recognised.
- The focus on the overall package can ensure integration between design, construction, finance and operation, avoiding the pitfalls of other, more fragmented approaches to the procurement and maintenance of new capital schemes.

Partners need to work towards common goals within a long-term relationship of openness, trust and compatibility. Private investment and partnership can add real value to the organisation's core business if the provider:

- Is focused on the long-term needs of the customer.
- Can translate those needs into an efficient design for the facility with maximum flexibility for future change.
- Specifies a solution that optimises the lifecycle costs of both the facility and the support services, thereby minimising cost.
- Works in partnership with the customer to deliver services aligned to (changing) needs.
- Enables the client organisation to maximise its efficiency and effectiveness, thereby adding real value rather than simply cutting costs.
- Offers a solution as part of a transaction that covers risks at minimum cost and is financed at the least rate of interest to provide both best value and a more affordable outcome.

Risk and private investment

The crucial criteria for assessing direct private sector involvement in capital scheme proposals are best value and risk transfer. The opportunity to transfer all risks inherent in the design, construction and operation of a new facility may be very tempting. However, a balance has to be struck between the two so that the client organisation should not be seeking the maximum risk transfer, but the most appropriate in securing best value. Risk transfer will always attract a cost. The principle of optimal risk transfer has an impact on value assessment, as any change in risk apportionment will have an impact on the total cost of the project and therefore on value for money achieved. In this instance, of course, best value is to be looked for in the full duration of private sector involvement, which, as we have seen, could be up to 30 years. Value in the context of facilities management services is therefore linked with the wider concern for best value in the total project. However, as the period of operation will far exceed that of design or construction, facilities management becomes a focus for best value and risk issues.

The contractual documentation required for private finance projects will deter or rule out those contractors who do not have a balance sheet able to cope with the contractual liabilities involved in creating the asset and operating a service on the back of it. While this is useful in the selection of suitable partners, the chosen contractor will look for profit margins that are commensurate with the risk. In turn, the risk issues that must be addressed in advance increase the complexity of the tendering process.

Problems with private investment and partnership

The potential benefits of private investment arrangements inevitably bring associated problems, including the following:

- The arrangements for private investment remain complex and therefore difficult to comprehend fully, as well as expensive to implement.
- The relative novelty of these schemes means that they suffer from the legal and financial complexities associated with any new type of transaction.
- The accounting complexities need to be resolved into a simpler set of principles – it is vital to make well-advised judgements concerning which party carries the asset in each case, as wrong decisions can prove costly and embarrassing.
- Few contractors are substantial enough or financially prepared to accept the risks; consequently, there may not be sufficient choice of contractors to ensure true competition and interested companies may enjoy premium pricing.
- Some contractors have limited their long-term risk exposure to notional liability for future defects – focus must therefore be centred on the long-term service issues rather than on the short-term construction project.
- The attractions of risk transfer may discourage its careful consideration on the twin bases of affordability and best value.
- Users may be especially intolerant of any deterioration in service and performance where it is known that the facilities have been organised with their long-term maintenance and operation in mind.

Conclusions

Public-private partnerships (PPPs) have become commonplace in many countries, including the UK where its particular enactment is the PFI. A new sector engaging in PPPs has emerged and is providing rewarding opportunities for construction companies and facilities management service providers. Private sector participation in one form or another is likely to be increasingly important for the financing, provision and management of capital scheme proposals within public sector bodies. It also has potential benefits for the private sector. Facilities management is a key element in all DBFO proposals, of which those schemes under the UK PFI are typical. Client organisations are free to consider many options, but they must always demonstrate rigour, especially in the areas of risk transfer and best value. It will also be important to ensure that appropriate priority is assigned between capital procurement, financing and facilities management aspects of project proposals. Ensuring that services can be maintained over the long term requires much 'up front' thinking and planning. This has had one unexpected benefit – it has forced project design and construction teams to confront lifecycle costs at the design stage. In this way, it has ensured that facilities management becomes a key input during early design as a strategy for delivery customer satisfaction and best value.

CHECKLIST

This checklist is intended to assist with the review and action planning process.

		Yes	**No**	**Action required**
1.	Is the organisation aware of the relevance and benefits of public-private partnerships to its own business, irrespective of whether it is a public or private sector body?	☐	☐	☐
2.	Where relevant, is the organisation aware of the nature of PPP/PFI projects in terms of project set-up, actors involved and mechanisms in regard to the handling of risk and finance?	☐	☐	☐
3.	Where relevant, is the organisation aware of the options for pricing the service created by the asset and how this will generate a return on the investment for the term of the concession?	☐	☐	☐
4.	Where relevant to UK organisations, have the requirements of the PFI been met in terms of considering facilities management provision?	☐	☐	☐
5.	Have the risks affecting partnership projects been noted and addressed?	☐	☐	☐
6.	Are the organisation's facilities management requirements properly reflected in the output specifications for partnership schemes?	☐	☐	☐
7.	Is the organisation aware of the balance between best value and risk transfer in assessing partnership proposals and the facilities management elements contained therein?	☐	☐	☐

16 Education, Training and Professional Development

Key issues

The following issues are covered in this chapter.

- Facilities management has emerged as the fastest growing profession within the breadth of the real estate and construction sector.

- Core competence in facilities management covers, amongst other things, real estate management, financial management, organisational management, innovation and change management, and human resources management.

- The necessity of the ICF should be a major factor in the drive to have personnel who are trained to act as competent client representatives, irrespective of whether or not services are outsourced.

- The organisation must be committed to the training and development of its workforce, especially, in this context, its facilities managers.

- The organisation should adopt recruitment policies that recognise the specialisation of facilities management, and seek individuals who have undergone appropriate education and training and who are prepared to undergo continuous professional development (CPD).

- Education and training in facilities management is available in the university sector, up to the level of Master of Science, with a larger number supporting research.

Introduction

The last five years have seen enormous advances in the facilities management profession in the UK and many other countries – except the USA, perhaps, where it has had a longer presence. Even so, it cannot yet be described as a fully established discipline in the way that architecture, civil engineering and surveying can. However, the rate at which the discipline and the sector have developed – and continue to develop – suggests that its status will continue to rise, bringing it to the point where it is on a virtual par with these other professions. The aim of this chapter is not to map the history of facilities management or the professional discipline that has emerged, but to discuss the educational, training and development framework and the needs of aspiring professionals and technicians seeking a career in the field. Since the subject of facilities management has come late to the broader real estate and construction curricula it may lack general agreement on its educational base and the professional training that should accompany or follow it. Nonetheless, facilities management has become recognised as a subject and discipline in its own right and one that can now be studied to postgraduate level in many universities around the world. From our perspective as authors – one an academic-researcher, the other a practitioner – we have tried to present an interpretation that is informative and purposeful, without attempting to steer the reader in a particular direction. As the various professional institutions evolve their approach to facilities management for the benefit of their membership, institutions dedicated to the discipline strive for their own recognition at the highest level. As authors, our approach is, we trust, one of objectivity and impartiality. In this connection, we freely discuss the needs and opportunities for education, training and professional development in facilities management, without trying to fit them into any institutional framework.

Backgrounds of facilities managers

Many of today's facilities managers are not graduates from schools or departments of facilities management. Instead, they are likely to have a real estate or construction-related discipline and career behind them. Architects, civil engineers, building services engineers, surveyors, builders and accountants have become today's facilities managers. For many, facilities management might have been seen as a new opportunity or, simply, a necessary role to perform in a rapidly changing world. Consequently, they may not have the background or experience for the job. That is not to say they are not performing well. Moreover, it does not follow that those from real estate or construction backgrounds are better equipped to undertake the work of a facilities manager. In fact, research has suggested that the three main attributes sought by employers of facilities managers are integrity, organisational skills and communication skills. Successful facilities managers are those who are able to combine knowledge and skill in estates-related matters with an understanding of organisations, people and processes. A good architect does not necessarily make a good facilities manager; understanding how a building works is not the same as ensuring that it is safe, secure and enjoyable for customers and/or end-users.

Facilities management is not just about looking after buildings. As the definition in Chapter 1 implies, it is the creation of an environment to support the primary function of the organisation. Knowing how people within an organisation make use of a building – moreover, how those people can perform at their best – is the key to understanding facilities management. For these reasons alone, it is possible to justify the need for specialised education and training in facilities management.

The organisation needs to be an informed client – again, see Chapter 1. As such, the ICF should be a major factor in the drive to have personnel who are trained to act as competent client representatives, irrespective of whether or not services are outsourced. Where organisations find expertise lacking they should adopt recruitment policies that recognise the specialisation of facilities management and then seek individuals who have undergone the appropriate education and training.

Growth of the professional discipline

For those who are engaged in facilities management, it will probably come as no surprise that it is the fastest growing professional discipline within the breadth of the real estate and construction sector. The last five years have, in particular, witnessed a breakthrough both in numbers of qualified persons and in an acceptance by clients, customers and other interests of facilities management as a profession demanding a separate identity and a clear recognition of the competence offered by both professionals and technicians.

Inevitably for a discipline that has grown out of the ranks of, *inter alia*, building services engineering, there is a strong belief in the need for a solid grounding in building services engineering, real estate (or property) management and/or contract management. These basic building blocks of the discipline cannot be denied, but today they are accompanied by several other subject areas that give both breadth and depth to facilities management. Taken together, they constitute the original core competences of facilities management.

Core competence in facilities management

Setting aside the historical background to the development of the discipline for one moment and, therefore, the particular competences that have been drawn in over the years, we can see that facilities management draws on a body of knowledge that spans science, engineering, the humanities and social science. Architecture, engineering, construction, technology, management, law and economics are the fields in which the foundations of its core competence were founded. Yet, facilities managers need to be able to take a physiological view of buildings – rather than a purely anatomical view – and this means a greater familiarity with softer issues than those of a technical, engineering nature. In practice, this means that facilities managers have to understand how buildings and other constructed facilities behave and function as environments to support people in their work (and in their homes). A fundamental characteristic of the environment is change, and so one of the main competences that facilities managers should have is an ability to manage change.

Other competences include organisational management, financial management and customer service. It is the interaction of these that establishes facilities management as a unique discipline. Traditionally, it may have been considered that a good education and training in one of the estates-related disciplines was enough, but those educated in one of those specialisations may well lack appreciation of organisational behaviour and human resources management, and how innovation and change can be managed effectively. Core competence in facilities management therefore covers:

- Real estate management – building performance, environmental services and workplace design.
- Financial management – accounting, finance, purchasing and supply, and legal aspects.
- Organisational management – organisational structure, behaviour, processes and systems.
- Innovation and change management – technology, ICT and information management.
- Human resources management – motivation, leadership, employment law, health and safety.

Studying facilities management

Many organisations and universities see facilities management as a serious subject for undergraduate and (post) graduate study. Even so, there are comparatively few degree courses worldwide, although that position is changing. Providing a basis for the study of facilities management in a way that is both rigorous and relevant to the needs of business and society at large really does require the support of universities, with practitioners making it clear that they value a university education. Of course, not all study is aimed at an initial qualification, no matter how high in academic terms it is placed. In the case of facilities management, there is a need to offer and encourage more open access for those who are intent on studying, but for whom formal entry qualifications do not exist.

Many universities and colleges recognise the need to provide in-service education for those already working full time in a facilities management capacity. The opportunity to undertake a degree programme on a part-time basis avoids the piecemeal approach of short courses that, collectively, can lack a coherent conceptual framework. Whether studying part time or full time, undertaking a structured programme of specialist study also allows facilities managers to share and compare experiences with fellow students to the benefit of all participants. Universities are also active in research and consultancy in various aspects of facilities management, and these activities feed back into the degree programmes and courses offered. This ensures that universities are abreast of the latest developments in what is a new and continually developing discipline. It is also possible to pursue doctoral research in a large number of universities, even though there may not be any taught (post) graduate courses in the same university.

Some university courses offer facilities management as an optional module or specialisation within broader undergraduate and (post) graduate programmes. Whilst the number of single degree programmes might be limited at present, the continuing growth in this sector will ensure that facilities management's voice is not lost.

Facilities management training and personal development

Many organisations invest significantly in the training and development of their personnel. We can think of training as being concerned primarily with the acquisition of new skills and extending individual capability, or updating existing skills and reinforcing individual capability – emphasis here is on the short to medium term. Development on the other hand is focused more on instilling interpersonal and other human-centred abilities and tends to follow a longer-term path. Additionally, we might see training as imparting detailed know-how, whilst development is concerned with broader, cross-cutting concepts. From this description, it should be clear that the two go together – training on its own is not enough.

Training in the private sector typically covers such areas as:

- Facilities operations management – budgeting, purchasing, costing centres, internal charging, critical success factors and key performance indicators
- Leading and motivating the facilities management team – human motivation theory and practice, and impact of organisational culture
- Optimising space usage and disposing of surplus space
- Managing change – coping with new legislation and the changing workplace
- Workplace productivity
- Technological innovation, ICT and systems
- Benchmarking costs and performance
- Service level agreements and their management
- Managing heating, cooling, comfort and energy costs
- Healthy buildings
- Performance-based partnering services contracting

Professional institutions have, to varying extents, recognised facilities management as an area into which some of their members have moved and in which opportunities for work and institutional membership exist. Architects, engineers, surveyors and builders have laid claim to facilities management, although none of these has a natural or automatic entitlement. A weakness would be if one were to believe that technical skills were all-important. The authors would contest that view, arguing that a broader base of skills is needed to cope with the many facets of facilities management today and into the future – see earlier comment.

In support of this view, we would point out that in the last few years IFMA has adapted its definition of facility management to reflect a broader range of interests and disciplines. Moreover, as a discipline that helps client organisations cope with change, it must involve people who understand softer issues. None of this is meant to imply that people with a good technical background cannot make good facilities managers, but it will require a mind that is able to adapt to new concepts and be capable of handling problems for which there may be no express formula or 'route map' to follow.

In Chapter 5, we examined a broad range of initiatives introduced by EastPoint, including its Training Sponsorship Scheme, which is aimed at developing the skills of its personnel. The scheme is used to motivate and encourage personnel to upgrade their skills continuously by attending accredited academic study on a part-time basis in their own time. Another of EastPoint's initiatives is an Open Learning Programme (OLP), which has been introduced company-wide to bring about a consistent approach to on-the-job training. Developing this in-house capability has led to significant, continuous cost savings and an upgrading in personnel training and on-the-job performance. Site-based property management training is now provided to all personnel using a technical manual and derivative open-learning workbooks – developed as part of EastPoint's mentoring approach to on-the-job training. The OLP covers a variety of subjects from customer service to personnel recruitment and selection.

Initially, twelve operational areas were identified and have been developed into workbook format for the OLP. Each workbook relates to sections in the EastPoint's technical manual, from customer service and quality, through building security, to financial analysis. The workbooks are produced for easy reading, cover a variety of topics and contain simple exercises to reinforce the learning process. Each exercise is designed to make the participant stop and think about a particular point or concept that is explained in the text.

New recruits enter the ongoing programme as soon as they join and are provided with their first workbook. Written assessments – arranged by the human resources department – are undertaken before the next workbook is distributed. At each property, a site-based professional is selected and appointed to be a coach or mentor and to assist frontline personnel in their self-study. There are also training sessions to reinforce learning for professional grades, enabling them to benefit through sharing practical work experience with peers. The satisfactory completion of the OLP is now included in the company's annual appraisal of employee performance.

Continuing professional development (CPD)

CPD (continuing professional development or continuous professional development) has become accepted as a necessary feature of holding a professional qualification, i.e. retaining membership of a professional institution. Our purpose in using this language to describe what should be welcomed by all as a perfectly reasonable way of keeping abreast of new developments is to draw attention to a common difficulty, even frustration, for professional institutions. Once qualified, many institutional members feel it unnecessary – for whatever reason – to give proper account of their ongoing learning and personal development. From a client perspective, it matters that the people it employees, directly or through agency, are competent in their work. Those who bother to be appraised of new developments should fear nothing, but this is, of course, a purist view. Most practitioners are busy people. Even so, this can be no excuse for failing to invest in an up-to-date understanding of their work and how it can be improved.

Fortunately, the past few years have seen an explosion in information through the world wide web and we can utilise this resource – much of it without cost – for personal benefit and gain. Unfortunately, some people will baulk at the mere mention of the web, claiming that it has nothing of value to offer. The short answer to this ill-informed view – there is no point digressing – is that the user is free to accept or reject information presented on the web. Much useful information is now freely available. That something should be without charge does not mean it is of inferior quality – 'paid for' content can be of poor quality. Ultimately, the user is the one to judge the quality of what is being received. It does not take a genius to recognise that something is not worth having – irrespective of the price tag. Equally, that same person should be able to recognise good, honest information and learning material. Unlike the legal expression, *caveat emptor* – let the buyer beware – which is used to warn us of the perils of purchasing anything, the web can offer us 'something for nothing'. Furthermore, the web has created entirely new models of business as well as a more efficient ICT infrastructure for ordinary business users.

In their attempt to promote their members' moves into facilities management, professional institutions encourage and mount courses to support CPD in the discipline. In this respect, the institutions are fulfilling a valuable role in ensuring that those members who are working in the field, or who may wish to do so, are receiving up-to-date training. Although useful, these efforts cannot substitute for a comprehensive and rigorous education, training and development programme. There is a need for facilities managers to be kept up-to-date in many areas, especially in health and safety matters where legislation is moving quickly. It is important, therefore, for facilities managers and key colleagues to have access to continuing education and information regarding current best practice.

The future for facilities managers

The enhanced status of facilities management within organisations has raised the profile of the facilities manager, and it is set to rise yet further as the discipline develops and its full potential is realised in practical and financial terms. The particular combination of skills required in a facilities manager means that suitably qualified managers can command increasingly high salaries. Under arrangements such as PPP including the UK's PFI – which seem likely to continue for a long time to come – the expertise of the facilities manager in the operational phase becomes invaluable. For this reason, well-qualified and experienced facilities managers may also become involved in private investment schemes in a consultancy capacity because of the detailed knowledge they possess about the services derived from facilities over their whole lifecycle.

Conclusions

Facilities management has emerged from an indistinct past to become the fastest growing profession in the broader real estate and construction sector. It owes its good fortune – if one can call it that – to the increasing awareness amongst real estate owners and users of the value that well-managed facilities can bring to the core business. At the same time, the discipline of facilities management has evolved to embrace softer issues, but without ignoring the engineering and science base that remains a cornerstone of the profession. In a continuously changing world, facilities management is likely to evolve in line with changes in corporate real estate management, legislation affecting employment and the workplace, especially health and safety, and the management of change. Whatever happens, distinct core competences must be present within those managing an organisation's facilities at any given time. Where they are not, retraining or recruitment of appropriate resources will be necessary. Facilities managers can earn recognised qualifications through many universities, institutions and centres. Facilities managers and those closest to them will need to keep abreast of developments in all areas of their work and be able to prove that they have done so.

CHECKLIST

This checklist is intended to assist with the review and action planning process.

	Yes	No	Action required
1. Is the organisation aware of the competences that must be instilled in their facilities management personnel for them to operate successfully?	☐	☐	☐
2. Has the organisation implemented a programme of training and development for its personnel that matches its strategic (business) objectives?	☐	☐	☐
3. Have the core competences required for the successful implementation of a facilities management strategy been identified and are they available within the organisation?	☐	☐	☐

	Yes	No	Action required
4. Are identified core competences brought into the organisation's criteria for the recruitment of facilities management personnel?	☐	☐	☐
5. Is the organisation aware of the extent of information that is freely available for supporting continuing professional development and has it satisfied itself as to the quality?	☐	☐	☐
6. Are there sufficient arrangements in place for continuing professional development, both for the organisation and its service providers?	☐	☐	☐
7. Is the organisation examining trends in the marketplace, so that it can introduce the most appropriate training and development to meet the challenges likely to be created by those trends?	☐	☐	☐

17 Innovation, Research and Development

Key issues

The following issues are covered in this chapter.

- Innovation is not the same as change management, but has a close relationship to it, with each supporting the other to a certain extent.

- Innovation is not invention – innovation is when an act, such as the implementation of a new method, product or service begins to have a positive impact on the environment.

- Innovation is not research and development – the latter provides the vehicle or capacity for enabling innovation to take place by providing answers to questions and solutions to problems.

- Facilities management represents a combination of disciplines focused on improving the quality of life and work – these disciplines should include research and development.

- Areas in which innovation is needed are many, but in focus here are those relating to flexible corporate real estate, healthy living, sustainable communities and tele-care in the home.

- The research and development challenges are many, but not beyond means – most of the challenges have to do with conventional attitudes and business models, none of which are immune from questioning or change.

- Delivering just some of the outcomes promised under the research themes would make a dramatic difference to the quality of life and work.

Introduction

Facilities management is testament to the notion that changes – particularly the introduction of new services and disciplines – can occur in business and that, consequently, there can be a positive impact upon the environment. Innovation is a process that has a close relationship with managing change – itself the subject of an earlier chapter. Many novel ways of dealing with estates-related services have been covered in this book, some of which are outcomes from organisations that are strongly focused on innovation. This is not some academic pursuit, but should be the mission of organisations to ensure that they keep abreast of important changes external to themselves – on the one hand – and to create and then satisfy new markets on the other hand. Increasingly, innovation is occurring as the result of formal research and development (R&D), not a process of trial and error. Recognition of facilities management as combining a number of disciplines does not preclude those of research or business development. On the contrary, these are key competences that must exist within the organisation or to which it must have direct access externally. This chapter explores some current concepts, which – in their desire to improve the quality of life and work – will require changes to be made to how things are done now as well as introducing entirely new ways. This will take the form of four themes, each equating to a distinct aspect of quality and performance improvement.

Change and innovation

Innovation is not some nebulous activity performed in laboratories – it is a process for helping an organisation, its customers and the wider society to benefit from something that is new. All organisations must have, otherwise they must create, a culture of innovation. This is necessary if they are to cope with future changes and, perhaps more importantly, pre-empt those shifts that exert unwarranted pressure on their organisation. Change management is about helping organisations to move from where they are today to where they want to be tomorrow – so too is innovation. The distinction is that change management can provide the context for enabling the results of research and development (R&D) to find their way into daily use. Whilst R&D is a key part of the innovation process, it is only one of three broad phases – see Fig. 17.1. The first of these identifies with business needs and the last with the commercial exploitation of the results of R&D. All too often, the efforts of R&D produce results that are not 'picked up' and so they fail to be implemented. Innovation, as a process, recognises that there must be a phase of implementation during which the results of R&D – in providing a solution to a problem identified earlier – can be successfully exploited. This usually means – if it is an in-house situation – that personnel will have to do things differently. Worse for them is that they may find their roles and responsibilities have to alter significantly. Making adjustments to the current organisation in order to exploit an innovation – be it a new product, working method or ICT system – will involve managing change – see Chapter 4.

Innovation and research and development

Research and development provides the vehicle for meeting challenges and for enabling innovation to take place; but it does not guarantee that

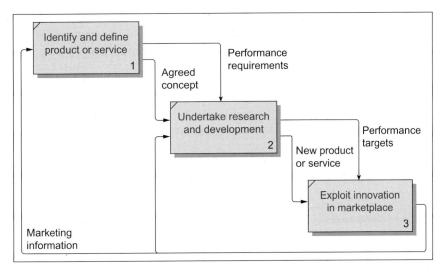

Fig. 17.1   Where R&D fits into the innovation process.

innovations will appear. The relationship between innovation, research and development and commercial exploitation are briefly discussed.

Innovation is not invention, although some things might be discovered or created by individuals in the normal course of their work; but neither is it serendipity. Innovation is when an act, such as the application of a new material or product, or the introduction of a new method, impacts positively on the environment. In other words, it is a process that enables something new or novel to be created. For innovation to succeed, it has to be formally recognised within the organisation. It is not a covert activity or moonlighting on company time. In most large corporations, innovation is the process by which they are able to retain and build market share, by bringing new products and services to the marketplace before their competitors. For this to happen there has to be an organisational structure and culture that encourages innovation across the board – everyone in the organisation is capable of something.

Innovation is not a department or unit with the organisation, although R&D personnel may need to be co-located. There is a distinction between making everyone in the organisation conscious of innovation and charging particular personnel with having to solve problems before a solution can be developed. No matter what money is spent on R&D it cannot be used as a reliable indicator of an organisation's propensity for innovation. Clearly, there is a relationship between the resources available to perform R&D and the chances of producing innovative products or services. In facilities management – taken in the broadest sense – there are considerable sums of money being spent on R&D. This is not intended as any kind of judgement on the efficacy of the R&D being performed or the innovation processes of which it forms a part, merely it is to observe that researchers are active in trying to find answers to questions and solutions to problems identified by their own or another organisation.

Initiatives that have resulted in R&D and which are current at the date of the publication of this book are wide-ranging. They include questions relating to organisational structure and culture, workplace productivity, security measures, other health and safety, and design of all-inclusive environments. It is unlikely that topics of worth are not currently under scrutiny. However, there is a lack of cohesion across the fields of research to the extent that, for example, cross-cutting issues are not well addressed. Since many of the problems are at the interfaces or arise because of an interaction or interdependence between two or more factors, it seems apposite to discuss R&D in the context of focus areas or themes.

Research and development themes

As implied above, there are so many areas in which to conduct relevant R&D that we might run the risk of providing little more than a catalogue of topics. In order to avoid this happening, we have focused on four areas where innovation is desperately needed and which must be supported by R&D if technological challenges and other barriers are to be overcome. The areas are concerned with living, working, health and community, and arise in the form they are presented because they are cross-cutting, multi-disciplinary and directed towards the needs of people.

These four areas translate into the themes of flexible corporate real estate, healthy living, sustainable communities and tele-care in the home, and are outlined below:

1. Flexible corporate real estate – providing highly serviced, re-configurable space that responds to the needs of different customers over short lifetimes.
2. Healthy buildings promoting future living – innovative solutions for delivering affordable, safe, adaptable homes.
3. Sustainable communities – workable sustainability concepts, real estate and infrastructure.
4. Tele-care in the home – utilising innovative housing and advanced ICT to deliver medical care.

Each of these themes is now discussed, including an indication of the problems to be solved by a coordinated R&D response.

Flexible corporate real estate

Businesses demand highly serviced workspaces and total flexibility. In response, industrialised building systems have been developed to provide the levels of engineering services and ICT that are needed in modern com-mercial buildings. Flexibility is generally claimed, but is often limited to changes in office layouts and workplace settings. Sometimes, flexibility can amount to little more than demountable internal partitioning and system furniture. Building systems that can offer re-configurable, serviced space, without adverse effects on the structure or services installations, would represent a breakthrough in space provision, reduce waste, raise profitability and avoid premature obsolescence. This implies designing building systems to provide a choice of multi-configurable components or products to shape not only the spaces of today, but also the spaces required tomorrow.

The manufacture of customised products from standardised components – the concept of mass-customisation – is a common approach in many industries in order to create variants of products that satisfy different customers' needs. To be competitive and remain so, especially in international markets, the real estate sector faces the challenge, amongst other things, of creating design concepts that take advantage of advanced manufacturing methods and that are adaptable to local conditions. The discipline of modularisation helps to identify how product variance, component lifecycles, maintenance and replacement costs and intervals can be used to create concepts for modular building systems that are adaptable to a variety of real estate needs. A more realistic account could thus be taken of the design life for various concepts and questions in regard to re-use and recovery. The research would also lead to significant transfer of technology from manufacturing into the real estate and construction sector.

Building obsolescence is a characteristic that can occur for many reasons, including technical limitations, premature failure and shifts in fashion. In their day, many buildings represented the (then) state of the art, but as time passed and the demands placed on them changed so did their usefulness and attraction. There is no guarantee that buildings and other facilities constructed today will not suffer a similar fate, unless they are deliberately designed with change in mind. But even that may not be enough. The increasing focus on whole life costs – primarily the concern for energy use over the operational phase of a building's life – brings into question some longstanding and basic assumptions. A design life of 50 or 60 years is rarely questioned, yet buildings designed 20 years ago may have reached technical (or another form of) obsolescence.

Present needs are not capable of extrapolation over decades. A plausible approach would be, therefore, to develop design concepts and real estate products that have deliberately defined lives more in step with the growth patterns of the businesses they are intended to support. This is likely to mean products that are easy to refurbish, re-configure and re-locate. This kind of flexibility most likely requires a redefinition of what it means to be a real estate owner, at least in the context outlined here. Ownership or rental will be too simplistic a decision when it is possible for organisations to offer total service packages that include all manner of support for the knowledge workers that are housed in their space.

The aim of the research required in this area is primarily to create manufactured modular products that provide a rapid response to the need for highly serviced, flexible space. The specific objectives would be to:

1. Define innovative service concepts that support business growth, whilst minimising risk exposure for businesses, especially SMEs.
2. Develop novel concepts for scaleable real estate solutions, based on high levels of service provision and re-configurable space.
3. Develop know-how to support the rapid deployment (and redeployment) of robust, state-of-the-art ICT infrastructures anywhere.
4. Devise workplace strategies that support building occupants in their work, making them more efficient and content with their conditions.

Figure 17.2 illustrates the relationship between these objectives.

Research should explore and define service concepts that adapt to, or better still anticipate, shifts in the marketplace and that provide low risk exposure for businesses, especially SMEs. The concept of networks of knowledge-based enterprises could be used to create access to human resources for selected industrial sectors – in terms of specialist skills and knowledge – so that both physical and virtual proximity are taken into consideration. The research should adopt an 'inside-out' strategy for defining end-products, relying heavily on the preferences of users to guide design decision-making. The nature of workplaces, as spaces that are conducive to productive knowledge-intensive activities, requires an indoor environment to match. Moreover, this must be capable of satisfying the various needs of all building occupants. The kind of real estate that is likely to satisfy these needs is highly ICT-serviced, re-configurable and re-locatable, matching the pattern of growth for knowledge businesses.

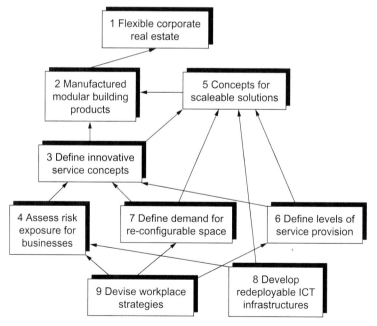

Fig. 17.2   Relationship between R&D objectives in achieving flexible corporate real estate.

The technical feasibility of these concepts will need to be fully explored including modularisation, methods of assembly, fixing and disassembly. The focus should be on how to produce real estate solutions in terms of designs that can be adapted according to product variance requirements. Additionally, they must allow for maintenance, replacement and upgrading to be done economically over the building lifecycle. ICT infrastructures will need to be designed and tested for their efficacy in supporting worker and organisational mobility.

A substantial proportion of new buildings will never experience the full service life for which they were designed. This is not a UK or even European phenomenon, but a global problem. Delivering business support is predicated on the use of many resources of which real estate is both obvious and primary. As such, real estate must provide an effective platform for businesses to develop and grow, so that flexibility – in the sense of adaptability – becomes paramount. The scale of the problem of creating flexible real estate products is enormous and is only likely to be tackled by a major push on the part of leading real estate developers, owners, users and providers. Overturning opinions in the real estate and construction sector that are fixated on permanent structures – albeit with scope for adaptation – which are built to last several lifetimes will not be easy. The task will, however, be made easier by demonstrable action on the part of major players in the sector, especially real estate developers and owners.

The areas of competence required for this research include, but are not restricted to:

- Workplace design
- Virtual design environments
- Modular building system concepts
- Modular building components
- Large-scale production of buildings
- Field-factory automation systems
- Control systems
- Mobile technology

Healthy buildings promoting future living

Housing is the fundamental right of all people, yet gross distortions in housing conditions and in the balance between supply and demand exist across the world. This situation is not peculiar to poor regions. Affluent countries fail to provide decent and affordable housing for all and this is an impediment to the advancement of modern and just societies. There are many excuses for this failure, but fewer for effecting workable solutions. A central theme is that housing must not impair the health of its occupants, yet there is evidence of ill-health from recurrent problems such as moisture penetration, emission of harmful chemicals and, inexcusably, lack of basic amenities. In the future, houses must do more than provide shelter and protection – they must contribute to a minimum standard of living for everyone and eliminate conditions that give rise to building-related illness. Furthermore, housing must not be used to define strata in society. All households must have access to modern services, and ICT in particular, otherwise the digital divide will become a reality for many people.

Maintaining control over the condition and functioning of homes and alerting occupants – and others with a legitimate interest – to the hidden dangers is fundamental to this thinking. Providing the means for monitoring and controlling the condition of buildings, especially housing, over the lifecycle would represent a major breakthrough in preventive maintenance and servicing of the built environment. Technology is already capable of providing many solutions, for example the introduction of embedded technology into factory produced components. However, the application outlined above needs careful examination, development and testing of prototypes and feedback from full-scale demonstrators. In this regard, the workability of any new approach and products is unlikely to be assured by scale-models – people's health is too important an issue for this kind of treatment. The scope of this research thus includes mechanisms for monitoring and control throughout the lifecycle, by the use of embedded technology. Access to information on the condition of one's home should be readily available and should be provided to authorised third parties. The use of embedded technology is not, however, confined to the occupancy phase. Tracking of components from manufacture through transportation and incorporation into the building can provide valuable histories for use in diagnostics and preventive measures. A term that could have been adopted here is that of 'smart homes'; however, this would not necessarily convey the importance of healthy homes and living. Another oft-quoted term is that of 'intelligent buildings'. Again, we have chosen to avoid its use, because of its strong association with 'technology push'.

Households change over time: they grow and contract and their tastes and requirements alter. Generally, homes stay much the same, apart from minor alteration and periodic redecoration. The lifecycles of households and homes could not be more out of step. Housing may be regarded as having to serve future generations, but when it fails to serve the present something has to be fundamentally wrong. Adaptation to new services and upgrading of the building fabric, services installations and interior fittings are needed for many homes. Retrofitting is an option for existing buildings. However, replacement with new buildings may be the only option where decay and obsolescence are too far advanced. Clearly, the mistakes that have led to this situation must be avoided in new buildings. For this reason, an implicit assumption is that the manufacture of customised products from standardised components – the concept of mass-customisation – will provide the platform for modularised house building on a major scale. This is needed if people are to have affordable, decent quality homes that are equipped for 21st century living. Moreover, homes must be capable of adaptation in a controlled and relatively easy way to provide different configurations of space to suit households at different stages in their development.

Often, people have to move to another home if the present does not satisfy needs. For many people, however, this may not be an option, either because they are unable to afford such a step or simply because they wish to remain within their community. In other words, housing provision must be driven by people's needs. The implications of this closer alignment of the needs of households with the provision of housing amount to a radical departure from traditional house building concepts in which largely conventional methods of construction can, quite literally, build in obsolescence. Furthermore, the speed with which new or replacement housing can be built is unlikely to be satisfied by a traditional construction response.

The primary aim is to produce adaptable, healthy homes that protect, support and stimulate occupants in their formal and informal activities. An implicit aim is to ensure that past mistakes in mass housing are not repeated. The specific objectives are to:

1. Define users' needs – housing developers, owner-occupiers and tenants – as a basis for developing housing concepts and support systems.
2. Develop housing solutions based on high levels of service provision, low energy consumption and re-configurable, extendable space.
3. Develop natural or passive methods for heating, cooling and ventilating that can be used alongside active systems and all necessary control regimes.
4. Develop methodologies for the correct selection of building materials, products and systems and the detection of harmful materials and potential emissions.
5. Develop systems using state-of-the-art sensing and navigational technology to support the tracking and interrogation of products and components, including support from internet-based cyber-agents.

Figure 17.3 illustrates the relationship between these objectives.

In spite of improved understanding of how to eliminate problems in buildings, especially multi-storey housing, building failures are all too prevalent. Much of the blame can be laid at the door of design teams in omitting to consider the broader implications of their work and in the lack of systematic feedback from projects past and present. The research should, therefore, re-engineer the process of design and production to include tools for the systematic gathering of performance data and for detecting potential failures. For example, the quality of the indoor environment can be assured through a variety of measures including, for example, methods for selecting the most appropriate components and for warning of the potential of harmful emissions.

Research should also examine the use of natural or passive methods for heating, cooling and ventilating the spaces within buildings so that the relationship between air quality and the energy used by more active methods can be better balanced. The efficient co-existence of these two approaches has to be determined so that effective monitoring and control strategies

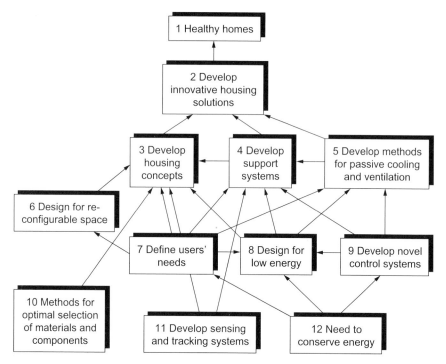

Fig. 17.3   Relationship between R&D objectives in achieving healthy buildings.

can be developed, ensuring that optimal comfort conditions are provided. The incorporation of embedded technology should be examined in the context of providing knowledge of how the building and its systems are functioning. The interconnectivity between different ICT infrastructures and standards for communication, for example *Ethernet, LonWorks, OSGi* and *Bluetooth*, are central to this approach and questions in regard to their deployment will need to be carefully examined. This has to operate in parallel with the ongoing development of industry standards for product information to provide data for embedded technology. The use of internet-based cyber-agents – 'search and do' agents – to assist in the coordination and control of the entire design, construction and facilities management process needs to be investigated. The aim should be to provide real-time support to occupants and other stakeholders such as maintenance crews.

The quality of housing in most countries is highly variable, with a significant proportion of dwellings lacking one or more basic amenities. A radical overhaul of the housing supply market is required if a serious impact is to be made. Traditional methods of house building have to be complemented by large-scale manufactured housing programmes through which affordable, decent quality homes that reflect owners' and occupants' preferences are produced on a wide area basis. Mobilising the supply chain to support such an ambitious, but vitally important, initiative will necessitate the inclusion of major industrial companies and the collaboration of large municipal authorities. Inevitably, this means that major players are needed, at least for the production, delivery, installation and commissioning of these products.

The areas of competence required for this research include, but are not restricted to:

- Occupant needs in healthy buildings
- Home automation
- Building automation
- Embedded technology – sensors and communications
- Building technology and quality assurance
- Modular building system concepts
- Modular building components
- Control systems
- Logistics
- Supply chain management

Sustainable communities

The concept of sustainable communities is not new. However, achievements are few and far between, with some questionable practices included in them. Advances in greener sources of energy, higher standards of building leading to substantial energy saving, and a perceivable shift in the attitude of people towards the environment bode well for a major push aimed at establishing workable sustainability concepts. Significant changes in demand and in the use of energy cannot, however, continue without further action or incentive. Demonstration of how entire communities can work successfully must be actively considered. It is not enough to show how novel concepts can work in a selection of specially commissioned 'show-houses'. Sustainable energy systems designed for large settlements must be implemented and must be clearly seen to work economically and socially, as well as technically. Demonstration seems to be one of the few ways in which it is possible to change people's attitudes to energy use and other activities that impact negatively on the environment.

Buildings are responsible for such a major proportion of energy consumption in any nation that it is an obvious and legitimate target for action. How they are designed and constructed is an important subject and one that cannot escape a root and branch review based on workable sustainability concepts. Realisation of *Kyoto* and European Community targets for CO_2 reduction and decreased energy consumption are only likely to be achieved by a concerted effort to implement new standards in design, construction, heating, power and waste disposal. Furthermore, such effort has to bring together a package of measures that can be tested, proven and released to the wider community. A coordinated action is necessary to avoid sub-optimal solutions emerging, where gains in one area are negated by losses in another. Balancing community interests will require that many trade-offs have to be considered and adjustments made to ensure an overall optimal solution. In this way, it will be possible to demonstrate a holistic approach to sustainability that could be then replicated across a wide geographical area.

This thinking is aimed at the challenge of designing and building entire communities where the environment is subject to proactive management. In most cases, this is likely to be targeted at the regeneration of existing communities; typically, those areas where communities are living in poorly maintained conditions. Although action is needed across a broad front, the main focus is operational energy-efficiency and, in particular, the use of materials having a low energy input requirement. The need is to reduce energy use to such a low level that by the addition of green sources of energy it is possible to provide a net gain to the wider community. This requires new design philosophies driven by the need to consider combinations of design concepts that minimise initial environmental impact and the longer-term consumption of resources.

The approach emphasises the ecological and economic dimensions of sustainability and also takes into consideration social and cultural questions. The emphasis is upon communities and, as such, a holistic account has to be taken of the planning and realisation of mixed use settlements, where housing is just one part – albeit an important one. In the case of urban regeneration, the intention must be to revitalise decaying areas, by offering decent, affordable housing incorporating space for work, health care, community services and shopping. Benefits from such regeneration are likely to include lower crime, improved health and a better economic base for the area. At the other end of the scale, recreational interests can be shaped to provide novel solutions to the need for new and greener sources of energy. The entire eco-system for settlements of up to 1 000 people has to be considered. On this scale, it may be possible to balance resource demands with renewable supplies of energy and to prove the viability of the concept of sustainable communities in which life can be seen to be as normal and unrestricting as possible.

The primary aims are to bring about achievable actions in reducing the impact of real estate and construction on the environment and to create a net contribution of energy to the wider community. The specific objectives are to:

1. Identify concepts for environmentally friendly design and construction that are achievable in practice, without detriment to owners' and occupiers' needs.
2. Define and develop knowledge management systems to support intelligent search for and analysis of appropriate know-how and technology in regard to sustainability.
3. Develop tools and techniques for generating, evaluating and synthesising design solutions based on whole life costs and minimal environmental impact.
4. Demonstrate the workability of the above concepts through full-scale buildings and infrastructure that minimise environmental consumption and that make a net contribution to the wider community's energy needs.

Figure 17.4 illustrates the relationship between these objectives.

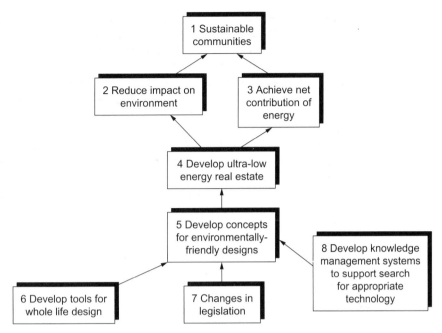

Fig. 17.4   Relationship between R&D objectives in achieving sustainable communities.

Legislative changes are pending and these should be examined to determine the timetable for conversion to practices that are consistent with the goals of sustainable development. Concepts for environmental design that minimise impact on the environment and the consumption of scarce resources in the construction of new buildings – as well as in the refurbishment of existing buildings – need to be investigated. This will require support from tools and techniques for selecting the most appropriate materials and components in terms of their whole life cost and environmental impact. These will require further support from knowledge bases used to select components that carry official environmental labelling, certifying their compliance with environmental codes, and offering advice on relevant financial or other incentives, for example tax breaks or rebates, for exceeding minimum code requirements.

Research is also needed to examine successful examples of combined heat and power, and district heating, concepts that have, for instance, stood the test of time in many towns and cities in Scandinavia. A further dimension that affects existing communities will be to devise strategies that strive to keep people in their homes until such time as they can be moved directly into new accommodation adjacent to their existing location. This approach will avoid breaking up the very communities that one is trying to retain.

Measures to advance sustainability concepts and to introduce them into the community cannot be expected to succeed on the back of piecemeal initiatives that address parts of a wider problem. The idea that one might bring about sustainable communities through a succession of minor measures that provide incentives to individual homeowners and occupiers is unrealistic. Wholesale change is required and, therefore, this can only be done on a scale that has the opportunity directly to influence entire communities. Another aspect is that of involving all the necessary expertise and other ingredients that are needed to turn a working concept into a real community. This can only be done on the scale of a major project in which demonstration on an equally large scale can be performed. Whilst there is little doubt that specific examples of novel technologies and approaches are scaleable, there is both a credibility and integration gap to fill. The project should aim for a full-scale community in order to demonstrate working concepts so that replication can take place. True breakthroughs in establishing lasting actions are only likely to occur if the scale is real and convincing for ordinary people, as much as it is for other stakeholders.

The areas of competence required for this research include, but are not restricted to:

- Building design for sustainability
- Engineering infrastructure
- Timber technology
- Modular building system concepts
- Fuel cell technology
- Photovoltaic technology
- Energy sources and management
- Energy systems infrastructure

Tele-care in the home

People are affected by their surroundings and, especially, by the condition of their homes. When people are healthy, a less than ideal setting may amount to little more than irritation; but when people are elderly and/or in poor health, conditions in the home can have a significant impact. Poor building conditions lead to poor health; conversely, good conditions can promote good health. The starting point for tele-care is a healthy building into which can be introduced medical and ancillary equipment to allow people to be treated and cared for in their own homes. There are sound economic as well as medical arguments for treating people in their own homes. However, this cannot take place without serious investment in both housing to suit and technology to enable medical care to be correctly received. Inevitably, this will mean that new buildings will have to be produced with such features and then maintained properly.

Retrofitting of the existing housing stock is also possible, but success is more likely when homes have been designed to take these features into account. Since an individual's needs are likely to be different to any other, a strategy for delivering technologically enhanced real estate is needed. The adaptation of homes to accept a range of support functions and care regimes will call for a rethink of how dwellings can be equipped or re-equipped to deal effectively with these challenges. One concern, amongst others, will be to minimise the impact upon the occupant/patient arising from changes to the original layout, functionality and appearance of the home. Furthermore, changes will need to be reversible if it is subsequently shown that an alternative arrangement is better suited.

The design of all-inclusive buildings and other facilities is a developing field, as opposed to an exact science in which all parameters are known. In addition to the provision of medical support, there is likely to be the need for homes that are responsive and which, as underscored above, do not adversely affect health. Many of the arguments and recommended solutions advanced for affordable, healthy homes would apply here, particularly in the context of enabling technology against the background of mass customised products that are economical, defect free and of a decent quality.

Homes equipped with ICT and medical apparatus could provide care, monitoring and education to patients who would otherwise have to be admitted to hospitals or other care facilities. Medical practitioners would be able to maintain continual contact with patients, enabling them to be treated in their own home and avoiding the trauma and expense of hospitalisation. The problem is one of designing and delivering both a home and a care environment – through the provision of modern, highly-serviced, ICT-enabled housing – that can accommodate the equipment required for home telemedicine. Given the right kind of setting and conditions, there is no reason why medical equipment that was previously found in health care centres and hospitals could not be adequately installed, protected and maintained in a person's home.

The development of mobile technology provides an important element in the provision of tele-care services, especially since mobility in the home is likely to be a key issue and one where the occupant/patient might face restrictions on movement. Another aspect of concern is coping with an ageing population and one where the proportion of older people will become increasingly significant in the coming years. The approach advocated offers a realistic alternative to moving people from their homes to health care centres and hospitals and then back again, and repeating the cycle many times over. The economic and social arguments are powerful, and there is sufficient technology to ensure this can be achieved. However, the latter has to be placed within a process that is purposely designed for tele-care purposes. It is not enough to graft it on to existing practices for procuring buildings that will house the elderly and/or people in poor health.

The primary aim of this project is to develop a range of innovative housing products that can provide a secure and safe environment into which tele-care services can be introduced. The specific objectives are to:

1. Define users' needs (i.e. housing developers, owner-occupiers, tenants and medical practitioners) as a basis for developing inclusive environments and support systems.

2. Develop housing solutions, based on high levels of service provision, low energy consumption and re-configurable, adaptable space.
3. Specify the characteristics of the indoor environment in terms of function, amenities, climate and support for medical and ancillary equipment.
4. Create branded products that are acceptable to national health departments and the medical professions and demonstrate this to all stakeholders, not least the elderly and infirm.

Figure 17.5 illustrates the relationship between these objectives.

The research necessitates extensive investigation of the means for delivering medical care in the home. It is not enough to scale down the facilities of a professional health care facility or to simply modify existing housing products. A detailed investigation of how elderly or infirm persons can be properly supported in their homes has to be undertaken. Questions of mobility and dependency will need to be addressed if housing solutions are to be real solutions to the needs of a growing proportion of the population. The interaction between such occupants and their surroundings needs careful examination so that workable solutions arise. It goes without saying that people should not be prisoners in their own home. The technical feasibility of the overall concept will need to be fully explored and this will extend to modularisation, methods of assembly, fixing and disassembly. Special attention will need to be paid to the added complexity arising from the incorporation of medical and ancillary equipment.

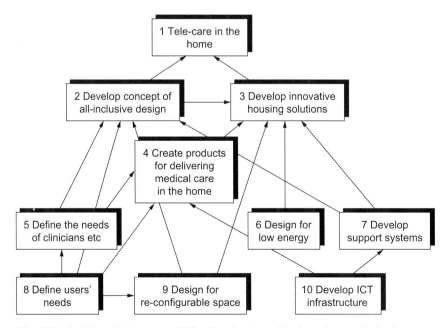

Fig. 17.5   Relationship between R&D objectives in achieving tele-care in the home.

The growing proportion of the population and, hence, the housing market that serves (or should serve) the elderly or infirm is in need of radical overhaul. Attempts to provide health care regimes for people in their own homes are, in many countries, generally limited to the well-off with little commercial interest in extending this to the social and mass housing sector. A concerted effort that would bring together the many interests, bodies and disciplines in this area is needed. The success of tele-care in the long run will depend largely upon how effective housing solutions are at catering for the needs of their occupants. This will require that the research results are adequately demonstrated so that practical solutions, as well as the concepts, can be replicated. Important too is that proprietary rights are not allowed to prevent the maximum penetration of tele-care housing products into the marketplace.

The areas of competence required for this research include, but are not restricted to:

- Design of inclusive environments
- Tele-care concepts
- Sensors and controls
- Telemedicine – equipment and communications
- Mobile technology

Conclusions

The need for innovative thinking and practices within organisations in any sector is generally recognised. This has, of course, to include facilities management, which combines many disciplines which bring their different skills and expertise to bear on solving problems to enable the quality of living and work to advance. Further research and development (R&D) is required, but not before precise needs have been identified and agreed. This chapter has attempted to show through examples – four of them in detail – the very kind of R&D that is required now to enable the quality of living and work to rise to more acceptable levels. Some longstanding conventions and assumptions must be challenged. These include questioning the rationale for building lifecycles that are out of step with the needs of some industrial and commercial real estate owners and users. Also of concern is the fragmented approach to dealing with sustainability – something that is talked about, yet for which there seem to be too few examples of real progress 'on the ground'. There are many other problems that must be solved. The most important of these is, arguably, the design, construction and management of buildings and other facilities to provide good quality conditions for living and work. Facilities management, in combining many disciplines, has the potential to deal competently with the cross-cutting issues that are involved. Experts with deep knowledge are needed, but they must be coordinated by others who are capable of seeing the bigger picture.

CHECKLIST

This checklist is intended to assist with the review and action planning process.

		Yes	No	Action required
1.	Has the organisation a recognised strategy or policy regarding innovation?	☐	☐	☐
2.	Is the organisation promoting a culture of innovation amongst its personnel?	☐	☐	☐
3.	Has the organisation a structured means for dealing with the process of innovation?	☐	☐	☐
4.	Has the organisation examined the case for accepting different lifecycles for its buildings and other facilities?	☐	☐	☐
5.	Has the organisation produced a strategy for dealing with the imperatives of energy-reduction and sustainability?	☐	☐	☐
6.	Are the buildings and other facilities owned or operated by the organisation truly 'fit for purpose' and, if not, are steps being taken to make them totally acceptable?	☐	☐	☐
7.	Is the organisation satisfied with the level of ICT support that it presently has and the arrangements for supporting personnel in their homes, as well as in their normal place of work?	☐	☐	☐

Appendix A

Glossary

accommodation strategy
An objective assessment of the space needs of an organisation and how these will be satisfied – see also space management.

action research
A branch of scientific discovery in which the research lifecycle is compressed to deal with subjects undergoing dynamic change; often involves iterations of key stages.

added value
Tangible gain from a decision, action or procedure that exceeds its monetary equivalent, e.g. a specified service might be performed at its most economical cost yet still provide further benefit from, say, the manner in which customers' other needs are satisfied – see also best value.

assets
Sufficient human, physical (e.g. property) and financial resources to enable an organisation to discharge its obligations under its charter or mission statement.

attitude surveys
A means for measuring the perceptions, expectations and experiences of people for the purpose of objective analysis.

audit (internal)
Measurement and verification of the practices, procedures, policies and decision-making within an organisation with the aim of improving its operational efficiency and effectiveness.

B2B
Business to business; a term used to describe the nature of electronic (web-based) commerce (transactions) – see also B2C below.

B2C
Business to consumer; a term used to describe the nature of electronic (web-based) commerce (transactions) – see also B2B above.

benchmarking
An external focus on an internal process to provide an objective comparison of performance or achievement.

best value
Relationship between cost/price and quality which is optimal for a given organisation or customer – not to be confused with lowest price.

business process re-engineering (BPR)
Fundamental rethinking and radical redesign of business processes to bring about dramatic improvements in performance.

CAFM
Computer-aided facilities management, where computer-aided design is integrated with database management to provide an environment in which the dynamic behaviour of an organisation can be planned, observed, modified and maintained.

change management
The process, tools and techniques to manage the people-side of business change to achieve a required outcome and to realise that change effectively within the social infrastructure of the workplace.

continual improvement
Recognising that today's performance is not enough to meet tomorrow's challenges – striving to raise standards.

contract management
Ensuring that service providers perform according to their commitments.

contracting out
A particular type of outsourcing, where work is undertaken by a contractor as opposed to being carried out in-house.

CSF
Critical success factors are those attributes of a service that determine whether or not its objectives and priorities have been met – see also key performance indicators.

customer-focus
Recognising that without customers there is no business and that they can be anyone with a legitimate interest in the organisation, e.g. own personnel, general public, funding agency, service providers and suppliers.

data integration
The principle that data are entered once only into a computer-based system enabling more than one application to share those same data.

de-layering
Removing supervisory or management grades within an organisation where there is no real or perceived benefit from their continuance. The effect is to flatten the hierarchy to bring the most senior managers closer to the customer.

disaster recovery
Planning of operations to take account of circumstances that would pose a significant threat to the organisation's continuation in the event of an incident – see also risk management.

document management
Control over the generation, distribution, storage and archiving of information, usually taken to mean a computer-based system.

downsizing
Reducing the scale of an operation or process to a level in keeping with the demands placed upon it.

EBITDA
Earnings before interest, taxes, depreciation and amortisation.

empowerment
Providing personnel (and others under one's control) with the ability to make decisions that will affect their own work and personal development; *synon.* effective delegation.

energy audit
Measurement of the amount, rate and cost of energy consumed in operating a facility in order to achieve acceptable conditions – usually contains a comparative element.

environmental audits
Assessment of the extent to which a system or organisation conforms with legislation and practices designed to protect the environment.

environmental protection
Taking steps to ensure that the consequences of actions, operations and processes do not harm or in any way pose a threat to the ecosystem.

EVA
Earned value added.

facilities audit
Determining the extent to which the provision of existing properties and other facilities match needs within an organisation – see also accommodation strategy and space management.

hazard assessment
Identification of a potentially dangerous or threatening occurrence and its subsequent assessment against legal requirements under health and safety legislation – see also risk assessment.

helpdesk
A point of contact for requesting information and action in response to a facilities-related need – does not have to be a physical location, but can be, for example, a telephone hotline.

human resources management (HRM)
More than a personnel function, HRM, as it is often known, takes account of the needs, motivations and welfare of people in order to help them realise their potential.

ICF
The informed client function, ICF, enables the organisation to strive for best value and total satisfaction in its facilities management by focusing on agreed core competences.

if ... then
Used in predicting the future; a type of conditional statement in which one event or occurrence triggers another, e.g. if global warming continues then governments will be forced to impose a carbon tax.

information management
An organised and structured approach to handling information and data so as to ensure that the right information is provided to the right people, at the right time and in the right format.

intelligent building
More than a building that has been 'wired-up', rather one that affords a high level of support for its users through the use of technology and a design that takes account of the inevitability of change – also referred to as technology-enhanced real estate.

intelligent client or customer
See informed client function, ICF.

Investors in People (IIP)
IIP is a national scheme for encouraging and rewarding innovations in the workplace that lead to personnel realising their potential.

Just-in-time (JIT)
Just-in-time delivery is regarded as one of the factors in the successful transformation of many industries. This lean production method ensures

that inventory levels are kept to a minimum thus lowering levels of waste and releasing cash flow.

KPI
Key performance indicators, KPIs, enable an organisation's effectiveness, in meeting its objectives, to be measured objectively. Usually, two or more KPIs will be linked to a critical success factor.

learning organisation
An entity that has as its underlying principle the will to learn from those outside and to use the knowledge it generates in doing business to help it improve its processes.

managing agent
Individual or organisation appointed to act on behalf of another to manage a service whose performance may be the subject of separate contracts.

mega trends
Tendency towards specified events in the future that are predicted to have a significant impact on the way we do things, e.g. governmental action on global warming that affects the way we live.

outsourcing
Placing one or more non-core services in the hands of an external organisation or contractor – see also contracting out.

partnering
A method of working with suppliers (and service providers) to enable both parties to share in the benefits arising from a close working relationship that strives for cooperation and improvement. This method can and should still contain a competitive element, but can be an effective counter to traditional adversarial working practices.

performance indicator
See KPI, key performance indicators.

PEST
Political, economic, social and technological; used to establish a framework around which discussion can focus on those external factors affecting an organisation.

PFI
The private finance initiative (PFI) is a type of public-private partnership used by successive UK governments to secure private investment in projects for public benefit – see also public-private partnership, PPP.

post-occupancy evaluation (POE)
Post-occupancy evaluation is a method for establishing the extent to which users are satisfied with their facilities and, by implication, how closely reality matches the brief. The term is perhaps inaccurate, since 'post' could imply that the occupants have moved out!

procurement
Used generally to refer to the process of inviting, selecting, awarding and paying for goods or services supplied to an organisation. This is nowadays taken to be part of an organisation's supply chain.

public-private partnership (PPP)
An arrangement where the public sector enters into an arrangement with the private sector to create an asset and/or service for public benefit, such as a school, hospital, road, bridge etc.

quality circle
An opportunity for personnel of different grades to meet informally, sometimes outside working hours, to discuss ways of improving the performance of their tasks and the effectiveness of their decision-making.

rightsizing
Establishing the most appropriate structure and resources for an organisation – see also downsizing.

risk assessment
Part of risk management wherein hazards, events or the likelihood of events occurring are identified and their impact evaluated.

risk management
Taken to include risk assessment, but extended to include dealing with the associated risks by the adoption of a given strategy. This can include, for example, holding the risk, transferring it or eliminating it altogether.

scenario analysis
A technique used by corporate strategists and planners to help them think in a structured way about the future by building different descriptions of how the future might be. In the process this may pinpoint key actions for the organisation if it is to secure its goals.

service level agreement (SLA)
An SLA deals with how the service specification shall be translated into actions that achieve the required result and will include the means for dealing with evaluation of performance, incentives and penalties.

service specification
Lays down what a specified service shall be and can be either prescriptive, where the process necessary to achieving a given result is outlined, or

performance-based, where the service provider is given outputs or measures that must be achieved.

sick building syndrome
A condition affecting the users of buildings that disappears after they stop using the building and which cannot be attributed to a specific factor; once identified, it is no longer sick building syndrome.

Six Sigma
A technique for improving customer satisfaction, profitability and competitiveness through a focus on the customer by the disciplined use of facts, data and statistical analysis – the term itself refers to a statistically-derived performance target.

smart homes
A term used to label housing in which technology is used to support occupants and other users – see also intelligent building.

space management
The process by which better use is made of available space, matched to needs. It ensures there is more intensive and extensive use of existing accommodation and that there is a reduction in the need to procure or acquire additional space, whilst maintaining flexibility in response to users' needs.

SWOT analysis
Strengths, weaknesses, opportunities and threats; a framework used to focus attention on the essential characteristics of an organisation; usually drawn as a cross, with each issue in a separate quadrant, where the aim is to list all possibilities and to examine any correlation between the lists.

tele-protection
The use of information and communications technology to support security and other measures aimed at safeguarding people and property.

total facilities management (TFM)
Total facilities management is where a single entity takes responsibility for all facets of facilities management. In reality, this entity may, however, subcontract some of the more specialist elements.

total quality management (TQM)
An approach to work where the aim is to do things right first time, every time. This has little to do with the administration of quality assurance schemes and has more to do with the motivation of individuals to give of their best and accept no compromises.

uncertainty
Events that cannot be foreseen or quantified, unlike a risk for which some assessment might be made – see also risk management.

value
Worth or utility; also a way of expressing the relationship between quality and cost – see best value.

workplace productivity
Concerned with the extent to which the working environment (surrounding an individual) contributes towards or detracts from the amount and/or quality of work undertaken.

Appendix B

Prevention of fraud and irregularity in the award and management of contracts

Definitions

Fraud may be defined as the use of deception with the intention of obtaining an advantage. Corruption is the giving or receiving of money, goods or services for favours provided. The risks of fraud and corruption can be reduced by awareness of their nature and good procurement practice.

Fraud should be deterred. Prevention is always preferable to detection, and strong preventive controls should therefore be applied.

Risks

Facilities management services have long been considered to carry a high risk of fraud, corruption and other irregularity. The frauds can take a number of forms, some involving collusion with the client organisation's personnel or agents.

One fraud risk is the 'ringing' of contracts, whereby a group of contractors conspires to form a ring for submitting tenders ostensibly in competition but, in fact, having arranged among themselves which firm will bid the lowest. Even the lowest tender will be overpriced. The aim of the ring will be to win the majority of the contracts available and share them.

Frauds can be perpetrated in the execution or pricing of work for new contracts. This can take a variety of forms from failure to perform to specification, to deliberate falsification of suppliers' invoices or labour records leading to overpayment for services. Maintenance contracts also provide opportunities for a contractor to claim for more work than has been done, with or without collusion.

The pricing of contracts not let by competitive tender carries the risk that costs may be deliberately overstated. This can be a particular problem in 'cost plus' contracts and in small value non-competitive contracts which can add up to large amounts of expenditure over the year.

Particular care needs to be taken about the acceptance of gifts, hospitality and other benefits, and to ensure there is no conflict of interest in the award of contracts.

Key principles of control

There are a number of basic principles of control to minimise the risk of fraud in estates-related services and facilities management procurement.

Separation of duties

Duties should be separated to ensure that no single member of staff has control over the award and procurement process for contracts. For example, there should be a separation of duties between ordering the work, certification and authorisation of payments. Failure to separate duties is one of the most common elements of fraud in this context.

Organisations should also ensure that all staff are aware of the risks of fraud and of their responsibilities for reporting any fraud or suspicions of fraud to the appropriate level of management. One option is to set up an internal fraud helpline.

Authorisation

All transactions or specified activities should be approved or sanctioned by a manager or other responsible person before they are undertaken. Limits for these authorisations should be specified. Authorisation seeks to ensure that proper responsibility is taken for all transactions and activities. Authorisation should ensure that delegated limits are complied with, and provide an independent scrutiny and consistency in the procurement process.

Competitive tendering

Contracts should normally be let by competition. A decision not to use competitive tendering should require a higher level of authority.

Regular supervision

There should be positive supervision of the procurement process including regular and unannounced checks of transactions. In addition, managers should carry out pre-commitment checks to confirm the need for the service, that the type of contract is appropriate, and that estimated costs are realistic.

Record-keeping

Appropriate records must be kept to enable every decision and transaction to be traced through the system. The requirement to keep proper records is an important deterrent to fraud.

Documentation

Standard documentation, in the sense of being uniform and consistent, can help to enforce conformity with procedures and legal requirements.

Budgetary control

Budgetary control matches resources and costs to responsibilities for objectives and outputs. Managers should be fully accountable for the achievement of their objectives and targets. Budgets should be closely linked to planning and review procedures to ensure that proposed expenditure is essential. This will help to minimise the risk of fraud.

Indicators of fraud

The following may indicate the occurrence of fraud in the tendering and award of contracts for estates-related services and facilities management:

- Contracts that do not make commercial sense
- Contracts that include special, but unnecessary, specifications that only a favoured supplier could meet
- Consistent use of single-source contracts
- Split ordering to circumvent contract conditions
- Contractors who are qualified and capable of tendering, but who do not do so for no apparent reason
- Unusual patterns of consistently high accuracy in estimating tender costs – this is used to deflect the attention of auditors and senior managers who tend to look for adverse rather than favourable variances
- Withdrawal, without obvious reason, of the lowest tenderer, who may then go on to become a subcontractor of a high tenderer
- Patterns in tenders from a group of firms, for example, fixed rotation of the lowest tender
- A contractor tendering substantially higher on some tenders with no logical cost justification
- Tender prices appearing to drop whenever a new tenderer submits a bid
- Obvious links between contractors tendering for these works, for example, companies sharing the same address, having the same directors, managers and professional advisers
- Acceptance of late tenders
- Disqualification of a suitable tenderer
- Change in tender after other tenders are opened, often by the drafting of deliberate mistakes into the initial tender
- Poor documentation of the contract awarding process
- Suppliers awarded contracts disproportionate to their size
- Contracts awarded to contractors with a poor performance record
- Unexplained changes in contract shortly after award
- Successful tenderer repeatedly subcontracting work to companies that submitted higher tenders
- A consistent pattern of the same winners and losers (from the tender lists)
- Undue patronage, by consistently favouring one firm or a small number of firms over others
- Close personal relationships between staff and suppliers

Table B.1 Risks and controls in the award of contracts.

Activity	Risk	Control
Scoping of contract	The contract specification is written in a manner which favours a particular supplier	Use of contract panel consisting of technical, end-user and purchasing representatives, to ensure that more than one person is involved in drawing up the specification.
Contract documentation	Conditions of contract are changed to accommodate a favoured supplier and/or exclude competitors who cannot meet the varied conditions	Standard contract conditions and specification to be used. Any variations to be approved by senior management.
Setting evaluation criteria	Original evaluating criteria are changed after the receipt of submissions to ensure that favoured suppliers are shortlisted	Use evaluation criteria as agreed by the contract panel prior to tendering. Where EU procurement directives apply, evaluation criteria are required to be stated in advance.
Selection of tenderers	The selection of a group of tenderers with a view to ensuring that the favoured tenderer will win	Selection by panel against clearly defined and objective criteria; where applicable, in accordance with the requirements of EU procurement directives.
Tendering	Contract rings – repeat orders using narrow source list Links between contractors – uncompetitive tendering	Firms should be selected by someone other than the member of staff commissioning the work. Widen the sourcing list by the introduction of new firms and examine tender records for a pattern of pricing and tenderers who have been awarded contracts. Check for links in names, addresses and telephone numbers plus tendering partners.
Tender evaluation	Collusion to ensure that the favoured supplier is chosen	Technical and commercial evaluation to be carried out independently by the contract panel.
Post-tender negotiations	Modification of favoured supplier's tender to ensure that it is successful	Where necessary, identify reasons for negotiation and negotiate with a minimum of two suppliers.
Single-source procurement	Overstating of prices	Competitive tendering and advance purchase planning. Tight budgetary control and a comprehensive system of price checking.

Table B.2   Risks and controls in the management of contracts.

Activity	Risk	Control
Contractual correspondence	Altering terms and conditions to suit favoured supplier	Contract terms and conditions will be the procurement team's responsibility and may not be altered without senior management approval.
Contract management	False claims for work not carried out or exaggerated claims for actual work done	Clear audit trail with written records. Authorisation of changes, by senior management, to original document. Site checks, random and systematic.
Claims negotiation	Assisting the contractor to justify claims	Claims negotiation should be carried out using professional advisers.
Certification of completion	Inadequate certification may lead to overpayments or payment for work not carried out	Clear separation of duties between ordering the work, certification and authorisation for payment. Ensure that certified documents are not returned to the originator.
Authorisation	Contract splitting to keep contract values under particular staff member's authorised financial limit	The splitting of contracts should not be allowed unless authorised by senior management. Managers' and supervisors' checks and sampling should be constructed to detect this.
Acceptance of documentation to support claims	Documentation has been modified or fabricated	Act on original documents. Do not accept copies/faxes. Do not accept use of correction fluids etc. without obtaining satisfactory explanation for any amendments.
Supervision	Payment for work not done and duplication. Failure to monitor daywork on site. Duplication of names on more than one return or 'ghost' workers. Work paid for under one contract and provided in a different format on another contract. Lack of separation of duties, failure to report gifts and hospitality or conflicts of interest.	Good site supervision and audit of site diary. Look for similar work in same building and enforce contract management controls. Separate duties; ensure hospitality rules are formulated and understood; have clear conduct and discipline code, including conflicts of interests and penalties; take disciplinary action against those staff who fail to declare a conflict of interest.
Security of documents	Duplication and manipulation of accountable documents	Restricted access to accountable documents, such as works and stores orders, tender documents and claim forms. Serial numbering should be used.

Declarations of interests

Staff and management should be required to declare any personal interests in proposed contracts, and appropriate administrative arrangements to facilitate this should be put in place. 'Relevant interests' for this purpose could include not only financial interests but also interests such as membership of public bodies or closed organisations. The duty to decline would also extend to the interests of persons closely connected with the manager or staff member, such as his or her spouse/partner and the close family of the individual or of the spouse/partner.

Risks and controls

A formal request to the tenderer to sign to the effect that no fraud or corrupt practice has occurred when developing the tender could be introduced at invitation to tender acknowledgement stage or at bid submission. This has two effects:

- *Deterrent* – the contractor is alerted to the fact that the client is aware of the risk of fraud and will be on the lookout for any evidence that it has occurred
- *Protective* – it ensures that should something fraudulent come to light there can be no excuse that the contractor was not aware of the policy of the client organisation.

Organisations will need to handle such a declaration with sensitivity so as not to impair good working relationships with suppliers or service providers. Tables B.1 and B.2 show the risks of which organisations should be aware, and suggested control factors that can be used to minimise the risk.

Adapted from *Estates and Building Services Procurement: Prevention of Fraud and Irregularity in the Award and Management of Contracts* (HM Treasury, 1996).

Appendix C

Risks involved in outsourcing

Planning to outsource

- Are the objectives for outsourcing correctly identified?
- Is the service to be outsourced adequately scoped and defined?
- Are the in-house costs of delivering the business to be outsourced adequately calculated?
- Will adequate competition be generated from credible contractors?
- Does the outsourced management team have the right number and mix of skills?

Shortlisting of potential contractors

- Are there appropriate evaluation criteria?
- Are there adequate safeguards against corruption or bias in the evaluation?
- Is there sufficient expertise on the evaluation team?

Negotiating contracts

- Are customers' needs translated into business requirements?
- Are measures of contractor performance defined?
- Are appropriate penalties for unsatisfactory contractor performance included in the contracts?
- Is the organisation's contract protected against the contractors making excessive profits?
- Are the contingency arrangements that would apply in the event of disasters defined?
- Are there adequate safeguards against the commercial failure of the contractor?
- Are termination arrangements specified?
- Are there adequate safeguards to protect the confidentiality of data?
- Are there appropriate arrangements for the control of assets?
- Are there plans for transferring staff in an orderly fashion?
- Is adequate audit access provided for in the contracts?

Tender assessment

- Have the evaluation criteria been tested thoroughly?
- Have the contractors' price proposals and their experience in delivering equivalent business been tested thoroughly?
- Are there safeguards against corruption or bias in the selection of contractors?
- Is there sufficient expertise in the evaluation teams?
- Are there safeguards against the possibility of legal challenge by contractors?

Contract award

- Are there adequate skills in the negotiating team?
- Is the significance of contract terms properly assessed?
- Are there safeguards against disruption to existing business prior to the handover of business to the successful contractors?

Contract management

- Are there adequate arrangements to manage the contracts after award, including performance monitoring and price-control mechanisms?

Adapted from *Outsourcing the Service Delivery Operations* (HMSO, 1996).

Appendix D

Contractual approach and terms

- The contract should normally be for a period of three to five years. Organisations may wish to include a provision for the option of extending this by a further one to two years.

- Organisations should ensure that contract documentation is consistent with the specification.

- Organisations, especially those in the public sector, should consider using the Chartered Institute of Purchasing and Supply (CIPS) model facilities management agreement and should ensure that their contract provisions are in line with the Central Unit on Procurement's (CUP) *Guidance Note 42* (CUP, 1993). The recently updated form of contract by the Chartered Institute of Building (CIOB) should also be considered.

- The contract should include provisions for:
  - organisations to retain ownership of, and access to, all relevant records and knowledge
  - the arrangements for another contractor to take over the service at short notice in the event of the financial failure of the contractor
  - the handling of changes in the organisation's requirements
  - full disclosure of all data via an open-book arrangement which gives the client organisation access to all the contractor's premises, systems, books and records
  - the organisation's right to check the qualifications and competences of the personnel the contractor proposes to use and to approve any appointment beforehand
  - requiring the contractor and any subcontractors to have in place quality assurance or quality management systems
  - contingency arrangements
  - the arrangements for the transfer of assets at the start and end of the contract
  - the mechanisms for dispute resolution
  - the arrangements for handover to a succeeding contractor at the end of the contract

- If the contract involves a one-off transfer of assets to the successful tenderer, it should include a clawback provision to allow the organisation to share the benefit if the contractor then sells them on. The contract should contain clear and precise terms which:
  - o detail the service levels and performance standards the contractor is required to meet
  - o define performance monitoring arrangements and the associated information requirements
  - o link payment to performance
  - o detail any remedies in the event of default of whatever nature

- Organisations may wish to guarantee the expected workload for the first few years of a contract, in order to generate enough interest from potential tenderers. If TUPE applies, the contract should stipulate that, at the end of the contract, the existing contractor will have to provide other tenderers with information about the staff who would transfer to them under this.

- The contract should set out the pricing regime:
  - o fixed price for items or tasks which can be defined fully
  - o variable price for those which cannot
  - o arrangements for sharing savings

- The payment structure should provide the contractor with an incentive to perform well, for example by:
  - o paying nothing until the required performance standards are met
  - o making subsequent payments dependent on the continued meeting of these standards
  - o structuring payments to provide incentives to improve performance
  - o making good identified failures at the contractor's cost
  - o recovery of costs incurred by organisations in rectifying poor performance
  - o the removal of particular services from the contractor
  - o in exceptional circumstances, the right to terminate the contract

- Client organisations should require appropriate third-party protection in the form of parent or associated company guarantees, performance bonds, and evidence of the appropriate insurance cover.

- The contract should normally reserve the client organisation's right to terminate the contract in the event of a change in the controlling interest in the contractor.

- The contract should ensure that the contractor cannot assign any part of the contract to a third party without the client organisation's agreement.

- Contracts should be consistent internally and with each other.

- The contract should be flexible enough to cope with any client-approved changes in user requirements over the course of the contract.

General conditions of contract for the provision of services

1. Definitions
2. Services
3. Recovery of sums due
4. Value added tax (VAT)
5. Bankruptcy
6. Racial discrimination
7. Transfer, sub-letting and subcontracting
8. Corrupt gifts and payments of commission
9. Drawings, specifications and other data
10. Use of documents, information etc.
11. Disclosure of information
12. Law
13. Arbitration
14. Official Secrets Act (condition that would not apply outside the public sector)
15. Security measures
16. Approval for admission to government premises and information about workpeople (condition that would not apply outside the public sector)
17. Observance of regulations
18. Safety
19. Accidents to contractors' servants or agents
20. Special health and safety hazards
21. Liability in respect of damage to government property (condition that would not apply outside the public sector)
22. Contractor's property
23. Intellectual property rights
24. Patents
25. Default
26. Insurance
27. Duty of care
28. Design liability
29. Issues of government property (condition that would not apply outside the public sector)
30. Personal injury and loss of property
31. Hours of work
32. Occupation of government premises (condition that would not apply outside the public sector)
33. Contractor's organisation
34. Break
35. Facilities provided
36. Duration of contracts
37. Variation of requirement
38. Contract documents
39. Amendments to contracts

40. Monitoring and liaison meetings
41. Price
42. Price fixing
43. Lead-in costs
44. Payment
45. Payment of subcontractors
46. Availability of information
47. National Audit Office access (condition that would not apply outside the public sector)
48. Transfer of responsibility
49. Quality assurance

Appendix E

Sections for a service level agreement (SLA)

1. Definitions
2. Services
3. Value added tax (VAT)
4. Subcontracting
5. Resolution of dispute
6. Default
7. Duty of care
8. Hours of work
9. Occupation of premises
10. Agreement holder's organisation
11. Break
12. Facilities provided
13. Terms of agreement
14. Variation of requirement
15. Agreement documentation
16. Amendments to agreement
17. Monitoring and liaison meetings
18. Price
19. Extensions
20. Allocation of costs
21. Transfer of responsibility

References and Bibliography

Aronoff, S. and Kaplan, A. (1995) *Total workplace performance: rethinking the office environment*. Ottawa: WDL Publications.

Barrett, P.S. and Baldry, D. (2003) *Facilities management: towards best practice*, 2nd edition. Oxford: Blackwell Publishing.

Bennett, J. and Jayes, S. (1998) *The seven pillars of partnering*. London: Thomas Telford.

CIRIA (1996) *Control of risk: a guide to the systematic management of risk from construction (SP125)*. London: Construction Industry Research and Information Association.

Clements-Croome, D. (ed.) (2000) *Creating the productive workplace*. London: Spon.

Gadde, L.-E. (1996) *Supplier management in the construction industry: working papers*. Gothenburg: Chalmers University of Technology.

Hofstede, G. (1991) *Cultures and organisations: software of the mind: intercultural cooperation and its importance for survival*. New York, NY: McGraw-Hill.

Kelly, J., Morledge, R. and Wilkinson, S. (2002) *Best value in construction*. Oxford: Blackwell Science.

Kelly, J., Male, S. and Drummond, G. (2004) *Value management of construction projects*. Oxford: Blackwell Publishing.

Kaplan, R.S. and Norton, D.P. (1996) *The balanced scorecard: translating strategy into action*. Boston, MA: Harvard Business School Press.

Leibfried, K.H.J. and McNair, C.J. (1994) *Benchmarking: a tool for continuous improvement*. London: HarperCollins.

Leiringer, R. (2003) *Technological innovations in the context of public-private partnership projects*. Doctoral Thesis, Stockholm: Department of Industrial Economics and Management, Royal Institute of Technology.

Pande, P.S., Neuman, R.P. and Cavanagh, R.R. (2000) *The six sigma way*. New York, NY: McGraw-Hill.

Rostron, J. (ed.) (1997) *Sick building syndrome: concepts, issues and practice*. London: Spon.

Stationery Office (2000) *Public private partnerships: the government's approach*. London: Stationery Office.

Thompson, P. and Warhurst, C. (eds.) (1998) *Workplaces of the future*. Basingstoke: Macmillan.

Williams, S. (2002) *Managing workplace stress*. London: John Wiley.

Index